A Fire to Kindle: Harris County School & Education Before 1950

I - Z

Mike Vance

Dos Dogs Press

Copyright © 2025 by Mike Vance

All rights reserved.

No portion of this book may be reproduced in any form without written permission from the publisher or author, except as permitted by U.S. copyright law.

Name: Vance, Mike 1959 – author

Title: A Fire to Kindle A – H

Identifiers LCCN

ISBN (hardback) 978-1-965272-12-1

ISBN (paperback) 978-1-965272-13-8

ISBN (ebook) 978-1-965272-14-5

Also by Mike Vance

Please enjoy these other titles by Mike Vance. They are available where books are sold and also at www.mikevancewriter.com

Non-Fiction

Undertold Texas Volume 1

Getting Away With Bloody Murder

Mud & Money: A Timeline of Houston History

Murder & Mayhem in Houston (with John Nova Lomax)

Houston Baseball: The Early Years, 1861-1961

Houston's Sporting Life

Stand-Up Stories: Tales from Behind the Microphone

Brenham

Fiction

The Devil's Lease

A Convenient Scapegoat

Wingo: The Remarkable Story of an Unremarkable Man

Wingo's Redemption

Zeke Gets Glasses. Jungleburgh Children's Reading Community (with John Swasey)

Contents

1. The Start of HISD — 1
2. Early African American Teachers — 3
3. Hygiene — 9
4. Schools I - K — 12
5. Schools L — 33
6. Schools M — 59
7. Schools N - O — 87
8. Schools P - Q — 96
9. Schools R — 114
10. Schools Sacred Heart – Southland — 128
11. Schools Southmayd - Sykes — 148
12. Schools T - V — 171
13. Schools Waller - Whittier — 181
14. Schools Willow - Z — 203
15. A Few Final Stories — 216
16. Acknowledgements — 222
Endnotes — 224

The Start of HISD

By 1921, the Independent School District of Houston was seriously struggling with the question of whether or not it was truly independent. Superintendent Horn wrote that the "question at issue is as to whether the city school system of Houston is merely one department of the city government, or whether instead it is a portion of the state school system of Texas." Urged by prominent citizens, direct governance of the schools had passed from the city supervisor to a school board shortly after the turn of the century, but clarity was still absent.[1]

Part of what prompted this soul searching was the fact that for the first time, the school district was larger than the city limits itself. Prior to this time, the area served was simply the footprint of Houston, but the district had recently added county district 25 "for school purposes only." That was an area that ran mostly north and northwest of Houston and included Sunset Heights, Sikes, Woodland, Dudley, Berry, Durkee, Harbor, Janowski, and Hohl schools.[2]

The arrangement of the schools with other city departments had changed over the years. There was no doubt that twenty years prior, it was on par with the fire department, police department, water, streets, parks, and even the scavenger department. The mayor and city commission held the purse strings and voted on every salary increase and major expenditure. That had changed, however.

The district now had its own money. Most of it came directly from the state as part of the Texas school tax system. There was also a local school district tax of fifty cents per hundred dollars valuation that had been levied and was dedicated to school use only.

"I do not believe that the average citizen or taxpayer of Houston would concede that the schools in which his children are to be educated are on the same plane as these other departments," Horn wrote. "However high may be his opinion of the importance of these departments."[3]

Yet there were still two large strings being held by whomever sat in the Houston mayor's office. The ping pong game that was the appointive versus elective board process had switched back to appointive, so the mayor had complete say over who managed school district affairs. He also had the "right to veto any financial action of the

Board, with the further provision that the Board may by a two-thirds vote override such veto action on the part of the mayor."

Horn pointed out that none of the six mayors who held office since the system had come into play had ever exercised the veto power, but it was a potential dangling sword nonetheless. He felt that a permanent resolution was needed, writing: "It is a question which sooner or later would have to be permanently settled if the schools of the city are to go forward. It is an impossibility for schools to be made the spoils of political warfare and still to retain their efficiency."[4]

When the schools were a city department, the offices were located in the City Hall and Market House Building on Market Square. Mike Vance Collection

With that as the backdrop, the Houston Independent School District incorporated on March 20, 1923, assuming some $2.3 million in city school bond debt. Faced with accommodating over 20,000 students in only 50 buildings, several operating on a split half-day system and 7,000 students without desks, drastic action was required. The plan to bring the Houston schools up to date centered around three multi-million dollar bond elections over the next six years. It would be the most transformative decade in the city's school history.[5]

Early African American Teachers

As United States troops occupied former slave territory during the Civil War, education for those freed from bondage often followed close on their heels. The Union Army occupied Fortress Monroe and Alexandria in Virginia over a year before the Emancipation Proclamation, but that did not stop the enslaved African Americans in those locales from working to organize schools for children and adults alike.

Lincoln's Emancipation ruling freed those enslaved in all territories of the rebellious states, and even as war raged, some federal commanders instituted schools for the newly freed Blacks. Top of the list was Massachusetts-born General Nathaniel P. Banks, a recent governor of his state, who had charge of the Gulf of Mexico coastal areas west of Pensacola. He ordered subordinates to set up a system of schools in and around New Orleans in March of 1864, and by that December, over 9,500 children and 2,000 adults were enrolled in 95 schools learning from 162 teachers. Newly freed laborers in many areas even demanded "educational clauses" in their work contracts with former plantation owners.[1]

It was June 19, 1865, before Texas slaves were officially notified of their new freedom, and the Freedmen's Bureau began to establish schools shortly thereafter. Like the experience in Virginia before them, Texas freed people clamored to learn. A pro-Union paper in Galveston observed that "We see fathers and mothers together with their grown-up children all anxiously engaged in the pursuit of knowledge."[2]

Many of the earliest teachers at these schools in the Houston area, as elsewhere across the south, were White female missionaries fresh from the northern states. Only five to ten percent of newly freed slaves had even the most basic knowledge of reading and writing, so there were few local candidates for the teaching positions. Still, the northern women caught a chilly reception from most Whites and even some Blacks. Records exist in other locations of what the benevolent Yankees took as ingratitude when the recently freed citizens preferred that their children be taught by fellow African Americans.[3]

By 1871, when the first attempt at universal free public education in Texas went into effect, there was a mixed slate of teachers. Miss Isabella B. Kent, a White woman, had overall charge of roughly 200 Black pupils at Gregory Institute, and an unnamed White male teacher was at the African American school in Fifth Ward. The instructor at the Black school in Second Ward, presiding over a "large attendance", was "a colored man recently from Mississippi." Within three years, White Houstonians' complaints about racially mixed faculties had prompted the Union general in charge of the city to hire four Black Gregory school teachers.[4]

The federal census of 1880 lists at least ten teachers of color in Harris County, and they offer a wide array of backgrounds. Emma Beuchley was 56-years-old and born in South Carolina with at least a decade stop in Alabama along the way. Such a history means that she was almost certainly born into bondage. Texas-born Annie B. Parker was a minister's wife, and their nephew, William Bradford, was also listed as a teacher in spite of being just fifteen years old. The teachers also included three married women in their twenties and four male heads of household, two of them as old as 45, southern-born, and likely with memories filled with decades of life as a slave.[5]

The variety of training noted among Black teachers around Houston speaks right to the heart of what would become a national debate over the type of educational system that best served African Americans. Dozens of normal schools, as teacher training colleges were known, opened around America in the 1800s, and shortly after the Civil War, separate but somewhat similar institutions began opening to train Black teachers. One of the first was Hampton in southeast Virginia. It was opened by the American Missionary Association in 1868 with Samuel Chapman Armstrong, a missionary's son and former Union general, as president.[6]

Armstrong built a school patterned after his father's work with the Polynesians in Hawaii. He set a curriculum that combined basic academics that would prepare a graduate to teach grade school and pass state teachers' exams with manual labor on the school farm. "A good labor record has often saved one from being dropped as incompetent," Armstrong wrote, adding "that very frequently the dull plodder at Hampton is the real leader of his people toward better things." Hampton's most famous alumnus was Booker T. Washington who would start his own school in Tuskegee, Alabama and carry on the same educational tradition.[7]

There are scholars, however, who question whether or not Samuel Armstrong had the best interest of African American society at heart. He was consistently adamant that the freedmen were not qualified to vote or hold office because they lacked "foresight, judgment and hard sense." In the 1870s, critical Black visitors noted separate seating for Blacks and Whites at graduation and portraits of Robert E. Lee and Andrew Johnson hanging in the school chapel. Graduates of Hampton and Tuskegee from the late 19th century were encouraged to be average, the critics contended, and to create a nation of average Black students who would be competent workers for White elites.[8]

Prairie View A&M opened in 1876 as the African American counterpart to the Texas Agricultural & Mechanical land grant college set up near Bryan. The curriculum at Prairie View was firmly in the Hampton-Tuskegee camp until 1901 when true college level liberal arts courses were added partly thanks to the advocacy of the Colored Teachers State Association of Texas that was formed there in 1884.[9]

A majority of White teachers in the Houston area during the second half of the 19th century and into the early 20th listed high school as their highest level of academic study, but there were no Texas high schools for African Americans until 1892. The normal school education, which would later become a university-level pursuit, was roughly equivalent to a high school degree at best. Some of the early Black colleges aspired to more, however.[10]

Unknown teacher. HHRC

The founders of Fisk University in Nashville, Tennessee, another institution backed by the American Missionary Association, vowed to have a school that offered the finest "not of Negro education, but of American education at its best." Fisk stressed the arts, raising needed building funds through a renowned group of touring student singers. Howard University in Washington, D.C. was founded in 1867, the same year as Fisk, by Union General Oliver O. Howard who was also the head of the Freedmen's Bureau. Within two years it was teaching liberal arts and medicine.[11]

By the mid-1890s, Houston's African American teachers included graduates of all of these schools along with Wilberforce in Ohio, the oldest historically Black college in the United States, normal schools in Atlanta and in Holly Springs, Mississippi, Texas' own Prairie View A&M and two schools in Jamaica - Calabar and Mico. The latter was chartered in 1836 by three British missionaries, the oldest Black college in the Western Hemisphere. The graduates of these schools did not generally hold bachelor's degrees, but many had gone on to earn permanent teaching certificates from the State of Texas.[12]

By the start of World War I, and after much debate and many published attacks between luminaries like Booker T. Washington and W.E.B. Du Bois, schools such as Hampton had seen the light and changed to a more academically-minded focus. It should be noted that Du Bois was not advocating for an overall uplift of the freedmen and their children either, but rather special dispensation for the most intellectually adept African Americans, a group he called the "talented tenth." Still, resentment over the Hampton concept burned within some Houston Blacks including local dentist C.T. Ewell who opined that "the schools here are under the control of some of the biggest Uncle Toms that you ever hope to see. They have put the Negroes here at a terrific disadvantage."[13]

It was an accusation that had some staying power among some of Houston's Blacks. In the early 20th century, James D. Ryan, the highly educated dean of Houston's Black education system and a leader at Trinity Church and the Elks Club, became a prime lightning rod for those who wanted faster integration and a better seat at the table. His lofty perch won him many friends among Houston's White business leadership, and to keep in their good graces, Ryan refused to rock the boat by aligning himself with protests. When he died in 1940, the *Informer* wrote that "unfortunately for his acclaim, he lived ten years too long."[14]

Most of the complaints seemed to be about whether or not African American school leaders could wring more equality out of a majestically unequal system. Judging by items in Houston's Black press, the undercurrent was always there, rearing its head at various controversies along what must have been a road of almost unending frustration.

Uneven teacher pay was always a concern. In "1882, Black male instructors received $42 a month as compared to $72 per month for White males, while Black females were paid $35 a month in contrast to White female teachers at $47.80 per month." There were some instances of equal pay when gender was taken into account. That same school year, H.C. Hardy, a Black principal with five years of service to the Houston schools, was paid $450 a year, the same salary as S. Allen, a White principal with the same service time. The difference was that Principal Allen was a woman.[15]

By 1884, there was an organization, the Colored Teachers State Association of Texas, formed to promote "fair distribution of funds and equal professional status." With only two Blacks remaining in the legislature after Reconstruction, it was a tall task.[16]

When the *Houston Informer,* an African American newspaper, came into being in 1919, teacher pay equality was one of its first editorial crusades. At the time, White grade school teachers were earning up to $1,200 a year depending on service time, compared to only $720 for some of their Black counterparts. Still, many of the African American teachers were reluctant to rock the boat for fear of dismissal. Other opportunities were quite limited. By 1930, well over 75% of all Black professional women in Houston were teachers. Numbers from that time showed that just over 60% of African American high school teachers in Houston district had degrees, but only about a quarter of those in elementary schools did.[17]

By 1924, Houston teachers of color averaged $1,096 in elementary positions and $1,291 in high school regardless of gender. When the Great Depression hit, though, Houston area teachers felt the pain. There was even a motion brought before the board to fire all female teachers and replace them with men who needed the work to support their families. The motion failed.[18]

Other austerity measures were implemented. School districts across America cut teacher salaries, and Houston was no exception. Teacher salaries were cut about 6% across the board, but White teachers making less than $1,000 a year were exempt while Black teachers were not. Several female African American teachers were put on half time or half year pay by HISD. That meant that they taught only half a day or half of the school year, and their salaries were adjusted downward accordingly. The largest number were married to men who also taught or were principals in the district and were deemed by the school board to make enough money to support their families, but several single women were effected, too. One woman was said to remark that "I'll quit my husband before I'll lose my job."[19]

The battle for equal pay for Black teachers played out across the south during the 1930s, moved along by several court cases brought by the NAACP and various Black teachers groups. One high profile victory on appeal was in Norfolk, Virginia featuring a legal team that included Thurgood Marshall. Even as the battle was being won, some of Houston's "old guard" Black teachers refused to endorse the fight. It took stringent appeals from *Informer* editor Carter Wesley, Negro Chamber of Commerce leaders, and Lulu White, the incoming head of the local NAACP and herself a former teacher, to eventually get the local teachers off the dime. When the legal challenges came to Texas, success was first achieved in Dallas in February of 1943 and in Houston a few weeks later. Standardized equal pay scales for all races did not become law in Texas until 1961.[20]

For all of the disadvantages handed to the Black teachers in Houston and Harris County, there was at least periodic lip service from the school bosses that "they have to contend with all the most unfavorable conditions which the White schools have, and with a great many more." Superintendent Horn lauded one teacher who taught Latin at the Colored High School. She took a year sabbatical at her own expense to go study in Rome before returning to teach in Houston. "How many White teachers could or would have accomplished this feat?" Horn asked. [21]

He wrote in his report of 1910 that: "It is my firm opinion that our Negro teachers, working under many very adverse circumstances, are doing faithful, earnest work, are making an honest effort to help their race, and are reaching results that are abundantly worth all that is paid for their schools." He neglected to note that "their schools" were getting hand-me-down books and equipment and far less money per pupil than their White counterparts.

Hygiene

W.H. Martin, the Harris County Physician, wrote to all county teachers on June 24, 1913 asking them to help in encouraging good habits and regular bathing among their students. After pointing out that the concept of cleanliness being next to Godliness was certainly nothing new, Martin continued rather apologetically.

"I realize that you teachers might feel that your functions and duties are multiplying alarmingly fast in this day of progress," he wrote. "However, it has become to be accepted by all thinking people that your influence is probably the most far-reaching in the life of the child; that impressions gained in the school room are the most lasting, and good habits formed there are the most fixed."[1]

As he advocated for individual drinking cups, dry shoes and socks, and regular brushing of teeth, notions that he acknowledged might be "a trifle radical", he went on to say that the county had adopted a plan for annual fumigation of the school rooms, adding that "the theory of the existence and the dissemination of germs is no longer a mooted question, but an accepted fact and the greatest fight that is being made in this country today is in perfecting means and measures to prevent their existence and render impossible their dissemination, and probably no measure is conducive of more good than that of educating individuals in the matter of taking precautions that science has demonstrated will be most beneficial in stamping out these little messengers of destruction." A nice but firm way of saying to keep it clean.

In Colonial America, common sentiment held that bathing stripped the body of the natural oils needed to keep it healthy. In fact, unlike several other religions, Christianity had no real teachings on the subject of keeping clean. Needless to say, much of Europe and America was an odiferous place, even with the occasional popularity of perfumes and toilet waters. It was the second half of the 19th century when things such as soap and more regular baths began to take a small hold in American lives. It started primarily with the wealthy, many of whom even went so far as to have a room installed in their homes for the practice, with fixed plumbing, no less.[2]

In rural America, however, there were virtually zero bathroom facilities. Those wanting to bathe carried water and poured it into a metal washtub. The family generally took turns using the same water. In winter, that might even take place indoors. The work-intensive aspect of the practice dictated that it was not a daily occurrence, even if some misguided soul wanted it to be.

The City of Houston schools were already on the hygiene bandwagon, and a certain part of what brought them there was the perception that early 20th century immigrants from Europe and Mexico were somehow less clean than those old guard Texans. It was still a need, however; one that was partially met by the progressive, charitable Settlement House Movement that came to the United States from England in the late 1880s with the idea to alleviate the conditions faced by not only immigrants, but the working poor, as well.[3]

The Settlement House at Rusk School about 1909. The free kindergarten is at left. HISD

Like other cities, Houston's Settlement House was started largely by middle and upper class White women who wanted to provide educational and social uplift for those most in need. At a time when few employment avenues were open to these women, it also gave them an outlet to do good work. The driver for the local movement was Sybil Campbell, a teacher at Rusk Elementary, who was inspired by a young girl she found sleeping on the school steps one rainy afternoon. She enlisted the Houston Woman's Club which had started a kindergarten in 1902 and wholeheartedly captured the devotion of women such as Alice Graham Baker and Estelle Sharp. The Rusk Settlement House opened in 1907, helping European immigrants, mainly Jewish refugees from Russia.[4]

The annual schools report authored in 1911 laid out particulars for the city's new state-of-the-art showplace school that was being erected for Rusk, an old frame building that had recently burned. "Bathing facilities are provided both for boys and for girls," the superintendent wrote. "The plans call for the widest possible use of the school plant by the people of the community."

All of this was to be done in concert with the Settlement House, by now firmly established in the old Settegast homestead located at the north end of the new Rusk campus alongside Buffalo Bayou just northeast of downtown. The focus soon shifted to the rapidly burgeoning Mexican immigrant community who were moving into Second Ward housing that often had no running water. It meant that the showers at the school were well utilized. Felix Fraga, who would go on to serve on the HISD School Board and Houston City Council, recounted that his family, with six boys, lived for a time in a tenement that had running water only in a kitchen sink. Fraga recalled many mornings of coming to school early in order to shower.[5]

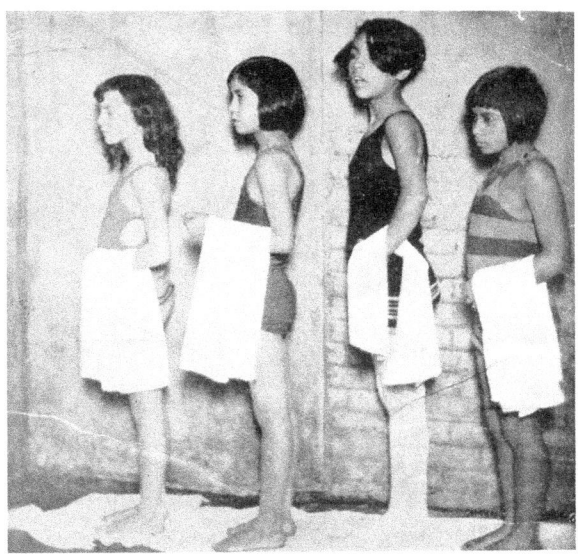

Girls wait for the "shower baths" at Anson Jones ES in 1935. HISD

Though showers became locker room staples in junior highs and high schools, few of the HISD elementary schools ever offered them, though the need among some of Houston's poor continued even after WWII. Sandy Reiser, whose mother worked at Longfellow Elementary in the 1940s, shared an account of one girl whose poor hygiene and dirt-encrusted body became so olfactorily offensive to others that a small group of teachers bathed her in a school bathroom and replaced the clothes that she had been wearing for weeks with secondhand items they had collected at their own expense.[6]

Schools I – K

IMMACULATE CONCEPTION

The parish school at Immaculate Conception was opened for about 70 students by the Congregation of the Sisters of Divine Providence on September 9, 1912, with four sisters. Originally, the school sat at the northeast corner of Capitol and Forest Hill. A convent, which was built in connection with the school at Magnolia Park, served as the community center not only for the four sisters teaching there but also for two missionaries who commuted about four miles by streetcar to Our Lady of Guadalupe School closer to downtown. The Immaculate Conception School closed in 1969.[1]

IMMACULATE HEART OF MARY

As more and more Mexican immigrants poured into Houston in the late 1910s and early 1920s, Our Lady of Guadalupe Church began to experience issues of overcrowding. Those Catholics in the new Magnolia Park neighborhoods rode the streetcar to Guadalupe until 1925 when the diocese created a new parish closer to their part of town. A two-story private home at 71st and Navigation served as the first chapel until, on November 8, 1926, a new building opened at 700 75th Street under the name of Immaculate Heart of Mary. The parish school serving the elementary grades followed in 1932 under the direction of the Sisters of Divine Providence who were already running both Guadalupe School and the nearby Immaculate Conception School. It remained in operation until 1998.[2]

IMMANUEL LUTHERAN SCHOOL

Immanuel was founded in 1927 adjacent to the church at 15th and Courtlandt in Houston Heights. Attendance was not limited to Lutherans, but there was a religious component to the curriculum. The school reduced operations to pre-school and early childhood education about 2011.[3]

INCARNATE WORD ACADEMY

Incarnate Word Academy, the oldest Catholic school in Houston, was founded in 1873 and is located at 609 Crawford Street where it shares a complex with Annunciation Church. As was the case with many of the early Catholic leaders in the Houston – Galveston area, Incarnate Word was founded by a French order, the Sisters of the Incarnate Word and Blessed Sacrament. They had come to Texas in 1852 and previously established schools at Brownsville and Victoria. It was from the latter that Mother M. Gabriel and two other sisters came to Houston, first operating out of a former monastery at Franklin and Caroline, before a building opened on a half-block facing Crawford at Capitol with first classes on January 3, 1874.[4]

The first building remained unfinished for some time, and the sisters lived and worked without much heat that winter since there was "neither plaster nor ceiling and the stars were easily seen through the roof." For their meager meals in the earliest days, they often relied on donations from neighbors.[5]

Just four years after opening, there were twelve sisters listed as teachers, and that number had increased to 20 by 1890. The enrollment gradually reached the neighborhood of 200 girls, both boarded and day-school, and has remained in that vicinity or slightly larger ever since. The teaching sisters continued to be brought almost exclusively from France and Ireland until the mid-1920s with their housing in a convent building adjoining the sanctuary of Annunciation.[6]

Incarnate Word originally took girls of all ages, offering English, German, writing, sewing, and music in addition to religious instruction. Science and higher mathematics were not available. As the enrollment grew, so did the campus. In the last few years of the 1890s, a two-story brick building containing an auditorium, music rooms, and a dining hall was completed at the corner of Jackson and Capitol. Constrained space brought elimination first of the boarding school and then the grammar school, making Incarnate Word into an all-girls high school.[7]

The original building that faced Crawford was in poor repair by the end of WWII, and in 1948 it was replaced with a three-story structure that contained more classrooms, a large cafeteria, and third floor housing for the sisters. The various outbuildings that had dotted the block were eliminated with the new construction. Sister Mary Paul Valdez wrote that it was a far cry "from the days when all the laundry was done in an old shed, a big, black pot heated over an open fire was used as a boiler and the flat irons were heated on a charcoal furnace."

The Nicholas Clayton-designed building demolished by the Sisters of the Incarnate Word in 2015. Laurie Feinswog photo

In 1984, when a new four-story school building, designed by McKittrick, Richardson, and Wallace, was completed, the academy trumpeted the fact that it still retained its beautiful 1905 red-brick Nicholas J. Clayton building, but by 2015, their stewardship of that historic structure was inconvenient, and it was demolished. It was the last Clayton building in the city and the second Clayton structure demolished by the sisters.[8]

INDEPENDENCE HEIGHTS SCHOOL
See Burrus

The "Independence Colored School" probably early 1930s. HCPL

INDIAN HILL SCHOOL

This was a short-lived school, likely a single teacher, in County District 31. In operation in the early 1910s, it was located east of Kuykendahl, possibly on Indian Hills Road, just south of the Montgomery County line.[9]

INDUSTRIAL E S

See Jacinto City ES

IRVINGTON SCHOOL

See Looscan

ISAACKS, E.M. "BOOGE" SCHOOL

Elisha Madison Isaacks, known as "Booge" in the neighborhood that would become the Humble area, had his name attached to a small school with twelve students for a four month course of study as early as 1887. Five years later, Isaacks was a trustee at the Dunman's Schoolhouse.[10]

ISAAC'S SCHOOL HOUSE

See Red Bluff

JACINTO CITY E S

Jacinto City Elementary, first known as Industrial Elementary after the Industrial Acres development of Frank Sharp, opened in 1944 to accommodate the rapidly expanding population of workers along the Ship Channel during WWII. The city incorporated at the end of the war, and today it is part of Galena Park ISD.[11]

JACKSON J H S, HOUSTON

One of the longtime junior high/middle schools that opened as part of the 1920s HISD construction flurry was the one named for Confederate General Stonewall Jackson. Dora Lantrip, principal of nearby Eastwood Elementary, arranged for the laying of the cornerstone, and the new building opened on a heavily wooded parcel in the 5100 block of Polk in February 1926 with 23 classrooms and a shop. Paved streets and gas lines leading to the school site were not yet in place, and a mule barn across the street had only recently given way to a stucco home.

Architectural detail on Jackson JHS. Laurie Feinswog photo

Jackson opened the same Monday as Lanier, George Washington, and Jack Yates. Most of the equipment and furniture was in place the first day, but the teaching staff was still being named at the last minute. Blanche Higginbotham moved from the assistant principal post at South End to take the reins at Jackson. Growth in the previously rural area was swift. Within a decade, there were 53 rooms at Jackson. C. F. Hartman took over as principal and stayed for 25 years, earning recognition when a new Southeast Houston Junior High sported his name. An annex was added in 1980, then rebuilt after a fire in 1999. Jackson's name was changed in 2016 to honor Yolanda Black Navarro.[12]

Caring For the School Buildings

Houston School Maintenance Department

For many years, schools both urban and rural relied on a janitor for maintenance and day-to-day operations. Many times, these custodians lived on or near schools grounds, sometimes even in a basement room. Overseeing the janitor corps was the head man at Central High School downtown. If more substantive repairs were needed for a school house, a suitable nearby tradesman was hired.[13]

For the 1904-05 school year, the city school board hired a carpenter full time in hopes that having someone on salary would save the district money overall. His "shop and headquarters consisted of any obscure corner of the basement of the building under repair; that he was contented to deposit his chest of tools wherever he chanced to be."[14]

As growth and complexity of schools increased, so too did the district maintenance staff. In 1905, school rooms were heated by a stove that could be operated by anyone with wood and a match. A decade later, the newer buildings contained "a heating system controlled through the thermostat method" that "may be in reality the highest and best type of its kind, and yet be totally ineffective so far as results are concerned, simply because of the lack of knowledge in the proper adjustments of its automatic features." The school board added Mr. E.P. Hiriart to be the "inspector and repairer of heating plants and plumbing."[15]

Hiriart was joining what had truly become an entire department. There were also four regular carpenters and two painters who were employed year round. As schools let out for the students, repair work increased. In the summer of 1915, the full-time staff was joined by two additional painters, "two boiler men, two stove repairers and three flue cleaners. In addition to these men we are also employing a number of workmen on special jobs, cement work, etc."

There was a repair department headquarters in a 30' x 30' room that contained a universal woodworking machine, a mortise, and a planer. The carpenters were said to be repairing furniture that otherwise would have become scrap. Space for these maintenance shops was still at a premium in the rapidly growing district. Near the carpenters' home was a paint shop "located in one of the shafts formerly designed as a pure air duct, leading to one of the furnaces."[16]

Adjustable Desks

"During the past year we have had adjustable desks installed in two of our buildings—complaints have been numerous... The most serious criticism is first, that they are not wholly mechanically correct. The adjustments are impractical and insecure. The attention required to hold them at any given adjustment is too constant.

"A room of such desks may be set to meet the requirements of a class at the beginning of a day and six hours later it is found that numbers of the same desks must be again adjusted. These complaints, however, may not be properly charged, in every instance, to the desk; but a mechanism that makes it so easy for a playful student to destroy the very essentials for which we are striving with his fingers or a pocketknife or a bicycle wrench is at least not fully perfected...

"The adjustable school desk at present is in just about that state of development as was the self-starter on the automobile five years ago. The self-starter has been made reasonably reliable within the past few years, and it is to be hoped that the adjustable desk will reach a similar degree of perfection within the next few years. For the present our plan is to equip our rooms for intermediate grade children with rigid desks, providing in each room a few that are above and a few that are below the standard size for the grade."

Houston City Schools Report 1914-15

Vacuum Cleaners

"After two years of experience and experiments with vacuum cleaners as an adjunct to our janitor service, I am forced to say that they have not proven thoroughly satisfactory in school room cleaning.

"School desks are a fixture upon the floors of a class room; they are firmly fastened; a vacuum cleaner brush must be used at about eight different angles around the feet of each desk, and when the end of an aisle is reached the hose must be dragged around the end of each row of desks and thrown over the tops before beginning the process of cleaning the next row. The usual time required for a janitor to clean a room with vacuum cleaners is approximately 25 to 30 minutes. If we figure on a basis of 25 minutes to a room it would take five hours for the cleaning of a 12-room building.

"A suggestion for the reduction of the time required for cleaning class rooms would be that in future, all class rooms be provided with air tubes, as well as those that might be conveniently located in hallways, where vacuum cleaners are installed. We find that vacuum cleaners are practical for open floor work, or where furniture may be early moved or shifted. They may be practicable for class rooms if the changes are made as suggested above."

Houston City Schools Report 1914-15

Thermostatic Heat

"A thermostatic, or automatically controlled heating and ventilating system is one of the luxuries of which we now boast in two buildings.

"These systems are designed so as to regulate the temperature and ventilation in each individual room. Large flues are so constructed as to lead from a central point of intake to a point of distribution in each room, the air being controlled by dampers or shut-offs, that supposedly work automatically after being driven by a forced draft fan over heated coils.

"The system of control is guided by pencil-sized pipe running like threads throughout the building, being moulded into the concrete as it is poured. These small pipes have a connection with the thermometers fastened to the sides of each wall, the thermometers being so constructed as to enable their sensitiveness to cause a reacting current of air to close or open the valves leading to and from the rooms to the central heating plant.

"Such systems were probably designed for uses where climatic conditions were such as to compel their users to keep all windows and doors of a building closed during the severity of winter and where conditions are such as to make an extreme measure of effort necessary for ordinary comfort.

"It is very likely that the cost for installing such a system as we have at the South End Junior High School, together with the preliminary preparations necessary for its reception, will approximate eight or ten per cent of the cost of the building itself.

"I do not feel that these systems are in fact automatic. Careful attention, as well as frequent adjustments, are necessary. The cost of upkeep and repair is excessive. High-priced and experienced mechanics alone can handle such plants.

"In a climate such as we enjoy, it is a matter of doubt with me as to the advisability of such heavy expenditures as are necessary for the plant and its installation, when we are so abundantly supplied with free air and have windows hung on weights.

"It is not a difficult matter to secure all the natural ventilation that we need, with all the protective measures against disagreeable drafts, and at a figure of cost that will save thousands of dollars to the city in each instance where one system might be figured against the other. I am firmly of the opinion that a properly figured steam plant, with low pressure boilers, could be made to meet our needs in every way."

Superintendent Paul W. Horn
Houston City Schools Report 1914-15

JACKSON J H S, PASADENA

Pasadena ISD was a latecomer to the junior high band wagon in 1937 when it opened one on land donated by the James Andrew Jackson family. It was located very near Kruse Elementary and Pasadena High, and the first Jackson JHS principal, W.J. Cole, referred to them as the "holy trinity" of Pasadena schools. It served the seventh, eighth, and ninth grades as the only junior high in the district until South Houston JHS opened ten years later. The old Jackson building was demolished sometime after 1980. Today there is a Jackson Intermediate School at 1020 East Thomas Street in Pasadena.[17]

Janowski School. HHRC

JANOWSKI SCHOOL

The Janowski family were immigrant farmers from Poland who settled in the area of Little White Oak Bayou about 1860. Building a prosperous farm and with smart land sales, Peter Janowski built first an 11-room house and then a small one-room school for his children and those of his neighbors on a quarter acre of land on East Montgomery Road, today's Fulton. He then donated it to the county. While it was being constructed, the county teacher held classes for the eight to ten students in the family's upstairs hallway.[18]

During the 1890s, Janowski was repeatedly the smallest school in County District 25, insured for $275 including furniture and getting only 1½ cords of wood for the winter. As the neighborhood grew, the old building was sold and a new one built and then expanded to two rooms for grades one through seven. Described as being in "run-down condition" when District 25 joined HISD, the school was closed when Burbank opened in 1927. Some years later, a new elementary school in the area was given the Janowski name.[19]

JEFFERSON E S

The pedigree of Jefferson Elementary is a very long one on Houston's northside. It started in 1883 as Little White Oak School, a wood building on East Montgomery Road that lasted only six years before moving about a mile northwest. That next building, named for County District 25 trustee S.T. Sykes, gave way in 1910 to a new three-story brick building at 4515 E. Montgomery Road, soon to be renamed Fulton Avenue, and very near the site of the original wooden building.[20]

The new brick school also came with a new name, Hillebrandt, honoring a more current member of the SD 25 board, though the old name of Sykes continued to linger in places for several years. Two years later, Hillebrandt was made a four-year high school serving the other eight schools and 1,500 plus students in the district. It was one of only three first-class high schools in the county program. With the expansion came athletic teams, a science lab, and facilities for domestic economy and manual training. There was even a program for children to get credit for work at home.

Old Thomas Jefferson School in 1952. Mike Vance Collection

When SD 25 became part of HISD, Hillebrandt had outlived its usefulness as a high school, but the new district put over $32,000 into building improvements for it to once again become an elementary school. It became Thomas Jefferson about 1927 after that name had been rejected as a replacement for South End High School, the city's educational palace that became San Jacinto High instead. In 1950, a new Jefferson Elementary was opened at 5000 Sharman, just around the corner.[21]

JOHNSTON J H S

When the HISD board was planning a new junior high for the area south of downtown and east of Main Street, a school called the Almeda Road school on the drawing board, they decided upon the name of progressive President Theodore Roosevelt. By the time the school opened in 1926 on ten acres at Cleburne and Almeda, the name had been changed to honor Albert Sidney Johnston, a West Point graduate who had served the Republic of Texas as Secretary of War and earned acclaim as a general in both the United States and Confederate armies. The change came after a storm of protest by elderly Confederate Veterans groups and their descendants.[22]

The lunchroom at the new Johnston JHS in 1926. HISD

The Greyhounds' first principal was William Moreland, who went on to become HISD superintendent during the turbulent times of the McCarthy and early Civil Rights eras. In 1956, due to changing demographics, the old Johnston building became a segregated African American school - William Miller Junior High. In the early 1970s, the school became the Contemporary Learning Center, operating until the 2010s. After three years in retirement, the Johnston name was reattached to a new junior high school at 10410 Manhattan in Meyerland. The purple and grey colors, the mascot, and the school song which called students to "be loyal to your cause," were revived, as well. It became a magnet for performing arts in 1985 and has since earned national recognition for courses in music, theatre, art, and dance. The Johnston name was removed in 2016 and the school renamed for the neighborhood in which it sits.[23]

JONES, ANSON E S

For roughly three quarters of a century, the Anson Jones school building was one of the most recognizable in Houston. Designed by top architect George E. Dickey and opened on April 8, 1893 at Elysian and Liberty (later Nance) in the Fifth Ward. The asymmetrical, three-story brick Richardson Romanesque landmark was part castle, part prison, and part Herman Munster's residence. This brick school was originally called the Elysian Street School.[24]

The Dickey building was not the first Elysian Street school on the site. A four-room frame structure had opened there about the start of the 1884-85 school year to replace the Fifth Ward School at Semmes and Providence that was "situated just upon the lines and in the switch-yards of several railroads, and surrounded by two or three sawmills." Almost immediately, the new Elysian Street school was in need of expansion. In less than five years, the situation became so dire that some fourth and fifth graders were sent to Hamilton Street School, and the first graders were divided into morning and afternoon sessions, attending school for only half the day. Two more rooms were added in 1890.[25]

The frame building was the site of an 1887 incident in which principal T.J. Patillo "flogged" a student named Joe Sick for badly misbehaving. When school ended, Sick's father and two friends were standing outside the building to give the same back to Patillo. Fortunately, City Constable Glass came to the rescue. Patillo was one of several top educators who oversaw Jones. Another was W.G. Smiley, and James B. Wolfe, head man there for 24 years, let favorite students ride his horse.[26]

The 1893 brick school came to be after the wooden Elysian Street School burned, forcing the students to attend classes at the City Market House for months. Superintendent W.S. Sutton dedicated the new brick building with an entreaty to avoid vandalism and act "as you would care for your home." It might have worked because for decades afterwards, school reports remarked on the cleanliness of Anson Jones School, a name that Elysian Street received about 1905. Opened with 12 rooms, additional class space was created in the basement within the first decade until it had 19 rooms by 1920.[27]

Anson Jones ES a few decades before Elysian Viaduct motorists sped past its classroom windows. HISD

Jones School became part of the growing Mexican American neighborhood, hosting a city-run community center where residents learned handicrafts, games, and staged Mexican plays. By the 1930s, the pupils were 96% Hispanic. In its final decade, many of the children came from the nearby Clayton Homes projects.[28]

In the 1950s, the elevated Elysian Street Viaduct was routed just a few feet outside of the school's upper stories, so close that passing classless motorists occasionally "flipped beer bottles through the classroom windows." Finally, in April 1967, the 449 students and 22 teachers boarded busses and moved to a new $700,000 Anson

Jones Elementary School at 2311 Canal that was trumpeted as a modern showplace. Though some of the children saw the sparkling new building as a "castle", at least a few children and teachers "blinked back tears."[29]

JONES, ANSON E S, BAYTOWN

The Anson Jones Elementary in Pelly opened in 1923, delayed until almost the end of the school year. The building had an Alamo-like facade and was the first brick school completed in GCCISD. When the opening finally took place that April, the children marched through the dirt streets from the "Barn" to their new digs. In 1938, Jones was the highest valued elementary in the district but with only six classrooms on six acres.[30]

JONES, J WILL E S

The old Charlotte Allen School, faced with new neighborhood demographics and overcrowding at Blackshear, was changed in 1956 by the HISD Board to an African American school honoring longtime director of music for the district's Black students. It operated as an elementary after serving briefly as an annex for Yates High School. It gained a 13-room annex and a courtyard in 1966 that reoriented the front of the school onto Stuart Street. The elementary operation at the location closed for good in the summer of 2009 after over a century.[31]

J. Will Jones: Music in Negro Schools

There are several giants of music who are closely related to Houston public schools, but the development of a music education program in the Black schools of HISD in the first place has one hero who stands above all others: Professor J. Will Jones. Born and raised in Texas, John William Jones' father, Henry, worked as a trained nurse in service to a private family, apparently earning enough to afford a decent education for his children. Records differ rather widely on Jones' birthdate, but sometime before the turn of the 20th century J. Will Jones was back in Houston, roughly 30 years old and living with his parents, after having trained at the School of Music at Allen University in Columbia, South Carolina, the New England Conservatory of Music in Boston, and Colorado University. Specifically, he had also studied piano and organ.[32]

In spite of his musical acumen, Jones was working as a railway mail clerk when Charles Atherton, principal of Colored High School, asked him to become the unofficial director of the high school glee club in 1904. Jones spent roughly eight weeks with the students, shaping a song program for the commencement and for other public appearances. He would continue in a similar role for 22 years before ever gaining a paycheck from the Houston school board. Principal Atherton, and his successor, James Ryan, compensated Jones from either the school's discretionary funds or out of their own pockets.

In 1926, E.E. Oberholtzer, superintendent of the newly formed HISD, named J. Will Jones Supervisor of Music in the Negro schools. He was faced with a challenging task. Music had never been part of the curriculum in the city's African American schools, so his first job was instructing the teachers how to instruct the students. Jones studied what the White schools were teaching and quickly figured out that modifications were needed; the Black schools didn't have the same facilities. At the start of his tenure, there were also some particularly harsh racial roadblocks. Only a few weeks after his appointment, Jones was ordered to avoid "new-fangled jazz numbers" and teach his charges "old plantation songs." Still, Jones persevered. [33]

Basing his instruction on a text and song book called the *Progressive Music Series*, Jones instituted an annual elementary songfest for the younger students beginning in 1933, a fifteen-day period at the start of December during which the youngsters put on programs at the four highest ranking Black schools: Washington, Yates, Wheatley, and Harper. In addition to a litany of relatively current songs from the book, every elementary school chorus was required to include one "Negro spiritual". For the high schools, Professor Jones utilized the same *Progressive Music Series* but added notation, progression, accent beats, and sketches of the composers' lives where he thought appropriate. The goal was, as the textbook preface read, to "grow a love for, and an intelligent appreciation of, the best in music."[34]

Jones enjoyed a long career and a lofty place among the Black schools of Houston. He died in 1946, having outlived his first wife and remarried to a fellow teacher. A few years after the integration of HISD, the school located on the site of the original Charlotte Allen School was renamed in Jones' honor. Perhaps his greater legacy is the parade of talented African American musicians that came out of HISD schools such as Arnett Cobb, Illinois Jacquet, Joe Sample and the Jazz Crusaders, and Archie Bell from Wheatley, Conrad Johnson and Jewel Brown from Yates, and many others all the way to Beyonce and Destiny's Child and the myriad of rap and hip hop stars from Houston.[35]

JUNKER'S COVE SCHOOL
See Middle Bayou

KAISER SCHOOL

Kaiser School was a small one-room building in the Klein area.[36]

KASHMERE GARDENS E S

Kashmere Gardens Elementary, opened at 4901 Lockwood in 1949, was a White neighborhood school serving a lower income area that lacked paved streets and city water. It gained regional and even some national notoriety when it became the first school in the district to desegregate, allowing seven Black first graders to enroll at the start of the 1960-61 school year even though a referendum on the issue had failed almost 2 to 1 the previous May. The pioneering four boys and three girls joined a student body that was predominantly White with a growing number of Hispanics, but were required to use a separate restroom located in the Kindergarten classroom.[37]

KATY SCHOOL

Katy, straddling Harris, Fort Bend, and Waller Counties, was originally known as Cane Island when it was a stop on the stage line between Harrisburg and San Felipe and later on the Texas Western Narrow Gauge Railway. It was when the Missouri, Kansas and Texas came through in the mid-1890s that settlement, largely by attracting Midwesterners, truly began to take off. The M-K-T is the source of one of the town's naming stories, the other being the wife of an early saloonkeeper. A school first opened in private homes, then by about 1898, a 32-foot square, frame school was built on Avenue A and Sixth Street. A brick schoolhouse opened in County District 42 with 98 students in 1909, and nine years later, the residents of Katy formed an independent school district. It was the second attempt at an ISD, the first positive vote in 1906 had been ruled unconstitutional because the district spanned multiple counties. The WWI-era vote spelled the end of small farm schools such as Dishman, Sills, Schlipf, and Cobb that dotted the area, much of it located outside Harris County.[38]

The brick school at Katy. HHRC

The original wooden building remained in use even after the brick school opened, housing the first and second grades for almost two decades until it was sold to a nearby church. The school had become a high school second class by 1912, and a new one-story elementary school wing was added in 1927. Shortly afterwards, the Stockdick and South Mayde rural schools were folded into Katy ISD. Two busses were added, one for a Harris County route and one in Waller County, and a gym was built in 1934. In the post-WWII years, the original Katy campus was abandoned in favor of other locations, and the old buildings were demolished with the gym being the last to go in 1988.

KATY COLORED SCHOOL

There was a small community of freed slaves in the area around today's Katy prior to the coming of the M'K-T Railroad in the 1890s, and more African American families arrived by the turn of the century, drawn by farming, ranching, and eventually, railroad jobs. A one-room schoolhouse for Blacks was opened near Cane Island Creek south of the town, and around the time Katy ISD came into being, a small building was erected across from Antioch Baptist Church on Danover Road. The school, run for over two decades by Odessa Punchard and two other teachers, served roughly 50 to 60 pupils in grades one through eight. It was replaced by a new structure on the same spot in 1953.[39]

KATY H S

When principal Minnie Bowers of Katy added two years of high school classes before the 1911-1912 school year, the upper classmen were still sharing a new brick building with the grammar school children. Brookshire began sending its high schoolers to Katy in 1927, the same year that a new elementary school wing was added at Katy campus. Addicks followed suit with its high school students in 1948. It swelled the enrollment, bringing the number of pupils in the high school to 123 by 1950, including 28 seniors. In those post-WWII years, with W.K. Russell as the high school principal, classes in vocational agriculture and homemaking were included with the academic basics. Football, for which Katy is so famous, came to campus in 1939, and three years later, the mascot was changed from the Kangaroos to the Tigers.[40]

KENNING SCHOOL

Kenning School, known by some as Wilson School, operated in the 1930s and 40s near the Crosby railroad section house, in a building provided at the expense of owner R.C.J. Kenning. Pupils above fifth grade moved to Barrett School in 1940, and the rest followed in 1947.[41]

KIDDOO ACADEMY

General Joseph Barr Kiddoo served as assistant administrator of the Freedmen's Bureau in Texas for less than a year. Though headquartered in Galveston, the school that bore his name was in Houston, and it lasted well beyond the January 1867 end of his tenure in the Lone Star State. Miss Hattie Daggett, one of the two missionary women overseeing some 130 students at Kiddoo School, wrote home that "our schools are large and flourishing beyond our expectations." The *Telegraph* commented two years later, however, on what they saw as the frustrating reality of a situation in which two young, idealistic women had to wrangle that many young children plus a "few old enough to be teaching instead of getting taught." The reporter opined that "they are not able to do so much work satisfactorily for such a vast number of young people who require the utmost and most unremitting attention in imparting to them the elements of a rudimentary education."[42]

General Joseph Kiddoo. Library of Congress

KINGSLEY SCHOOL

Margaret Hamacher Kingsley opened a private school for pre-school children at her home, 790 Elwood, in 1926. Soon after, she added grades one and two. After Mrs. Kingsley's death in 1936, the operation, with enrollment fluctuating between 14 and 40 pupils was taken over by Mrs. J.M. Finck.[43]

KINKAID SCHOOL

Houston High graduate Margaret Hunter had been teaching at Hawthorne School in First Ward when she wed William Kinkaid, and promptly lost her job due to the Houston school's prohibition against married teachers. She responded by opening a kindergarten in her dining room. After a two-year hiatus during which she gave birth to her second child, Kinkaid reopened in her two-story home at San Jacinto and Elgin in 1906. Eventually, the family moved out, giving the home over to the school completely, but by 1923, with 100 students in six grades being taught by ten people, the well-to-do parents began exploring options for a more permanent campus. A board of trustees was formed and were a true who's who of Houston business: R. L. Blaffer, Chairman of the Humble Oil and Refining Company; E. L. Neville of the First National Bank; Burke Baker of Seaboard Life Insurance Company; H. E. Wiess, President of the Humble Oil and Refining Company; and Will Clayton, founder of Anderson-Clayton Cotton Brokers.[44]

The new directors raised $175,000, and a new five-acre campus with a Spanish style one-story building opened on the south side of Richmond at Graustark. Though it was nicely equipped with 25 classrooms, there was not a proper lunchroom. Students ate outdoors in good weather and at their desks otherwise. Athletics were encouraged along with academics and other extra-curricular activities, but the large tree in the middle of the school's football field was a great embarrassment to the coach. One weekend, he and the school's caretaker cut it down, and though he waited to be fired, Mrs. Kinkaid never spoke a word about it.

By 1934, Kinkaid had added tenth and eleventh grades, but class size was kept low and standards for teachers high, attracting the children of many of Houston's elite. One who did not choose to leave public school in favor of Kinkaid was Dr. Denton Cooley who adamantly told his mother that he would remain with his friends rather than "go to that school with all those sissy boys." In spite of that, the school prospered. Margaret Kinkaid remained at the helm until 1951, retiring shortly before her death. The school moved to its present forty-acre campus in Piney Point Village in the fall of 1957. In the history of the institution's first 115 years, while it developed a national reputation as an elite day school, Kinkaid had only five headmasters.[45]

Study hall at Kinkaid circa 1950. Courtesy Kinkaid School

Teacher Marriages

Kinkaid School, the oldest secular private school in Houston, traces its founding story to the fact that Margaret Kinkaid loved teaching but was unemployable due to her status as a married woman. The city schools' Annual Report for 1904, the year of Kinkaid's opening, included Rule 11 regarding teacher employment: "No teacher shall resign without giving fifteen days' written notice to the Superintendent, in default of which all compensation for that length of time shall be forfeited. The marriage of any lady teacher during the scholastic year shall be considered a resignation and cancellation of her contract without further notice."

The vast majority of school districts around the nation forbade female teachers from marrying or "other unseemly behavior." By the late 1930s, when the popular young Alvin schoolteacher Lesta King got married, that district dismissed her the moment her transgression was discovered. At the start of the following term, however, she found a job in HISD which had dropped its objection to married women teachers after a need for instructors overtook any moral concerns about what a fully life-informed woman might convey to her charges. Mrs. King went on to enjoy a decades long career in Houston schools.[46]

KIRBY SCHOOL
See Cage

KLEIN E S
After the Rural High School No. 1 building burned at the start of 1940, the elementary and high school received separate buildings on the same campus.

KLEIN H S
The community of Klein is named for Adam and Fredericka Klein who eloped from their native Obendorf, Germany at the start of the 1850s, ending up in northwest Harris County. From the small start around a store and homestead, today the name graces a school district that educates over 50,000 children. The original Klein High School began in 1928 as Rural High School Number 1, formed when County Districts 1, 2, 3, 9, and 47 merged to provide a high school opportunity for 350 White students in the area. African American students in the new district attended the Kohrville Colored School which went through grade nine.

In February 1938, residents voted to create Klein ISD, and the school received the name of Klein High. The original consolidated school building burned on January 3, 1940 and was rebuilt as a high school and an elementary school at the same site on Spring-Cypress Road near Steubner-Airline, behind the location of today's Klein ISD administration offices. The building had electric lights and bubbling drinking fountains, but no telephones in the years prior to WWII. The Bears moved to a new home at Louetta and Steubner-Airline to start the school year in 1963.[47]

Rural High School No. 1 in Klein

KOLBE SCHOOL
See Big Cypress

KOHRVILLE COLORED SCHOOL
The community of Kohrville is near Highway 249 and Spring-Cypress Road. It draws its name from a White German postmaster and store owner named Paul Kohrmann who arrived in the 1870s, but there was a population of freed slaves, many moving from Alabama and Mississippi, prior to that time. These families had settled in the Bottoms, an area along Cypress Creek, but when frequent flooding became a problem the community moved closer to Boudreaux Road. The initial school was on land donated by Willis Woods, and it remained in the Bottoms necessitating some children to walk as much as five or six miles each way for the three to five months term of school.[48]

County District 1 first built a schoolhouse for White students, but the Kohrville Colored School was a county school by 1886. By the 1890s, the school was located at the present intersection of Spring-Cypress and Kohrville-Huffsmith Roads. When the White schools of the Klein area were consolidated into Rural High School #1 in 1928, the plan was to make the students move to the old building in the town of Louetta, though eventually the building came to the Kohrville site instead, later being portioned into two rooms. The final Kohrville Negro School, roughly 24' x 60' in size, was constructed in 1948 and continued to be used until integration took hold in Klein ISD in the mid-1960s. After three decade's use as a community center and then as a storage building, the Kohrville School was moved to the Klein Museum complex in spring of 2000.⁴⁹

KOHRVILLE SCHOOL

The Kohrville community along present day Highway 249 derives its name from German immigrants Paul and Agnes Tautenhahn Kohrmann who opened a general store there in the 1870s. County District 1 had a one-room school for the White students in operation before 1884. The school continued operating as a small rural operation until all the area school were consolidated in 1928 into Rural High School #1 which became Klein ISD.⁵⁰

KOTHMAN SCHOOL

Kothman School, on the south side of Louetta not far west of today's I-45, was operating at least by 1892. Named for Henry Kothman, it was one of two schools in County District 3, one of the districts that was combined into Rural HS No. 1 in 1928.⁵¹

KRAHL SCHOOL

Following almost a decade of teaching at Longfellow and Dow schools in Houston, Mary Lighfoot married W.F. Krahl, disqualifying her from that career. Beginning in the 1890s, she then operated a private school in her home for children in the first five grades. Teachers later remarked on her modern methods at the little school that moved from Chenevert to Dennis Street and then to San Jacinto, saying she taught phonics, though she did not use that terminology. The school closed after Mrs. Krahl's death in 1917.⁵²

KRENEK SCHOOL

The first attempt at building a school on Krenek land outside Crosby was destroyed by the 1900 storm before students could even being classes. A second building fared better, sitting at what is now Krenek Road and Bohemian Hall Road. It was merged into Crosby School in fall of 1925.⁵³

KRUSE SCHOOL

See Pasadena School

Schools L

LA ESCUELA MEXICANA "HIDALGO"

The Hidalgo Escuela Mexicana was a private, tuition-based school that operated in Magnolia Park for at least a brief while in the latter 1920s. Unlike the public schools, this institution was not as adamant that students discard their Mexican customs and Americanize.[1]

LA PORTE COLORED SCHOOL

The town of La Porte was sneaking up on 20 years old when a school was formed for the handful of African American children who lived in the area. In 1909, such an institution began operating at the Black Baptist church on the north side of town. A few years later, the Methodist church in that neighborhood sold a building on North Fifth Street to the newly formed La Porte ISD, and that served as the city's Black school until 1943. Viola DeWalt taught grades one through six in the single room for over three decades. The two-room building that was moved next door to the other small schoolhouse was originally the school in Morgan's Point, then had served as the first and second grade classrooms at the White La Porte School. A new brick school named in honor of Ms. DeWalt opened in La Porte in 1953, serving through eighth grade. It operated until La Porte ISD was integrated in 1963. The two frame buildings on North Fifth were still in existence in the early 21st century, and were being preserved.[2]

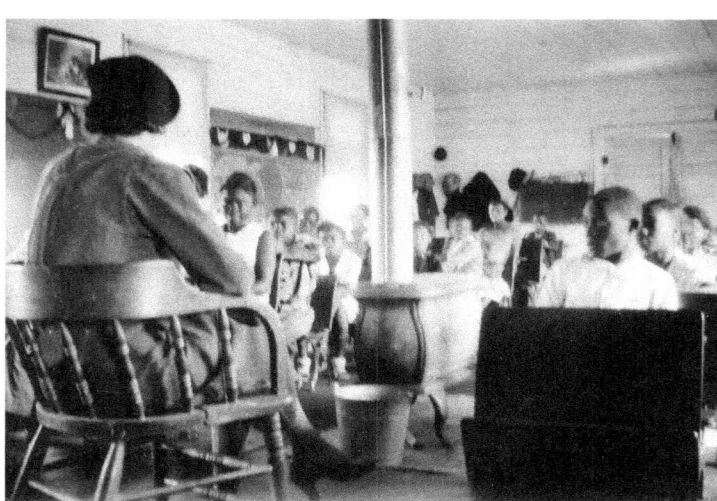
La Porte Colored School that became DeWalt. HCPL

LA PORTE E S

In 1940, when the entire student population of La Porte ISD was less than 750, a one-story elementary school opened next to the three-story school building at Broadway and C Streets. The older building continued to house the higher grades. An additional wing was added to the 1940 building eight years later. A modern La Porte ES sits at the southern end of the old school complex today.[3]

LA PORTE SCHOOL

La Porte began as a real estate venture by a group of Denver businessmen in 1892 and grew quickly. The city was incorporated the same year, and a railroad from downtown Houston was chartered, as well. Also that first year, Bay View School was replaced in the county treasurer's ledgers by La Porte, though no money was expended until 1893 when a building at Main and Fourth Streets belonging to A.B. Prince was loaned for school use. After three years, the city built a two-story, four-room school at the corner of Second and C, and it was the seat of education in the town for two decades. It started small, though soon the curriculum included two years of high school work, and facilities sported a library plus maps and a globe. By the end of its run, the rooms were so overcrowded, that some of the younger students went to class in the Christian Church one street over. In 1916, La Porte ISD opened a three-story brick building on Broadway and C to serve all grades. A portion of that building still remains today.[4]

The Prince Building in La Porte where classes met. La Porte Bay Area Heritage Society

LA PORTE H S

La Porte was offering high school courses in the early 1900s, but the students shared a building with all other grades, first in the old downtown, then after 1916, at the three-story building constructed at Broadway and C Street. The top floor was an auditorium that held up to 500 people, over four times the total number of pupils in the district. In 1943, when a hurricane passed directly up Galveston Bay with no advance warning due to wartime security concerns, the top two floors were damaged so badly that it was rebuilt as a single-story. By that time, the elementary grades had a nearby building of their own, so the remaining portion of the 1916 structure was for the high school and junior high only. When WWII ended, a new high school building and a gym/auditorium were constructed next to the original school. Three years later, a new junior high went up, and the 1916 first floor began duty as a cafeteria. It was the first time that all three levels of school for White students in La Porte had their own buildings. The present location of La Porte High opened on Fairmont Parkway in 1959, and the junior high took over the old campus.[5]

The three-story La Porte high school. La Porte Bay Area Heritage Society

LAIRD SCHOOL

Laird was re-chartered under the new school law of 1876 with A. Laird as one of the trustees. Nothing else was found.[6]

LAMAR E S, BAYTOWN

The large bond issue of 1929 in GCCISD provided for Lamar Elementary, and it came online a few years later with eight rooms. Faced with "overflowing conditions" for its 377 students, the school received additional land in 1950 for an expansion. Today, a modern Lamar campus is located at 816 N. Pruett in Baytown.[7]

LAMAR, MIRABEAU B. H S

For many years, a local joke quipped that River Oaks Boulevard had a country club at each end. To be sure, the high school that opened at 3325 Westheimer in 1937 had roughly 1,300 students not only from River Oaks but from Bellaire, West University, Montrose, and Southampton, neighborhoods that were largely upper middle class and better. Even the architectural design was done by a sort of local dream team, led by John Staub, known for dozens of River Oaks houses, and including Harry Payne, Louis Glover, and Lamar Q. Cato who, with Alfred Finn, would go on to design several Art Deco buildings on the U of H campus. Though Kenneth Franzheim's name appears in places, he is not noted in files as having done any work. In a large irony, the mascot chosen for the school named after the Texas Republic's chief advocate of native Indian extermination, was the Redskins. That was changed to a less politically charged Texans in the 2010s.[8]

Lamar boasts scores of notable ex-students, especially in the arenas of entertainment and literature, including Paula Prentiss, Robert Foxworth, Jaclyn Smith, Tommy Tune, Francie Mendenhall, Gene R. Wolfe, Kelly Rowland, Tommy Sands, Lauren Anderson, Linda Ellerbee, Lisa Hartman-Black, and James Lee Burke. It also has one of the most active alumni groups of any high school in America, an organization that raised $3 million of non-HISD money, led by Ned Holmes, to renovate the school with a special emphasis on the well-known auditorium with the distinctive relief map of Texas on its outer wall. Today the diverse campus is on better financial footing than most Houston high schools, thanks to booster organizations and alumni. With an enrollment that once topped 3,400, it is one of the largest high schools in the state. Lamar has been home to an International Baccalaureate magnet program since 1982.[9]

The Lamar Redskins beat the Odessa Bronchos at Rice Stadium to bring the 1953 football title to Houston. The star player (with football) was All-State tailback Walter Fondren III who went on play at the University of Texas. HHRC, Houston Post Collection

Houston Public School Stadium

Houston school officials were noting the inadequacy of athletic facilities as early as 1912 when Superintendent Horn wrote this: "The High School athletic work is not one-tenth of what it ought to be, or of what it could readily be made if we had a suitable athletic field. The football team has to rent a field which is inconvenient and unsuited; the baseball team has no place for practicing or for holding its games; the track team has no place for its meets, and its place for practicing is hardly better than none."[10]

After the city was gifted with Hermann Park, which opened in 1914, Horn angled to place an athletic field there, writing: "It is to be greatly hoped that in the development of Hermann Park by our city this special need will not be overlooked." There were some baseball fields located in the far southern reach of Hermann Park that would eventually become Texas Medical Center land, but it did not adequately meet the district's needs. Instead, the Houston schools continued to be a renter until 1928.[11]

In that year, HISD athletics purchased the old West End Park from the St. Louis Cardinals when that baseball club's Houston Buffs farm team moved to the new Buff Stadium along what is now the Gulf Freeway. Local high school teams had been playing there for years, but the benefits of being a property owner instead of a tenant came as a welcome financial relief.

School officials still wanted a proper stadium for its most popular sport, football. On September 19, 1930, just as another season was getting underway, Houston newspapers ran an artist's conception of just such a venue located on the northeast quadrant of Memorial and Waugh in what is today Spotts Park. The seating bowl was a perfect half oval, truncated behind the middle of each end zone. A track circled the football field, and a large parking lot had multiple entrances off Memorial Drive. Committees continued to study the idea through at least 1933 with both HISD and the City of Houston flirting with this proposed municipal stadium. The timing and realities of the Great Depression, however, ensured that the first shovel of dirt was never turned.[12]

In the late 1930s, after watching federal stimulus money used locally for projects from the Coliseum and Music Hall to the San Jacinto Monument to Houston's new City Hall, some HISD power brokers were inspired to again talk about construction of a high school athletic stadium and fieldhouse, this time near the new southeast side campus of the University of Houston. "Holger Jeppesen, school board member and chairman of the school athletic committee, has promoted the project of a high school stadium for several years, and his efforts apparently have met with success," the *Chronicle* announced.[13]

The HISD Stadium and Fieldhouse under construction. Courtesy Fretz Construction

It was HISD under Superintendent Oberholtzer that had started the university in the first place, and in March 1940, they spent a little over $75,000 to purchase roughly 58 acres of heavily wooded land from the Settegast Estate. Adding another small parcel shortly afterward, the district had a site that today is bounded by Scott, Wheeler, Holman, and Cullen, the latter then being known as St. Bernard.[14]

Armed with a loan of $550,000 from the U.S. government's Reconstruction Finance Corporation, the wheels began to turn. Longtime HISD architectural collaborator Harry D. Payne was tapped to design, and Houston's

Fretz Construction was hired with an original target date set for the start of football season in 1941. It would not happen. In July of that year, Payne told the press that they were at least two months behind schedule due to unusually heavy summer rains. That was followed by a late-September hurricane and the Japanese bombing of Pearl Harbor.[15]

The football stadium and the multi-story fieldhouse were constructed simultaneously. As Fretz worked on the stadium, Woodruff Construction built the basketball facility that sat just beyond the south end zone. Both had Art Deco design elements, and the stadium towers that sat parallel with the goal lines would prove to be a landmark feature of the campus.

The inaugural football game took place on September 18, 1942, and the Lamar Redskins ripped Dallas' Adamson High School by a score of 26-7 in front of a capacity crowd of 14,500. Papers noted that the seating capacity could be expanded by closing in the end zones, something that did not happen until the American Football League's Houston Oilers arrived in 1960. The stadium's largest ever attendance was for the AFL title game in 1962. One of the more interesting events ever held at the Public School Athletic Stadium took place in the opening months when the War Department staged a five night demonstration to give Houstonians, through drills and mock battles, a glimpse of the American war effort.[16]

In 1958, HISD renamed the football venue Jeppesen Stadium in honor of the man who had pushed so hard for its construction. In 1980, now owned by the university instead of HISD, the stadium was renamed once again, this time for Corbin Robertson who had worked and donated to renovate it on behalf of the Cougars.

The Fieldhouse was demolished in 1996 to make room for an expanded football scoreboard area, and the Houston Public School Athletic Stadium, by then judged to be a decrepit relic, fell to the wrecking ball in December 2012. The Cougars' current football stadium stands on the same site.[17]

LAMAR E S

Mirabeau Lamar, the second President of the Republic of Texas, first got his name on a Houston school that was opened in 1909 to relieve dire overcrowding at the Fifth Ward's Sherman Elementary. It replaced previous rented buildings on Freeman Street and Montgomery Avenue. The first principal was Nona Leigh Ammerman, sister to County Judge A.E. Ammerman who would also go on to be Houston mayor. Together with the Mother's Club and a dozen or so good faculty members, she created a school that received frequent commendation for its cleanliness and efficiency, all the way down to the flowers blooming by the doors.

Crowding was soon an issue at Lamar, and a wooden temporary building was brought in as enrollment topped 570. Still, principal Ammerman went the extra mile, overseeing a Saturday class for "backward pupils" and offering a supervised playground seven days a week. She retired in 1928 to care for her ailing mother.[18]

Lamar ES in the sunshine. HHRC

A new Lamar went up in 1963. Eventually, Lamar and Lee, the latter of which had opened to relieve overcrowding at Lamar, were replaced by the new Kettleson Elementary next door as part of HISD's Rebuild 2002 program.

In the early 21st century, picturesque old oak trees still circled the block of green space bounded by Quitman, Chestnut, Gentry, and Henry. They had been planted around what had been a barren campus when Lamar Elementary opened there. Andrew Jackson Maxey, who moved to Houston to work on the Main Street Viaduct, had taken a job as custodian at Lamar ES where he helped plant the young trees, part of efforts that would earn him accolades as best janitor at a White school in 1913. Eventually Maxey bought three duplexes along Gentry Street, one for himself and two that he rented to single teachers at the school. His grandson, Orie Clark, himself an HISD teacher, recalled playing on the twisting, turning fire escape slides at the old schoolhouse.[19]

LANE, ELLEN B SCHOOL

Lane School, which sat at Aldine Bender and Aldine Westfield, originated with a bond to consolidate four county schools that passed on 18 June 1932. It was the town's first attempt at a high school, and the two-story building opened in 1933 with 12 classrooms and an auditorium serving grades one through nine. Grades 10 and 11 were added about a year later. Previously high school students from Aldine had to go into Houston to Jeff Davis. Presumably they paid. Lane was at capacity when it opened, and records seem to suggest that the high school campus moved to the SMN Marrs site in 1934 and that a class of nine graduated in May 1934. The name later changed to Aldine HS and was at another location by 1948.

LANGFORD SCHOOL

Canadian-born Anna Langford, a single woman in her 50s, ran a small private school from 1905 to 1912 at 2211 Providence in Fifth Ward.[20]

LANGSTON SCHOOL

Second Ward Colored School began under the revised public school law by renting the Mt. Zion Baptist Church on German Street to the east of downtown. Seventy-two pupils were noted by Superintendent Smith in 1877. The principal, and one of the two teachers, was Charles E. Johnson, a young South Carolina-born White man who was boarding with a nearby Black family in 1880. The enrollment at the rented church soon topped 100, and before 1887, the city had purchased a building at what would become 2317 Canal when German street was renamed during WWI. The top grade at the school rose from fourth to seventh just after the turn of the century. Among the teachers at Second Ward Colored was Pauline Gray, the wife of prominent attorney J. Vance Lewis.[21]

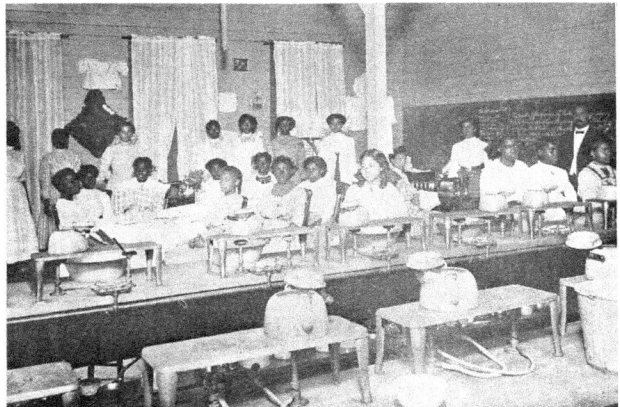

Cooking class at Langston ES in early 1900s. HISD

Around 1902, the school was renamed to honor John Mercer Langston, a mixed race man whom many believe to have been, in 1855, the first African American to win elective office in the United States. He was also an abolitionist, community organizer and, briefly, the first Black Congressman from Virginia. The school newly named for him hit a peak enrollment past 450 students during the first three decades of the century, all crowded into what eventually became a dozen rooms in the old frame building. It was, at times, the largest enrollment of any Black school in the city. A new brick Langston rose courtesy of a 1920s bond election, but a decade later industrialization and the building of Navigation Blvd. had wiped out much of the African American neighborhood that ran along Buffalo Bayou. Student population at Langston was only 127 with three teachers in 1934. The school closed, but the Langston name was moved across the bayou to Brackenridge in 1955. The old property on Canal Street was listed for sale by HISD in February 1963.[22]

LANIER J H S

Of all the renaming controversies that embroiled HISD in 2016, perhaps none of them was more bitter than that over Sidney Lanier Middle School that opened with 34 classrooms at the corner of Westheimer and Woodhead in 1926. Lanier, the man, was derided by name change advocates as a racist Confederate, though the truth is that he was known in life as a teacher and poet who "rejoiced" at the end of slavery. What was not mentioned during the debates was that the school was originally slated to honor Abraham Lincoln until loud protests by surviving Confederates and their descendants got the name changed to something that would "be loyal to our own heroes of the South." The nation's political savior would not have his name on a Houston school for decades, and then it would be on a segregated African American building.[23]

The library at Lanier JHS shortly after opening. HISD

Miss Pearl Tallman was the first principal at Sidney Lanier, and the "silk stocking" junior high that served the Montrose neighborhoods and River Oaks was a showplace from the start. The mascot was the Purple Pup, and the school newspaper that bore the same name was printed with purple ink. The Hogg family donated some of the oak, cypress, and pecan trees that shaded the new campus. A decade after its opening, the enrollment hit 1,600, and the school had ballooned to 64 classrooms, a science lab, two home economics laboratories, two art rooms, two music rooms, a library, gymnasium, swimming pool, and an auditorium that held one thousand people. Among the dozens of famous Purple Pups are Texas Governor Mark White, heart surgery pioneer Denton Cooley, newsman extraordinaire Walter Cronkite, journalist Linda Ellerbee, Houston Mayor Fred Hofheinz, and Astrodome architect S.I. Morris.[24]

Starting the Vanguard program for gifted students in 1973, Lanier continued its reputation as a public school with the academics of a private institution over which Houston parents competed to send their children. The building itself underwent an extensive restoration at the start of the 21st century. Wood was restored, brass and marble repolished. The auditorium was rehabilitated to possess "the charm of a 19th-century Viennese opera house." And in a bit of almost unremarked irony, Sidney Lanier's name was replaced in 2016 by that of former Houston Mayor Bob Lanier, a man who provoked many controversies of his own by torpedoing the city's best chance at a comprehensive rail plan, profiting from the Savings & Loan Crisis and highway rerouting, and being the key figure in the destruction, or gentrification, of Freedmen's Town, Houston's most historic African American neighborhood.[25]

LANTRIP E S

Dora Lantrip was the principal of Eastwood Elementary School when it opened at 100 Telephone Road in 1916. She had been teaching sixth and seventh grade arithmetic in Houston schools for some years. The school she took over was a Spanish style collection of buildings done on the cottage plan, something that had been tried at Montrose Elementary just prior. William A. Wilson, who developed the Eastwood neighborhood, donated five acres to the city for school use, knowing a gleaming new elementary helped sell houses to young families. Even as the school opened, additional cottage units were being added, and by 1920, it offered 14 rooms. Enrollment at Eastwood Elementary peaked at well over 800 pupils around 1930.[26]

The original beauty of Lantrip ES. HISD

Over the next quarter century, the school took on the personality of its principal. During WWI, Lantrip had the front yard planted in flowers and the backyard in vegetables, but it was her inquisitive wanderlust that had the biggest impact. Showing an interest in travel since childhood, she spanned the world during her tenure at Eastwood. Sometimes combining her trips with a chance to study at a faraway university, Lantrip visited Peru, Brazil, Russia, Australia, Paraguay, Alaska, and destinations in Europe, Asia, and Africa. With each trip, she brought back souvenirs and costumes, teaching about her experiences and creating a museum of sorts that lined the halls of the school.[27]

Dora Lantrip retired in 1942, and after her death in 1951, the campus was renamed in her honor. The historic school underwent a major redo in the early 2000s, with much of the beautiful original structure being demolished, but not all. The main building was restored and other architectural elements, including a Spanish style fireplace donated by Ima Hogg in the 1920s, were incorporated into the new construction. Today Lantrip offers an environmental science magnet program, echoing the plantings that adorned the campus a century ago.[28]

The Story Hour Movement

The Annual Report of Houston schools of 1907 – 08 was effusive in praise of a national educational trend that had taken hold in the Bayou City: "The story hour movement in Houston has grown from a small beginning, three years ago, when a few children were gathered at the library on Saturday mornings at 10 o'clock. They came eagerly, week after week, to listen to stories held as a precious heritage by the human race, and which have been repeated by one generation to another in all lands, among all tribes, since the world of men began. Only stories of the highest value were desired, and this lofty standard continuing is the ideal also of the Story Hour League. Houston holds the proud record of the most successful city in Texas in the story hour movement, and inquiries have frequently been made of those interested here, by teachers, librarians and club women elsewhere, as to the Houston way."

A dozen or more Houston elementary school teachers stepped up to organize story hours at their campuses which included Sherman, Lubbock, Reagan, Merkel, Beauchamp Springs, Dow, Anson Jones, Rusk, and Austin. Another story hour was set up at the DePelchin Faith Home. Julia Ideson, the city's top public librarian, held sessions at the new Carnegie Library & Lyceum downtown and worked with school officials, and volunteers giving "freely of their time and energy" all worked toward the goal of holding a story hour at "each public school building every week during the coming season."[29]

Among the leading advocates of Story Hour Leagues across America was the imminent 19th century scholar Charles Elliot Norton of Harvard, who penned this call to action: "To make good reading more attractive than bad... Selections should be specially chosen with reference to the culture of the imagination. The imagination is the supreme intellectual faculty, and yet it is of all the one which receives least attention in our common systems of education."

A committee of several teachers along with librarian Ideson arrived unanimously at a list of fifty stories. Most of the selections came from books such as Grimm's Household Stories, Hans Christian Andersen, Brown's Book of Saints and Friendly Beasts, or Lang's Fairy Books which were differentiated by colors of crimson, brown, green, red, pink, yellow, orange, or blue. There were stories drawn from Russian, Spanish, and Italian, plus enduring classics including: Aladdin, or The Wonderful Lamp, Ali Baba and the Forty Thieves, The Elves and the Shoemaker, Hansel and Gretel, The Pied Piper, Rapunzel, Rumper-Stilts-Kin, and Snow White and Rose Red. Other titles are less known today such as: How the Hermit Helped Win the King's Daughter, Jack, My Hedgehog, Pinkel, the Thief, St. Launomaur's Cow, and St. Rigobert's Dinner.

LEE'S SCHOOL

Lee was one of the original county schools registered under the new Texas Constitution's public school laws in 1876. Part of District 8, Lee changed to Hargrave's by the mid-1880s and perhaps had a series of name changes before the Lee moniker disappeared by 1894.[30]

LEE, ROBERT E E S

Lee Elementary opened in the 2100 block of South Street at Henry, next to a vast expanse of green space near the Southern Pacific Hospital, in 1919 to serve a portion of the Fifth Ward. The single-story Spanish style school with eight classrooms cost just over $50,000. Within the year, officials were asking for four more classrooms and an auditorium to be added, and some of that was achieved in the middle 1920s. The campus closed in 2002, and after sitting empty for a decade and threatened with demolition, Lee was saved by Harris County. Operated by Neighborhood Centers, Inc., today the lovely building alongside I-45 is the Leonel Castillo Community Center providing a variety of services to the Near Northside.[31]

Lee ES on Houston's near northside. HISD

LEE, ROBERT E H S, BAYTOWN

Oil was booming in the 1920s-era Tri-Cities, specifically the growing Humble Oil Refinery, and the taxes the companies paid into the Goose Creek School District meant new and expanded buildings. The crown jewel of that growth was the Art Deco and Spanish Harry Payne-designed Lee High School that opened at 1809 Market Street in Baytown in the fall of 1928. The school took over as the high school for all three of the communities that would later become Baytown, with an auditorium that served as a center for civic activities. The Ganders athletic teams became a rallying point for the entire area. It was a large campus on 14 acres with 40 classrooms by the end of the 1930s. Beginning in 1934, Lee Junior College operated night classes on the campus until they gained their own home in the early 1950s. The main building fell victim to arson in April 1987 but was rebuilt in the original style.[32]

The rebuilt Baytown Lee. Mike Vance photo

LILY WHITE SCHOOL

Lily White was a Black community often described as being located on the Missouri, Kansas and Texas Railroad Line at Post Oak Road, though the village pre-dated the 1893 stretch of railroad by at least a decade and a half. The true location of the cluster of homes and the church, cemetery, and school was closer to modern Westview Drive, a tiny easternmost portion of which was originally Lily White Road. The small African American school at Lily White was a community center, used as the site for political barbeques in the mid-1880s for Black and White voters who also used the occasion for dancing and target shooting. Martin Stewart taught at the school for much of the late 19th century earning $29 a month for teaching a student population that sometimes numbered less than a dozen African American children. Among the teachers that followed him at the District 27 school was Mabel Wesley. The segregated Lily White School continued operations after the formation of Spring Branch ISD, and the teacher used a district-owned station wagon to pick up and drop off some of her students every school day. The school sessions continued until at least the mid-1960s.[33]

LITTLE CYPRESS SCHOOL
See Winkler's

LITTLE GREEN'S BAYOU COLORED SCHOOL
Not much is known about this single-room school that operated in District 16 along with the Clinton schools and a few others in the mid-1890s.[34]

LITTLE YORK SCHOOL
The busy north Houston thoroughfare of the same name originally led to the small village of Little York and is the only remnant of the town. The rural community was centered near where Little York Road intersects with Airline Drive. It had been established in the late 19th century and was surrounded by truck farms raising fruits and vegetables to sell in Houston. Many of the small farmers were Sicilian immigrants. By 1910, the school there was big enough for two teachers, and by the WWI yet another had been added at the brick building in District 25. Little York School was still in operation in 1959.[35]

LOCKETT J H S
See Booker T. Washington HS

LOCKHART E S
The mid-century modern building at 3501 Southmore was built as Beth Yeshurun Educational Building in 1949 by Finger and Rustay architects. It was later repurposed into an HISD school.[36]

LOMAX SCHOOL
Today Lomax School Road in La Porte, northwest of downtown, runs from North H to North P Street and a Lomax Elementary School carries on the name after a decades long gap. The community had been started by R.A. Lomax in 1895, only a few years after neighboring La Porte, and it had its own one-room school in County

District 13, serving grades one through eight. When La Porte ISD opened its three-story school in 1916, students at Lomax were bussed there, yet the Lomax schoolhouse was still used as a voting place in 1922. Whether any classes were being held there is unknown. The community itself was absorbed into its bigger neighbor in the 1940s, but in the 1950s, residents voted to de-annex. The area became part of La Porte once and for all in 1980.[37]

LONGFELLOW E S

When Superintendent Smith made his visits to several local schools on opening day 1877 with a reporter in tow, the Third Ward School, under the care of Misses C.G. Forshey and M.T. Reddish, had roughly 100 students from first to sixth grades. Like the vast majority of city schools, the quarters were rented. Within five years, it had relocated to another rented building on the west side of Austin between Lamar and Dallas, but the space was cramped. Kate Albert had 108 first and second graders packed into her room. Jennie Rowlett had 40 third graders. The answer for this and other Houston ward schools was a new large city-owned building. The new school in Third Ward, christened to honor the poet Henry Wadsworth Longfellow, opened at Bell and Chartres around Thanksgiving 1888. It had six classrooms plus a "bell room" that was soon converted to class space.[38]

Wood frame Longfellow School. HISD

Teachers Albert and Rowlett were among those moving into the new quarters. In addition to the students from Austin Street, others transferred from Taylor and from among grade school children who had been placed in the high school. An underground cistern supplied drinking water at Longfellow, transferred to six buckets with shared dippers. A large central stove gave heat for over 330 pupils. An annex was added to the growing school in 1903, but it was still crowded with close to 500 pupils. By 1907, when Frank Black was principal at Longfellow, the district reports were regularly calling for a new building to replace the remaining 1880s frame structures serving the White students. A fire at Rusk moved it to the top of the group, but Longfellow soon got its turn. The new Longfellow building which, combined with the grounds, cost roughly $90,000, opened down the street at 2209 Chartres at Webster during the 1912-13 school year. It was roughly a duplicate of Crockett

Elementary, and employed fourteen regular teachers. The Mothers Club helped with the new campus by fitting out a teachers' restroom and planting trees around the yard. Some Chamber of Commerce-sponsored seeds given to the pupils helped create a garden worthy of note.[39]

A 1920s bond issue brought more rooms to Longfellow utilizing an addition and the ground level floor which was called the basement since most classrooms were up the large front steps. A cafeteria was placed on the basement level, as well. Longfellow had a nurse's office, but not an everyday nurse, so emergencies sometimes fell to the teachers. That included one 1940s occurrence in which a girl's finger was accidentally cut off. Teachers put it in ice and drove her to the nearby St. Joseph's Hospital.[40]

By the time Lavinia Namendorf was principal in the late 1930s and into the 40s, the neighborhood around Longfellow had declined into poverty, changed ethnically in the segregated district, and gained more industrial buildings. The school finally closed, but the Longfellow name was revived, living on at a new building in Braeswood Place, west of the Astrodome.[41]

Polio

Poliomyelitis had been plaguing humanity since before recorded time, but little was known of it. The first epidemic outbreaks, events that filled every parent's heart with aching panic, would not become commonplace until around the start of the 20th century, jumping to prominence with a 1916 occurrence in Brooklyn that took over 2,000 young lives.

The newfound awareness of the disease might have been a contributing factor to a major civic improvement. Water chlorination on a citywide basis began in Jersey City and Chicago in 1908 with Youngstown, Ohio being the first to inject chlorine gas into the water just two years later. When the federal government set maximum bacterial standards for drinking water, it dramatically increased the practice nationwide. By the 1930s, drinking water-borne diseases in the U.S. were almost eliminated. Also eliminated from water supplies were diluted amounts of the poliovirus that might have allowed infants to develop an immunity. As an ironic result of the better water, the frequency of polio outbreaks may have increased, with the average age for contracting the disease rising from the first year of life to between 5 and 9 years old.[42]

There was no cure, only treatments of symptoms that ran from common sense to the downright bizarre. Polio was highly contagious and spread most often through contact with fecal matter of an infected person during a relatively brief window before and after their first symptoms. It thrived in hot climates and areas with poor sanitation. When this last fact became known over the years following WWII, it brought a focus on the many drainage ditches around Houston and Harris County where school children loved to play. Not only Houston, which had been treating wastewater for decades, but smaller cities such as Bellaire, West University, and many others began to worry and act upon the amount of raw sewage that was entering the bayou system at their hands.[43]

The contagious aspect had been known and feared for some time. Quarantines had taken place in Houston schools before. Typical was one 1927 case that placed 27 students in the low first grade into home confinement. While the diseased pupil was entering treatment, the classmates were kept away for nine days. City health officer Dr. A.H. Flickwir conferred with Dr. C.C. Pierce, assistant surgeon general at the United States Public Health Service, and other doctors to determine when the outcasts would be safely allowed to return to school.[44]

At its height, throughout most of the 1940s and 50s, polio epidemics were a worldwide scourge. About a half million people globally were killed or paralyzed by the virus every year at its peak. In the United States the number of those paralyzed topped out at 22,000 annually. Every summer, parents observed their children with hawk-like focus, knowing all the same that if the worst happened, they were helpless to do much about it. Local newspapers even noted the number of new cases, sometimes with relief, such as when there was only a single new victim in Bellaire during one May week of 1948.[45]

Sometimes the paralysis confined a person to an iron lung, immobilized for months or forever, kept alive by mechanical breathing. Others were fitted with leg braces and crutches and sent back out in the world. In schools that were often filled with daunting flights of stairs, it became a burden born by those children. For example, at Longfellow Elementary on the southeast side of downtown, the polio stricken, those who had Down's Syndrome, and students with any other mobility or coordination issues were placed in the Orthopedic Class in a special basement room, united by the common need for easy, stair-free access. They had little contact with their fellow students.[46]

The Orthopedic Class at Longfellow ES. Courtesy Sandy Rieser

An injectable and an oral vaccine were released in the late 1950s with dramatic effects. By 1961, the number of new polio cases in the United States had dropped to just 161, and the last American outbreak occurred in 1979. The developer of the vaccine, Dr. Jonas Salk, was honored on a postage stamp. Due to the enormous number of cases in the United States, it was those affected by polio who in large part pushed for reforms contained in the Americans with Disabilities Act in order that they might fully take part in society.[47]

LOOSCAN E S

The school at 3600 Robertson opened in 1936 as Irvington Elementary, but shortly afterwards it was christened to honor Adele Briscoe Looscan, a remarkable Houston woman who was descended from the founder of Harrisburg and whose father, a San Jacinto veteran, was the first chief administrator of Harris County. Her own achievements included founding the first women's club in Texas, writing articles on Texas history, being a charter member of the Texas State Historical Association, serving in the leadership of the Daughters of the Republic of Texas, and being a major supporter of the Houston Public Library to which she bequeathed her personal library of 1,500 books. In addition to the school, a branch of the Houston library also bears her name.[48]

LOVE E S

Already growing by leaps and bounds, new construction in the Houston Heights Annex, which rose between Railroad and Nashua south of 16th Street, brought even more residents into the area. A one-room wooden building on Lowell Street first met the need in the middle 1910s. A decade later, the small school needed relief, and in 1927, a new brick building was opened at what is today 13th and Shepherd. At first, the building had only four classrooms for 87 students, though the "beautiful" campus covered seven acres and boasted 209 trees: pines, oaks, elms, and hickories. It was named for William G. Love, a former Heights mayor and school board member, Harris County District Attorney, judge and personal attorney for Governors Ma and Pa Ferguson. Two additional rooms were added to the building soon after its opening.[49]

In the 1930s, many elementary schools offered some form of student government, but Love's was different, with its five grades modeled after a small city. The halls were given street names, and various classes took on duties including fire department, toy shop, little theatre, telegraph station, bank and even a broadcasting station. The most famous Love Elementary student, newsman Dan Rather, came along a decade or so later. As for the little frame school building that was Lowell Street School on the west side of the street between 14th and 15th, it was still standing, just barely, in 2018.[50]

A 1921 photo of Lowell Street School held in front of the building in the 2010s. J.R. Gonzales photo

LOWELL STREET SCHOOL

See Love E S

LOWER BRAYS BAYOU

Lower Brays Bayou School was located in County District 22 in the 1890s. Its exact location is unknown at this time.[51]

LUBBOCK E S

In 1906, city school officials were looking for relief for Rusk School in the Second Ward with an added goal of possibly doing away with the two-room Oak Lawn School. The answer was an eight-room building at the corner of Sampson and Harrisburg named in honor of early Houstonian and former Texas governor Francis Lubbock. The building was completed so late in the following school year that classes did not begin there until the fall of 1907. As was the case in many Houston schools, complaints soon followed. One of five recently completed brick buildings, Lubbock was not well-lighted, not "fire-proof", and offered no assembly room. Within five years, it was so over-crowded that two basement rooms were converted to classroom use and two wooden shacks brought onto the grounds. It, along with Travis Elementary, had indoor bathrooms that could not be used since the city had not yet extended sewer connection close enough to the campus.[52]

Lubbock ES near the time of its opening. HISD

By September 1913, Principal J.J. Boone had received a large annex, big enough to boost the faculty size to fifteen. An inspection by Mrs. Presley K. Ewing that year still found concerns including the lack of a school nurse, no adjustable desks so that most children found their seating either too large or too cramped, and no drinking fountains. There were four wash stands for girls and four for boys, each with a shared drinking cup. As Mrs. Ewing pointed out, 579 sets of lips "drink from these eight germ-laden cups." Still, the Mothers Club had supplied a piano, Victrola, manual training and gymnasium equipment, two sets of encyclopedias, and had paid $30 to plant oak trees around the block. By the early 1920s, Lubbock, with yet another eight-room annex added, was becoming more Hispanic as Mexican immigrants found homes in the area. By WWII, a majority of its pupils were of Mexican descent. Lubbock closed in 1969 and was subsequently demolished. The lot sat vacant for decades, though neighboring institution Champ Burger and some of the live oaks planted over a century before thrived on. The new METRO rail down Harrisburg and neighborhood gentrification brought new construction to the block in 2016.[53]

Indoor Toilets

Though stone toilets have existed for millennia, including some primitive water-flushing models that could be found in today's Pakistan, India, Greece, and Scotland some 4,500 years ago, the modern toilet we know and love has only been a widespread fixture in American bathrooms for about 100 years. At the dawn of the 20th century, even the fanciest of Houston schools relied on multiple outhouses located at the rear of the property to answer the call of necessity for student and teacher alike.[54]

For centuries, the wealthier urban dwellers had relied on outhouses, chamber pots, an open air back lot, or a small enclosed space with a removable pot that was literally a "water closet." Scots watchmaker Alexander Cumming patented the first modern toilet improvement in 1775, an S trap that created a constant pool of water in the bowl.

Many of the major steps toward the flushing apparatus that we recognize today took place in Victorian Britain, not the least of which was the push for more sophisticated sewer systems to combat cholera. Grand hotels in both Europe and America were among the first to advertise these indoor luxuries, though guests generally had to go to the basement to find them. In England in 1885, Thomas Twyford introduced a vitreous china bowl as an improvement over earthenware predecessors, and English china concerns including Wedgewood and Doulton soon joined the act. Toilet paper in the form of a roll of tearable sheets showed up in Britain, too, but it took the American Scott brothers to successfully market it. Then in 1891, Thomas Crapper & Sons patented a valve and siphon design that marked a giant leap forward in flushing. They also opened a plumbing showroom, not to mention adding a word or two to the English lexicon.[55]

In the first decade of the 1900s, flush toilets with an overhead tank became extremely popular in the United States with companies like Eljer and Sloan leading the way. Though it would be the 1920s before most city building codes called for indoor toilets, their adoption in Houston and Harris County schools took place in the years prior to WWI.

It was not solely a matter of convenience. School officials understood that sickness led to absenteeism and therefore poor grades. Specifically, dysentery, typhoid, and tuberculosis were problems in rural Harris County. The biggest culprit was hookworm, a parasitic infection that can cause intestinal cramps, fever, weight loss, and anemia among other symptoms. Described as "prevalent in the Southern States," it was often contracted through bare feet in areas where the soil contained traces of feces, and poorly managed outhouses used by a few dozen children created just such a situation.[56]

It fell to the teacher, the sole authority in many isolated county schools, to clean them and minimize odor by dumping in powdered quick lime every morning, and occasionally stirring it in. In 1914, mindful of these health issues, the Harris County School Superintendent wrote of methods to cut down on dust in the schools, increase medical inspections, and install "odorless, germ-proof indoor toilets", a bold claim indeed. Because most county schools were far away from city sewer lines, the toilets consisted of a rectangular white enameled bowl with a vent behind it and a 20-gallon septic tank buried below ground.[57]

Old basement toilets at a Houston elementary school. HISD

The City of Houston schools had gotten a head start on bringing some of the school toilet facilities indoors. Rather surprisingly, the introduction of indoor plumbing was one of the rare instances where the White and Black schools benefitted almost simultaneously. Once an initial round of plumbing improvements were meted out to several White schools, when new sewer lines were extended to the blocks where schools stood, the upgrades seem to have been performed regardless of the school's racial orientation. In an era of such profound racial inequality and institutionalized segregation, it is certainly noteworthy.

Fannin School, in a "silk stocking" district of town, got a new indoor toilet system for the girls in March 1911. At about the same time or shortly thereafter, indoor toilets were added at the all-White Longfellow, Austin, Hawthorne, Dow, Sherman Elementary Schools, and in the High School where it was part of an addition. Also benefitting during the same three-or-four-year period were Colored High School and the African American Gregory Elementary that served the Freedmens Town area of Fourth Ward.[58]

By 1917, the year the United States entered WWI, more sewer lines had been run to the suburbs such as East End and West End. The city report recommended toilet systems for a total of seven schools at a cost of $9,950. Four of the schools were Black and three White. The report two years later showed some of that work had been completed at places such as Abbott and Thompson schools in West End, Lubbock and Fullerton in East End, and the African American Emancipation Park School, later called Blackshear, in Third Ward.[59]

Just like the new-fangled indoor toilets in the luxury hotels some 30 years prior, the lavatories in Houston schools were also mostly located in the basements. Given the problems with basements in wet Houston, many schools had what were in reality half basements with dirt floors. The Houston high school building constructed around 1894 had basement "water closets" for girls, male teachers, female teachers, and the boys got both water closets and urinals. These seem to have been hooked up to a septic system, however. As the real indoor restrooms were added, many of the schools also finally had a cement floor put in the basement.[60]

LUCKIE E S

The six-room, two-story wooden school named for Black educator Charles W. Luckie opened in 1908 at 1004 Palmer between McKinney and Lamar to relieve crowding at Douglass. The principal was J.N. Dodson, a graduate of Wilberforce University, and he stayed in that job until his death in 1921. During his tenure, the school was noted as being the best kept among African American campuses in the district. Janitor Bailey Sparks was singled out for recognition multiple times, and comments on the many beds of blooming flowers were noted in the schools reports. On February 5, 1918, a fire destroyed the wooden building, and for about a year students attended classes at the Boynton Chapel M.E. Church. In 1919, a new brick building opened, notable for a Black school in the city at the time. The school prospered under new head J.P. Jones. By 1934, it had a faculty of twelve. Luckie closed during WWII, and for a time served as the administration building for Houston's African American schools. Sold along with several HISD properties in 1962, it was the home of a plumbing supply company, then in 1992 was purchased for $65,000 by Calico Tees screen-printing company. The latest owner is Mario Figueroa, the artist known as Gonzo247. His plans are for a studio, event, and green space serving the East End.[61]

This impressive wood frame Luckie School was lost to fire in 1918. HISD

LUTHERAN HIGH SCHOOL

Lutheran High School opened at 6901 Woodridge Street in southeast Houston in 1949. It split into a north and south campus in the early 1980s, both of which remain.[62]

LYNCHBURG SCHOOL

Nathaniel Lynch bought land in Austin's Colony near the confluence of Buffalo Bayou and the San Jacinto River in 1822, moving upstream a few years later and platting a town. His ferry operation played a crucial role in the Texas Revolution. In the years before the Civil War, six steamboats a day stopped at Lynchburg, and the shipyards were busy with repairs and new construction of sailing vessels that plied the bay. The population was 1851 in the 1860 census with African Americans slightly outnumbering Anglos. The war brought even more area activity to the shipyards plus an ammunition operation. The town boasted a post office, saloons, stores, and, prior to 1876, a school for White inhabitants on that side of the river. An early school trustee was Alvin P. Tompkins who operated a hotel there.

Lynchburg School in the 1910s. HHRC

By the dawn of the 20th century, the White school in Lynchburg was located on the south side of the Crosby Road, today's Independence Parkway, where the road bends west toward the ferry landing. Attendance was in the neighborhood of 30 children, and there were other schools across the water at the little town of San Jacinto. The county report of 1910 opined that three frame buildings "is too many buildings for the number of children in the district, yet on account of the dangers in crossing the San Jacinto River, the trustees have deemed it wise to construct three buildings, rather than that the children should have to undertake the dangers in crossing the river each day." Hurricanes regularly preyed hard on Lynchburg, and the 1915 storm depleted the local population to fewer than 75 people. When the Deer Park ISD was created, Lynchburg children fell under their purview, and by the mid-1930s, the schoolhouse was quiet. Though the town itself is gone, the Lynchburg Ferry still operates today.[63]

LYNCHBURG COLORED SCHOOL

District 17 did operate a school for African Americans in Lynchburg, starting at least as early as 1886, though it is possible that the county-paid teacher was working in a privately owned room. The parents might have been employed in any number of business operations along the waterways. The school itself was always small, and in the 1890s was only paying a teacher for a three month term. By 1905, there were just four students.[64]

Schools M

MACGREGOR E S

Southmore Elementary School bounded by Crawford, LaBranch, Wentworth, and Rosedale was opened in early 1922 and renamed in honor of New England-born businessman and civic leader Henry F. MacGregor in 1930. The lot dwarfed the school, taking up the entire block and then some. Initially a drive ran through the playground portion of the campus, but that was removed for the obvious safety concerns about motor vehicles driving through a children's play area. The school opened with Principal Lucille Gregg and five additional teachers for about 100 pupils. By the mid-1930s, the original building had been enlarged to 22 classrooms plus a kindergarten and auditorium-lunchroom for an enrollment that had swollen to 687. "Miss Lucie," as Gregg was known served the first 22 years as principal until her death in 1944.

Located in a prospering South End neighborhood, the student body gave back to the city at large during the Depression. "Each year each classroom takes care of a needy family. They send food and clothing and toys for the little children," one report noted. In addition, they brought old clothes to donate throughout the term. MacGregor was one of the first three HISD schools to integrate when that finally took place during the 1960-61 school year. There was one single Black student, Jacquelyn Sibley. Today the Museum District campus, with no remnant of the original building, is a Music and Science magnet. Therein lies a small irony since the 1922 request for a piano at the school was denied.[1]

The expansive playground at MacGregor ES with the school in the distance.
HISD

Physical Education

Children have always played, but as far as schools were concerned, it was not always a worthwhile use of a student's time. Though the first official American gym teacher was hired in Massachusetts in the 1820s, importing the idea from his native Germany, it was far from the norm. The generally accepted idea in the 19th century was that kids could run at recess or on their own time. Even more than that, in a mostly rural United States, the majority of youngsters got all the exercise they needed through farm work.[2]

The Northern European idea of gymnastic exercise was certainly not absent from Houston in the 1800s. The Turnverein was a popular downtown club organized by German immigrants where they participated in organized tumbling, gymnastics, calisthenics and, later, bowling. The Turners, as they were called, also became advocates of P.E. in schools.[3]

There was also national influence for greater physical activity in youth. When President Theodore Roosevelt took office in 1901, he brought with him a devotion to a vigorous life filled with physical activity. T.R. was a fan of horseback riding, boxing, and reveled in gymnastics. He also loved, and saved, the game of football, which put him squarely in the American mainstream. The post-Civil War years were a time during which team sports were exploding in popularity. Baseball and football were ubiquitous, and basketball began to rise in the 1890s thanks to the support of thousands of YMCA locations.[4]

It was 1908 when Houston Superintendent Horn weighed in on the subject, coming down firmly on the side of physical education. "Just why anybody should have imagined that it is worth while to develop him mentally but not physically or morally, is a thing which future students of education will find it difficult to explain," Horn wrote. "The boy whose mind is loaded down with Latin, Greek and mathematics, and with other subjects of the college or university curriculum, but who is physically or morally a wreck, is not one who is capable of doing a great work for the State, and is not a product of which our schools have a right to be proud."[5]

Indoor baseball city champs from Austin ES. HISD

A program was initiated in city schools, and by 1910, Robert W. Keeton, the new P. E. Director for the district, felt there was enough data to give a solid evaluation. One of the first topics he addressed was athlete eligibility, what would later be termed "No Pass, No Play". Decrying this "age when the public is investing so much money in professional baseball", Keeton stressed that "to win at all hazards" was not the ideal that Houston needed to be instilling in its youth.[6]

Even before the start of the 1909-10 school year, the boys at Houston High School had suited up and started practice, but there was a fly in that eager ointment. Keeton wrote to Horn "that there had been on the team at least four boys who had had no right whatever to be there, but who were making a pretense of going to school for no other reason than to play football." He set up a system of honor points with a student earning four points for an A, two for a B, all the way down to losing four points for a failing grade. Conduct was also considered. If a student did not maintain three honor points each month, they did not play competitive sports.[7]

Keeton also believed in fair play. Referring to an interscholastic track meet hosted by A&M College, he stressed that "there must be some method of handicapping or classifying the entries in events, so that all will have an opportunity to compete, with some show of winning."[8]

Facilities were another problem in the early days of physical education and athletics. The high school was in the middle of downtown, and the city had to pay the owners of the Houston Buffs baseball club for use of West End Park as a practice and game venue. Rent "was almost prohibitive." The high school did at least own a gymnasium, opening that in December 1909. The school posted a winning record that school year in every interscholastic sport except football.[9]

The grade schools also had teams and competition for both boys and girls. A female director of girls P.E. was added in 1909. Local business including Mistrot-Munn Department Store, Teetshorn Book Company, Guarantee Life, United Bank, and Bullock Decorative Company sponsored trophies for the winning schools. City school officials felt that the games "were of great value in enabling the establishing of a feeling of confidence and friendship between the players, and in eliminating intense rivalry and a feeling of social inequality, which existed between the schools of the different sections of the city."[10]

In 1912, the Harris County schools joined in the fun and games. County Superintendent L. L. Pugh called for "Systematic, physical exercises should be given daily. The child spends a large part of his school hours in a sitting posture. The result of this extended physical inactivity at a period of life when he needs motion to enhance growth and general vigor is retarded blood circulation and insufficient respiration."[11]

Pugh was quite specific. No doubt after studying outside sources, he wrote that exercise be given at 10:00 AM and 2:00 PM every day, and he ordered teachers to "lower the windows from the top and open the doors so that the air of the room will be completely changed." In addition to the games used in the city schools, Pugh suggested tennis, swinging clubs to strengthen arms, marching, dancing, chin ups "and combative games in the yard." He was most concerned about the children "who do not play vigorously or do not play at all unless urged."

In 1913, the county began holding athletic meets for competition between the small common schools in "football, volley ball, basket ball, fast running, high jumping, running broad jump, potato race, and girls' relay race." Both at the Fullerton and Harrisburg meets, domestic science pupils prepared lunch for everyone attending, and Pugh reported that the atmosphere was "crowded full of glorious life. It was a great feast for those who relish things of the heart, to see the five hundred boys and girls in their childish glee as they played and raced with that abandonment and spontaneity that is only the gift of youth."[12]

As the decade wore on, other activities joined the big four of football, baseball, basketball and track in the Houston city schools, too. Volleyball was introduced in 1910 and hailed as "the ideal schoolyard game." Many campuses formed intra-school volleyball leagues. "One school had twenty teams of six players each, while another school had every girl, excepting two, above the fourth grade playing regularly on a team."

Indoor baseball, played in the school gym, was another regular activity. Soccer had been added by 1918. All together there were over 1,200 city grade schoolers taking part in team sports.[13]

Both Robert Keeton and his successor, J.K. Staples, were fond of calisthenics as a way to improve posture, increase lung and heart activity and develop "the habits of obedience to command and concentration of attention." Keeton recalled overhearing two teachers observing their pupils at play remark: "I never saw Mary hustle before."[14]

Hamilton JHS students perform calisthenics in the school gym. HISD

Staples was even more of a stickler. He took Keeton's in-room exercise periods of two and eight minutes and turned them on their ear. Staples wanted to see quantifiable metrics on posture improvement and set a competition among the city's grade schools. He even suggested in one lengthy report that Houston look to Brookline, Massachusetts as an example of low mortality rate and well-organized municipal exercise. He claimed that by following in Brookline's well-balanced footsteps, there would be a saving of 407 lives a year.[15]

Even more disturbing was the report that was released shortly after World War I's end. The War Department admitted that "one out of every three drafted individuals was highly unfit for combat." The federal government responded with legislation mandating P.E. in public schools for the first time. The frivolity of the Roaring Twenties and the financial straits of the Great Depression eroded that resolve, though, and after WWII came another dire revelation. This time it was nearly half of all draftees who were either rejected or had to be placed in non-combat roles.[16]

MAGNOLIA CITY SCHOOL
See Franklin ES

MAGNOLIA PARK J H S
See Edison JHS

MAGNOLIA PARK SCHOOL
See Franklin ES

MALE AND FEMALE SELECT SCHOOL
Tennessee-born James S. Burnett's Male and Female Select School "was among the most prosperous of Houston's private schools." He also operated a night school for young men.[17]

MANN, HORACE J H S
The Goose Creek High School, which was built after students had been attending classes in the rented YMCA, was turned into Horace Mann Junior High in 1928. Bond issues in 1929 and 1937 funded additions for the building at 610 South Pruett Street. The original building was replaced by a new facility at 310 South Highway 146 in the 1993-94 school year.[18]

MANNAZANK SCHOOLHOUSE
This name surfaces in two separate generations for a school along the San Jacinto River. Not surprisingly, the spelling of the name varies radically. The first time it appears is in relation to Sarah Penn who started a Sunday school in her home near present day Crosby in 1839. Both Chuck Chandler and William Hardt, a fine historian of Texas Methodists, transcribe the name of both her school and the nearby church as Manayunk. Penn's Meeting House, named for Sarah's husband David, was a polling place on the river in 1841. The *Texas Wesleyan Banner* describes her operation in 1850 as "a very good week-day school." Attaching a general, secular curriculum there requires some presumption.[19]

The name appears again over 30 years later with indications that it may have been a short lived name for the school in Lynchburg, or it might have been a different school in the area. The location up river at the old Penn's Meeting House would certainly qualify. A.P. Tompkins is a trustee of both Lynchburg and Mannazank in the mid-1880s, but the other trustees listed for those schools are different men.[20]

MARKET HOUSE SCHOOL
As the Houston city school system was building the new high school building in the 1890s, and at various other points of need in the late 19th century, a portion of the Market House and City Hall on today's Market Square was used for classrooms. Though reports called it "a poor make shift," as many as six rooms accommodated over 300 sixth and seventh grade students at the high water mark in 1893-94.[21]

MARRS, STARLIN MARION NEWBERRY SCHOOL
See Aldine HS

MARSHALL J H S

Houston's city schools got into the junior high business when Northside and South End Junior High Schools opened in 1914. The affluent south side of town got the better end of things initially, more classrooms and amenities, but in 1916, a separate gymnasium and swimming pool building was added to the Northside campus at Noble and Cochran. An adjoining city park and library also improved things. The inaugural seventh, eighth, and ninth graders were overseen by H.N. Shofstal and a staff of ten teachers, but the school grew rapidly. Neighborhood civic clubs and the city's newspapers worked to fill the library shelves. Many of the students chose vocational programs offered there. By the time the name was changed to John Marshall in 1926, there were some 30 faculty and 900 pupils. First a west wing and then an east wing were added. Principal J.L. McReynolds took over around that time, moving from nearby Sherman Elementary. A decade later, he was in charge of 57 teachers at the school and 1,500 students. From an early date in the school's history, Marshall was described as a "melting pot" with pupils who were native to "Mexico, Italy, Germany, France, Spain, Ireland and Holland." It was also a district pioneer in the use of a counselor and a visiting teacher to go to students' homes. The original Marshall buildings were demolished in the 1980s. The soccer field now occupies the ground which housed the 1913 construction. Only the columns from the old Carnegie Library live on at Castillo Park. The school itself is alive and flourishing as the Marshall Fine Arts Academy.[22]

North Side JHS soon after opening. HISD

The Advent of Junior High Schools

The first junior high school in the United States opened in Columbus, Ohio in 1909 with another following in Berkeley, California within the year. Like the set up in Houston, Harris County, and elsewhere around the country, grade school had previously lasted through eighth grade, with students moving on to what was then three more years of high school in the Bayou City. The trouble was that a large percentage of youngsters considered their school careers to be over after eighth grade.[23]

Educators on the college level had been calling for an improved curriculum in public schools for years. In an 1893 report, the National Education Association had come out in favor of academic study beginning during the last years of elementary school. It coincided with a groundbreaking book by psychologist G. Stanley Hall that posited that adolescence was a particular time of "storm and stress" with children changing radically physically, mentally, emotionally, socially, and morally. Anyone who has ever parented a an early-teenager can back him up. Psychologist Hall called for individualized attention for children in this volatile age group, a dream that ultimately led to a move from junior highs to middle schools. That tweak to the system was still decades down the road, however.

The larger Houston city schools had moved to a departmental plan of instruction in the fall of 1905. That meant beginning in fifth grade, students no longer had a single teacher for the entire school day. Instead, they would see one teacher for English, another for math, and so the day unfolded. Three years into the plan, there were still complaints from all quarters, but the school remained committed with "no disposition whatever to return to the system of instruction by grades." Superintendent Horn cited the biggest problem as the "tendency for the teacher to lose personal touch with the children."[24]

When Houston began looking to add junior high schools, however, the greatest goal was not concern for individual students by any stretch. It was viewed as a way to frugally address severe overcrowding at the city's lone high school. It was landlocked on a single downtown block and could not physically be expanded any further than it had. Citizens wanted a new high school for Houston, but could not agree how to divide it in a city that was growing in all directions of the compass. Some suggested segregating the White students by gender, but if that route was chosen, which gender would get punished with the old building? Others wanted a classical school and a technical school, but that ran contrary to the concept of a well-rounded education.[25]

Instead, the school board believed that the new educational idea of a junior high school, or two of them, had many advantages. By building in both the north and south suburbs of town, students could stay closer to home for at least another year or two "without in any way interfering with the democratic ideal of having all the children of the town together during the last years of their high school course." It would also allow more of that special attention at a crucial time in childhood development.

The curriculum for junior high would incorporate "two parallel lines of work. One is the four-year course leading to the University, as we now have it, with the opportunity to elect work in Manual Training and Domestic Science, if the pupils should so desire. The other should consist in shorter, semi-vocational work, of two years duration, for those who will probably be under the necessity of dropping out at the end of that time."[26]

Though everything proceeded as planned, there was still some slight hedging of bets on this new educational experiment. Just before the city's first junior high schools opened in September 1913, Paul Horn again felt the need to justify their construction. His report that year certainly contained the descriptions of these "elegant" and "fire-proof" new buildings that boasted the most modern systems for heat, light, and ventilation and came complete with auditoriums, gymnasiums, study halls, laboratories, manual training and domestic science facilities, libraries, club rooms, and top flight swimming pools, one completed and one planned.[27]

The junior high school experiment in Houston was one of the first and strongest commitments in the nation, and it drew notice. Horn's annual report in 1915 was republished in the *Elementary School Journal*, and he commented that he had fielded calls "from Maine to California." Among the advice he offered his fellow administrators was to use methods of teaching and discipline that were more mature than grade school, but not as much as high school, that a junior high was neither fish nor fowl when comparing it to those other levels, that elective courses should be offered and that, when a student merited promotion to high school work, they should get it.[28]

By 1918, the City of Houston had annexed Houston Heights, and with it came an entire school system suddenly absorbed into the city schools. It gave the city three high schools: Central, Heights, and Colored, and four junior highs at North Side, South End, Heights, and West End which started out in Brunner I.S.D.. According to the thought process of the day, that meant Houston had seven high school buildings.[29]

That year, six years into the junior high experience, Houston continued to note an uptick in the number of high school graduates, and they credited the junior highs with looking after the students' need to "build for a future." They were managing to keep pupils in school longer. Still, the Superintendent admitted that it had not accomplished all of the desired goals.[30]

Part of Horn's frustration was with high school teachers and principals who looked upon the work of teaching seventh graders, formerly something that was squarely ensconced in grade school, as being as difficult but less important than teaching ninth or eleventh graders. He opined early on that it was not always easy to get teachers "to understand fully just what they are trying to do." Still the district was fully committed and would not go back. "Houston schools are working out the realization of the junior high school ideal," Horn wrote. "They are in the process of pressing forward to it, rather than in that of having attained it." He also added a note of realism:

"Its growth may be somewhat slow." That was yet more reinforcement to something he had written five years prior: "School systems do not ordinarily grow by revolution or by miracle."³¹

MASONIC HALL SCHOOLS

When the Masons of Holland Lodge No. 1, the oldest such body in Texas, built their new building at the northeast corner of Main and Capitol in 1852, the lower floor was set aside to be rented for school use. Such was the importance that lodge members placed on education. The first school located there was an academy run by A.W. Boyd and H. Moore, and the pupils included some children of the Masons. James Bolinger was schoolmaster there in 1857. Schools continued in the space until the lodge temple burned in October 1862. A new, larger Holland Lodge was erected on the same spot, and its second floor served for at least a year in the late 1870s as the home of Houston's public high school. A plaque noting that latter achievement was for many years affixed to the building.³²

MCDONALD SCHOOL

See Berry School

McGEE SCHOOL

David McGee, a freed slave who had been a Blacksmith during bondage, bought about 370 acres of land located near the present day Briar Forest Drive, in an area around where it today crosses Highway 6 and Eldridge. It was part of a tremendous growth in the African American population in West Harris County after the Civil War. The immediate area along San Felipe Road back toward Piney Point to the east was over 60% Black by 1870. The men were almost all working in agriculture or lumber, several as teamsters hauling logs. McGee Chapel Baptist Church opened in 1869, and a small school followed in the area within the decade.³³

McGHEE SCHOOL

This school that sat off Market Street in in Channelview was named for Joseph McGhee, a Black farmer who donated land and helped build a small school upon it sometime prior to 1916. Seven grades attended the 26' x 30' one room building in County District 18, learning from a single teacher. Attendance was not large by the 1930s, with total scholastic population between 9 and 17 pupils a year. The school ceased operation in 1942, and the Channelview ISD, by then suburban rather than rural, became an all-White operation for almost a quarter century. The McGhee building still exists, located behind the DeZavala Elementary School at Crockett and 1st Street.[34]

MCGOWEN E S

McGowen Elementary School opened in the fall of 1916 at 3415 Lyons Avenue at Gregg, serving White children in the Fifth Ward. It opened with six rooms, but had grown to 12 by 1920. It was described as being in good condition, but in need of more ground, an auditorium, and additional plumbing. In January 1927, Wheatley High School was established in the building, and McGowen Elementary ceased to exist.[35]

MEADOWBROOK SCHOOL

See Bonner

MEMORIAL E S

The precursor to Memorial Elementary was a one-room schoolhouse at Birdsall and Washington that was donated to the City of Houston by G.T. Roberts in 1915. That first year, the lone teacher at the Roberts School had forty-two pupils. Even though the nearby community of Brunner had a combination elementary and junior high school at the time, as well, the West End had such an influx of population that in 1921 Mr. Roberts paid $58,000 for the old Red Cross Building at Camp Logan, which had closed two years before, and the school moved there, filling out eleven classrooms. That location remained the elementary school until the HISD bond issue of 1926 when a site for the new school building was procured with a combination of $10,607.32 from the district and a donation of some land by philanthropist Will Hogg. Hogg's real estate company had purchased a great deal of land in the area back in 1923 with the plan being to expand his recently built subdivision of River Oaks, but within the year, he and his partners had come to support the idea of establishing a large Memorial Park on the site, and they sold just over 1,500 acres to the city at cost. The school site was a remnant of his purchases. Though the initial thought was to name the school at 6401 Arnot for Hogg, its benefactor, there was already a Hogg Junior High named for his father, the late governor. So, the new campus, like the adjacent new park, was named as a Memorial to those soldiers who had trained on that same spot before giving their lives in the recent World War. The P.T.A. placed a brass "Memorial Tablet" in the corner stone in honor of the nearly 1,000 Camp Logan soldiers who had been killed in battle.[36]

MERKEL SCHOOL

Merkel Hall was a four-room brick building at 615 Pinckney Street at Freeman in Fifth Ward. The city rented all or a portion of it for multiple years beginning about 1904 to handle overflow from Dow and Sherman Schools. The building belonged to the family of Richard Merkel, a son of German immigrant Joe Merkel who owned a large post-Civil War private park on the south side of Buffalo Bayou. A portion of that land, called Merkel's Grove, lives on today as Tony Marron Park.[37]

MESSIAH LUTHERAN SCHOOL

This small religious school was operating by 1932 at the intersection of Rose and Roy near the affiliated church. Messiah merged with Trinity Lutheran Day School in 1970. The buildings appear to still be intact, but today it is an early childhood school.[38]

Students at Middle Bayou School.
Courtesy Jean West

MIDDLE BAYOU SCHOOL

Junker's Cove was listed as a pre-1876 school that became Middle Bayou shortly thereafter. By the mid-1880s, Middle Bayou is listed in County District 13, sitting south of Red Bluff, in or immediately adjacent to what is today the Armand Bayou Nature Center. Trustees of the district were given the green light to sell the old Middle Bayou building in 1913. The lead school trustee for decades salvaged many of the one-room school's contents. Miraculously preserved by family members for over a century, they were donated to the Heritage Society in 2018 for display in the Kellum-Noble House.[39]

MILAM E S

See West End High

MILBY, CHARLES H S

As early as 1919, Houston school officials were asking about provisions for a high school in the East End "probably somewhere out on Harrisburg Road." The cost was expected to be a quarter of a million dollars. In the planning stages, it was referenced as Eastwood High, but when it finally opened on Broadway at Wilson in March 1926, it sat well past that neighborhood. The campus was named for Charles H. Milby, a civic minded businessman, hotelier, Ship Channel booster, and resident of the east side of town. It replaced the old Harrisburg High in the area that was annexed to HISD and the city of Houston the same year. The school opened with 11 classrooms, two science labs, a home economics lab, library, gymnasium, auditorium, and cafeteria. Not long afterwards, a bond issue allowed the addition of a swimming pool and eight more classrooms. Other additions followed.[40]

The first principal of Milby, W.K. Stevenson, stayed in his post for over a decade, presiding over the children of mostly blue collar workers, many from the nearby maritime and railroad businesses. The neighborhood remained similar economically, even as the influx of Mexican immigrants began to dominate the southeast part of town. Many elected officials from Houston have been Milby grads including Bob Gammage, Frank Mancuso, Mario Gallegos, Gordon Quan, and Carol Alvarado. Other alums run the gamut from wrestler Gorgeous George to murderer Andrea Yates.

Milby HS circa 1930. HISD

Milby reached a peak enrollment in the early 1990s with over 3,600 students, but today, as a science magnet, its population is much more manageable. In 2014, ground was broken on an enormous new building project to create a new, state of the art Milby High, fortunately with the preservation of the oldest portion of the 1926 main building.[41]

More Football Rioting

Perhaps the decade of the 1930s was a particularly violent one for fans of Houston high school football, or maybe it was simply coincidence. When Austin High's Mustangs went up 14-0 on Milby at Buff Stadium on the night of November 2, 1939, the football Buffaloes' captain protested that field judge Ivan Reid had gotten in the way of Milby's defense, allowing the Austin player to make it to the end zone. After curse words allegedly flew from the Milby player's mouth, he was ejected. Following the game, a large crowd surrounded a building under the stands calling for field judge Reid's head. The trouble escalated into a full-fledged riot that the *Post* called "probably the longest ever staged after a Houston high school game." The superlative might have been warranted since an estimated 300 people were involved, and the melee lasted for a full hour. Perhaps as many as 30 HPD officers arrived to break it up, but before that happened a Milby pep squad girl was trampled and another young woman bit a teacher's hand while defending her boyfriend. Of the twelve arrested, seven were students (four from Milby, two from Austin, and one from Jeff Davis), and five were not. Only one of those charged got a fine of $15. The rest were treated to a stern lecture from the judge. Reaction from HISD officials was less hysterical than the incident at the beginning of the decade with board member Holger Jeppesen warning that "If conditions of this kind continue, all we can do is take football away from the students." Needless to say, they did not.[42]

MILLER, DORIS SCHOOL
See Woodcrest

MILLER J H S
The classic mid-1920s building at 1906 Cleburne became a segregated Black junior high school named for educator William E. Miller in the late 1950s after they moved Johnston Junior High, along with the name, to Meyerland.

MILLS COLORED SCHOOL
Immediately southeast of the town of Cypress Top, near the intersection of Hempstead Highway and Skinner Road, was the "Mills Colored School District #6" property that adjoined land belonging to the Solomon family in February 1928. In addition to the Solomons, there are a few other African American households in the area in 1930.[43]

MILO'S SCHOOLHOUSE

Milo's Schoolhouse, named for trustee William Milo, was listed in the original 1876 county schools ledger. Within six years, the school had been moved, the land sold, and the money transferred to the Rose Hill School Community.[44]

MINNETEX SCHOOL

Minnetex was a small, short-lived school in District 45 with Mykawa that sat northeast of the intersection of Almeda-Genoa and Cullen during the 1913-14 time frame. It was named after a land development of Morris Workman who had moved from Minnesota. In spite of his northern roots, Workman deeded the land with a clause to revert to his family if it ceased to be used for school purposes, or "if any persons of African descent are allowed to attend school on any of the land covered by the deed."[45]

MISS BELL'S SCHOOL

Miss Bell, who ran a "Select School for Girls" that opened in 1870 was very possibly the Isabella Bell, born in Maine, who was living in the household of Frederick and Charlotte Allen Rice that year. Her school was one of many that sought to "make 'ladies' of their pupils.[46]

MISS BROWNE'S SCHOOL

Easily one of the most respected and longest tenured of the pre-public school era institutions was Miss Browne's Young Ladies School. Mary B. Browne had started her school about 1860 on Franklin near Caroline by St. Vincent de Paul Church. Shortly after the close of the Civil War, she moved the operation to a "more healthy" and "more worthy" large, new house-like building she had constructed at McKinney and Crawford that was "remote from the city noise.". Several of the other faculty and half a dozen domestic servants lived there with the Irish-born Miss Browne. The teachers offered the girls courses found in the "solid branches of an English education" along with French, German, music, and drawing for tuition in the four to six dollar a month range. Board was provided for out of town pupils. The most fashionable young ladies in Houston attended Miss Browne's including Adele Looscan along with daughters and future wives of some of the city's business elite. Miss Browne was remembered by her former charges as "rather stalwart of figure, she always wore a loose fitting gown, made with a short cape falling about her shoulders. This costume was usually gray, but for formal occasions it was always black." Discipline and respect were expected and it was recalled that "Each morning we had to answer roll call by giving the number of hours we had studied for the day's work. Miss Browne finally closed her school in 1889 and moved to St. Louis where she died "at a ripe age."[47]

This ad for Miss Browne's School ran in the 1877-78 Houston city directory.

MISS EICHLER'S UNIVERSITY

Not a university at all, but rather a popular kindergarten at Christ Church Cathedral by German-bred Jenny Eichler who had moved to Houston from New York. Miss Eichler, known for demanding discipline, taught several notable students in the years prior to WWI including Howard Hughes, Dudley Sharp, and Ella Rice.[48]

MISS SHEPLER'S SCHOOL

Miss Blanche Shepler ran a private school for first graders only in a small rent house at the rear of the lot at 1718 Dart in First Ward. The school opened about 1902 with Miss C. Shepler at the helm, but her sister took over in September 1904 and operated it for fourteen straight years. Annual enrollment was near forty, and the students left knowing their ABCs forward and backward, multiplication tables through 12, and they could read and write. Miss Shepler left teaching to go to work as a clerk at a furniture company.[49]

MISS WALDO'S SCHOOL

Culturally accomplished sisters Mary, Lula, and Virginia Waldo ran a college preparatory school for some of Houston's more privileged girls. Mary Waldo, a graduate of the Sorbonne, started it in 1903 and was soon joined by her sisters, both alumni of Smith College. The sisters had rigorous admission standards for students from sixth through eleventh grades. The school closed in 1914, and Mary subsequently taught French at Kinkaid then became dean of girls at the new Lamar High School. Virginia moved to teach at the Hockaday School in Dallas.[50]

MONTROSE E S

The longtime site of HSPVA at 4011 Stanford, previously Connor Street, was originally Montrose Elementary. The neighborhood around it was developed beginning in 1910 by J.W. Link who sought to build a streetcar suburb, a "great residential addition" as he called it. Anchoring the new area that stretched Houston's limits was Montrose Boulevard, a true north-south axis lined with palm trees and graced by Link's own mansion and others. The city owned land for a new elementary, donated by Link, less than a year after the first houses went up. A cottage acquired in the Lubbock School land purchase was hauled to the site by a two-horse truck and used for the first classroom. Sixty-one pupils of the first four grades arrived in 1914 under the tutelage of Miss Emily McKinney as principal. That building was later relocated on the campus and employed first as the janitor's residence then a Boy Scout house.[51]

A new modern school was already in the works. The style was a patio design with mostly single story units forming a square and opening onto a covered colonnade that surrounded a courtyard. The first side of the square opened in 1916, and more units were soon added, proudly echoing "the form of building done by many of the Mexicans of the better class in the southwest." Rice Institute's William Ward Watkin led the architectural work. By 1922, there were twelve permanent classrooms and four temporary buildings, and within a decade an auditorium-play-lunchroom and more class space was added. Long after they were grown, former Montrose pupils recalled mosaic tile benches at each corner of the courtyard, oiled hardwood floors and a lone second story room for upper classmen.[52]

Montrose, along with Lantrip and Taylor, were built in the cottage style. This photo shows Montrose students on the play patio. HISD

The Montrose neighborhoods were home to many upper middle class families during the early decades, and they were an involved group. On February 27, 1919, the school's parents sent a telegram to President Woodrow Wilson alerting him that "The Montrose PTA most heartily endorses your news regarding the League of Nations." At the dawn of the 1930s, the concerned parents were vocal enough to get a traffic light installed at the intersection of Connor and West Alabama. The area around the school was considered in decline by the 1960s with an aging population and many vacant houses that became homes to artists, musicians, bikers and hippies before becoming the center of Houston's LGBT population by the late 1970s. Montrose Elementary was demolished at the start of the 1980s to make way for HSPVA.[53]

Mothers' Clubs

"Your Superintendent is still of the opinion, as expressed in previous reports, that the Mothers' Clubs are probably the most helpful of all the special features connected with the Houston schools," wrote Houston's Paul W. Horn. "Thousands of dollars have been raised in the last few years and expended by these organizations, mostly for objects for which public money could not at the time be spent."[54]

It was the Mothers' Clubs, beginning at Fannin Elementary in 1904, that had started the practice of serving nutritious lunches to school children, but "Houston's noble band of civic workers" did much more besides. Beautification of the school grounds was a major task, turning a patch of dirt or spotty grass into "pretty and inviting flower gardens."[55]

They also bought the latest technological advancements for the schools their children attended, furnishing stereopticons for a number of schools and "graphophones with records of music of a high classic order" to "enable children to get in touch with the best music." Additionally, the mothers donated the usual books, globes, maps, and even an occasional piano.[56]

The clubs flourished in both the city and county schools, and though they started earlier in the White schools, many of the African American schools were not far behind. Colored High School, Douglass, Gregory, Bruce, Crawford, Luckie, Harper, and Booker T. Washington Elementary Schools all had Mothers' Clubs of their own by 1913, focusing on things such as kitchen equipment, pianos, sewing machines, shade trees, and picture framing.[57]

It was out of the Mothers' Clubs that the Council of Parent-Teacher Associations grew. Formed in 1907, the council served as "a clearing house of ideas for the Mothers Clubs of the entire city." They wished to create a "unity of home, school and community; thus aiding in the four-fold development of the child, physical, mental, spiritual and moral." By the early 1920s, the clubs were not only buying Victrolas and moving picture machines, but raising money to pay assistants at the new kindergartens, supply first aid kits and clinic supplies, build sidewalks and in one case, pay for a yard man.[58]

These dour faces from a newspaper photograph are purported to be the Montrose ES PTA in 1914. Mike Vance Collection

Like many organizations, however, Houston's PTA went through a major rift that led to the formation of a rival. The catalyst was progressive ideas including the radical notion of allowing women, who couldn't yet vote, to serve on the school board.

The issue came to a head when Mary Ellen "Mamie" Ewing, the forward-thinking wife of a prominent judge and president of the organization, led a walkout of 25 like-minded women after a "spirited discussion" at a PTA meeting held at First Presbyterian Church in the late spring of 1913. Mrs. George Heyer remained behind with the more "standpat" members who were not concerned about having their interests represented on the school board.[59]

Mrs. Ewing and her supporters quickly established the United Mothers Council, and the members of that new group asked that their names be removed from PTA roles and that their membership dues be returned. There were no teachers represented in the new group. Mrs. Ewing told the newspapers that she felt those teachers were "dominated by powers higher up" in the school system and were not free to voice their mind. In spite of that, the new Council promised to have every school in the city represented within their membership.

"We believe in the freedom of persons to vote their honest convictions," Mrs. Ewing said. "And it was because I do believe in that very thing that I declined to embarrass the school teachers of the city by allowing my name to go before the association as a candidate for the presidency."[60]

Mamie Ewing would continue to be a strong advocate for the best in public education for several years. The UMC asked to be consulted on the construction of new schools so that "the new buildings be erected with a view of affording greater comfort and efficiency." They furnished both school officials and the newspapers with a dozen requirements that included a school clinic, teachers restrooms, vacuum cleaners with attachments to clean under seats, drinking fountains, adjustable chairs and desks, sanitary toilets, adjustable window shades, and playgrounds. Much of what they requested soon became school district policy.

MOONEY'S SCHOOL

Two of the three election managers for this turn of the 20th century school in County District 1 were are John and George Mooney. It may have been a briefly used name for Kohrville School.⁶¹

MOONSHINE HILL SCHOOL

See Woodward School

MORGAN SCHOOL

See Fidelity

MORGAN'S POINT SCHOOL

County District 13 established a school at Morgan's Point sometime around 1907. Prior to that, students had to travel to La Porte "through all kinds of weather and over unimproved roads… As an illustration it was estimated at the time that one young lady whose home is at the Point and who graduated from the La Porte High School in 1905, had walked a total of over 8,000 miles during her school life to earn her diploma." ⁶²

MOUNT GILLIAN SCHOOL

Mount Gillian was an African American Houston public school that consisted of one or two rented rooms at a Baptist church of the same name. It appeared during or immediately after WWI and operated until 1936, though the location's description had changed from "out on Baker Street" to 219 Kemp. Mount Gillian, also shown as Mount Gilead in some later records, served the Dawson-Lunnon Community founded by Mike and Margarette Lunnon who had come to Houston in the 1850s as slaves of Rufus Cage, Sr., father of the later school board president. In 2017, the site of the school and church, just east of what was later the sprawling Hughes Tool complex, was overgrown, and the exact stretch of Kemp Street where it stood no longer exits.⁶³

MOUNT HOUSTON

In September 1912, William Dermody sold three lots in the Village of Mount Houston to the county for use as a school in District 48. It was still operating in the early 1930s before merging with East Houston School.[64]

MOUNT PILGRIM

A Black school in County District 25 in the middle-1890s that was likely the smallest one in that crowded district just north of the Houston city limits. Not much is known about the school or whether it was connected to a church. The current Mt. Pilgrim Baptist Church in Independence Heights claims 1925 as its founding date.[65]

MOUNT PLEASANT SCHOOL

Mount Pleasant was an African American school in District 21 with Bender School. It appears in various county records from 1886 to 1895, but likely was in operation on either side of those dates. It is possible that it operated at a church location.[66]

MRS. ANDREWS' SCHOOL

In October 1837, only months after the first lots in Houston were sold, Mrs. E. A. Andrews gave notice that she will open a school "principally for young ladies, yet a few boys under the age of 12 years will be received until further notice. The various branches of English education will be taught." The house in which it was conducted was reported to be "the one where President Houston had formerly lived" and where her husband, who painted miniature portraits, had his studio."[67]

MRS. CAPSHAW'S SCHOOL

Mrs. M.L. Capshaw was teaching Black students at the African Methodist Church in 1858, several years before Emancipation. Unfortunately, little else is known beyond the announcement that her school would resume in November 1858.[68]

MRS. HAMILTON'S SCHOOL

Mrs. Hamilton advertised a school for children under ten at a rate of four dollars a month, opening in July 1838. This is perhaps the school that Dilue Rose Harris recalled when she noted a teacher named Mr. Hambleton that same year. Given the propensity for husband and wife teachers, it is a possibility that this is the couple. Harris, writing many decades later, recollected a two-room plank wood building with no glass in the windows and no shutter for the door. Desks and seats were boards laid across barrels and nail kegs. The girls' room, at least, had a wood floor.[69]

MRS. NOBLE'S SCHOOL

For several weeks in early 1851, the *Telegraph and Texas Register* ran the following ad: "Mrs. Z.M. Noble and Miss C.A. Kelly will open a School on Monday, Feb. 10th, at a large, airy and commodious house... universally known as the late residence of N.K. Kellum, for the instruction of Misses generally, and Masters under the age of twelve, in the various branches of an English education, with Drawing, Painting, Worsted Embroidery, and Music if required. Pupils wishing to board with the Teachers, can be accommodated."[70]

This 1890s image of the still extant Kellum-Noble House includes Zerviah Noble herself at lower left. Mike Vance Collection

Zerviah Metcalf Robinson Kelly Noble had come from Connecticut to Texas as a widow in 1846, bringing her daughter, Catherine Kelly. After remarrying to Abram Noble, a widower with five children of his own, the combined family moved to the Nathaniel Kellum Place, a tract of land on Buffalo Bayou that held a comfortable two-story, verandaed home and farming and business operations including a brickyard where materials to build the house originated. Only a few days after Noble purchased the property, his wife ran the above notice.[71]

She had received her own education at Bacon Academy and taught in Connecticut before moving away. Her school initially met in the southeast room of the large house, but eventually an addition was connected to the south side of the building exclusively for school purposes. Her former students recalled Mrs. Noble as a "very capable and thorough teacher," and one added "I think I accomplished more in one year under her tutorage than at any other period of my school life." Textbooks at the Noble school were the McGuffey primer, speller, and reader. While most students lived in the neighborhood, a few came from as far away as the present day Medical Center area, necessitating a boarding arrangement.[72]

Edwin Bonewitz as a schoolboy. He wrote extensively about his grandmother's time attending school in the Noble House.

Her daughter, Catherine, married Hungarian-born A.A. Szabo, but died in 1866 at age 31, leaving her mother to carry on the school without her. When Texas introduced public education in 1871, Mrs. Noble brought her school into the new system. In the fall of 1872, she had 36 students with room for more. She continued under that law and under the subsequent one, with the schoolroom at her house being part of the city system until 1881. The Kellum-Noble House remained her residence until her death in 1894. Also living there was her granddaughter, Eloise Szabo, who became a teacher, as well. As for the house itself, it is today the oldest surviving building constructed in Houston and can be seen at the Heritage Society at Sam Houston Park.[73]

Women on the School Board

In spring of 1904, Houston Mayor Andrew Jackson's nominations to the city's school board ran into a bit of difficulty. Jackson expected business as usual, sending the names of three businessmen for the post, but local women's groups felt the time was right for some female representation on the board. They managed to get the ear of a majority of City Council members who refused to appoint two of the mayor's appointees. A fine bit of lobbying in a time when women were not allowed to vote. For his part, Mayor Jackson simply renominated the two men, Dr. S.C. Red and Edgar Watkins, and, one week later, they were approved.[74]

For good measure, Jackson reported to city council that women were not even legally eligible to serve as school trustees. Judge Noah Allen was called upon to share his views, and offered a lengthy citation of why it would be perfectly legal for women to serve. The ladies groups vowed to press their claim. The battle would not prove easy.[75]

Two mayors and nine years down the road, the issue still sought traction. That emerged via a letter to the newspapers from Mrs. Presley K. Ewing, the head of the United Mothers' Club, charging that the all-male school board was blatantly derelict in its duties. The group of mothers, many of whom had been members of the official inspection committee for some time, had submitted a long list of problems and neglect at the city's schools. Adding women to the school board, Mrs. Ewing suggested, would bring great attention to such details and better results.

Many Houston men agreed, albeit not out of a burning desire to foster equality. One such gentleman wrote: "I would heartily endorse a law requiring the whole of 100% of the positions under the Public School system to be filled by women... The main reason for this is that no matter how unruly a child may be, the soft tender appeal to the child from a woman's voice has ninety-nine times out of a hundred a better effect than the harsh, abrupt, stern command of a man... Every child looks to the gentler sex, the women to guide it to its destiny."[76]

Dr. S.C. Red, the same man who had almost lost his school board spot to a woman back in 1904, published a response that was not so supportive. Red was a highly respected member of the community with impeccable medical credentials. He was in the midst of a 17-year run of service on the school board, but he was having none of Mrs. Ewing's rabble rousing, calling her claims of negligence "grossly exaggerated."[77]

Mamie Ewing responded immediately. As it had with the entire exchange, the *Post* carried the battle verbatim along with a certified response from the five women who had inspected the schools testifying that there was not a shred of exaggeration in their report. Mrs. Ewing added that the women "are charitable enough to think (Red's remarks were) through ignorance as it is in keeping with some of the members of the School Board to know nothing of what they speak concerning the schools."[78]

She was far from done.

"Dr. S. C. Red has had a disturbing nightmare," she wrote. "He evidently sees in the vision of women on the school board a disappearance of himself and similar ornaments. Dr. Red treats it as a fundamental "that women should simply rely on men like babies on their mothers. A man who is inspired that way in this progressive day, face to face with the great independent work being done by women in the world, writes himself down as so antiquated that he ought in justice to the spirit of the age retire from public service. Dr. Red says, in his opinion, that 'the sanitary condition of the Houston Public Schools are as good as they are in any public school buildings in cities of equal size.' ... It means if you have a vile smelling, unforgivable stench in your own home, be comfortable and don't bother if your neighbor has one equally bad. Ye gods, what a philosopher!"[79]

Though Mamie Ewing won the war of words, Houston Mayor Ben Campbell made it clear that he had no intention of adding women to the school board. Instead, he offered to create a three-member Women's Advisory Board, adding that "The school system is the most important branch of the city government. It has the disbursement of funds aggregating from $350,000 to $375,000 a year. The present board is made up of good business men."[80]

Mrs. Ewing and the United Mothers' Club evidently felt that there was more than one way to skin the proverbial cat. The ladies believed that a majority of Houstonians would welcome a female point of view on the school board, so they set out to get a petition under the new home rule act that would force the question. The threshold needed was ten percent of "qualified voters of the city," and Mayor Campbell was happy to oblige should the signatures be gathered.[81]

Two months later, Mrs. Ewing presented 1,909 names, nearly twice the 1,036 signatures that were required. Moreover, the petition not only asked for women on the school board, but called for direct election of all the trustees, as well. The Labor Council, a powerful force in Progressive Era Houston, backed the measure which landed on the October ballot as the Eleventh Amendment.[82]

Mamie Ewing

Before the vote, however, there was more gasoline to be thrown on the fire. The arsonist was Rufus Cage, president of the Houston School Board. In his annual report which coincided with the start of the new school year, Cage addressed the matter at hand thusly: "During the past year there has been some effort made to have women appointed as members of the School Board, the claim being made that female influence is needed in the schools and that women are more efficient than men so far as the proper housekeeping of the schools is concerned, meaning by this, as I understand it, that women are more capable of looking after the cleanliness and sanitary condition of the school, the proper care of the grounds, and other matters of this nature. We now have 283 women and 60 men teachers in the schools, and as they have direct charge of the buildings and grounds, it would seem that the female influence is already fully represented. The Board has special charge of the business management of the schools, and I think that even women will concede that, as a rule, men are more capable in this department."[83]

Mamie Ewing would not let these comments pass.

"Oh, what a travesty!" she wrote to the newspapers. "Women will never be satisfied with the fact that some schools in other cities are in worse condition than ours; they would deplore that fact, while they exerted every effort to make our own schools perfect. Do you think perfection too good for your bright boy and your bright girl?"

As the election approached, voters began to weigh in. Neighborhood meetings were held on the South Side and at the new Dow School in Sixth Ward. At the latter, Superintendent Horn spoke against the city charter amendment asserting that electing trustees would "plunge the board into politics." Mayor Campbell and former Mayor Horace Baldwin Rice were both opposed while G. J. Palmer and County Treasurer Charlton, both former school board members, reminded people that there had been a previous time when school trustees were elected. Charlton preferred that system.[84]

Sixth Ward resident George Adams was "fiery" in support of the amendment. "More than 90 percent of the persons who are molding the future of children in this city are women," he said. "You are glad to have it so."[85]

On Wednesday, October 15, Houston voters decided on a total of 29 amendments to the city charter. Only three of them failed, and one of those was number eleven. It lost by 441 votes, the biggest losing margin of the day, even worse than the amendment to raise the salaries of city commissioners. Among the things passing that day were free textbooks for city schools, an eight hour work day, and city ownership of public utilities.

Politics can be fleeting, however. A new mayor brought a new outlook. By the time that the more progressive J.J. Pastoriza took office in 1917, an elective school board had once again become the law in Houston. That in turn led to the first two female members of the body, Mrs. Charles Scholibo, who had been P.T.A. president at South End Junior High, and Mrs. Frank B. Dwyer, a past president of the Dow P.T.A. and current parliamentarian for the citywide organization. Though the barrier had finally tumbled, it would be another 50 years before a woman was elected to a position other than school board trustee in Houston.[86]

The two pioneers took office on Monday night, May 28, 1917, bringing "the first deft touch of womanly fingers." They did not sit silently in their first meeting, either. Mrs. Scholibo objected to the idea of suspending Domestic Science and Manual Training classes, and Mrs. Dwyer took part in the discussion of various school buildings, showing "intimate knowledge of many of them which she had visited as a member of the Mothers' Clubs."

MRS. SATOR'S SCHOOL

A Mrs. Sator was conducting a public school at Beauchamp Springs under the Reconstruction-era law with about 35 students learning in both English and German.[87]

MRS. TUCKER'S SCHOOL

During, and seemingly before, the Reconstruction-era school period, a Mrs. Tucker was teaching a school for White boys and girls "in Abbott's Prairie on Slaughter Pen Ditch," today's Country Club Bayou.[88]

MYKAWA SCHOOL

One of the few century-old county school buildings extant in 2025 was the orange-brick Mykawa School that sat on Almeda-Genoa Road just west of Mykawa Road. The town that it once served was named for Shinpei Mykawa, a Japanese immigrant who was among those who brought improved rice growing techniques to the Houston area just after 1900. He was killed in a farm accident in 1907, one year before the community that bears his name got a post office. By at least 1910, it also had a school in County District 45. The building standing today was erected in 1923 to replace the frame structure. As of 2025, the building was not rehabilitated, but the grounds were being used for agriculture education.[89]

Mykawa School building empty but somewhat maintained in the 2010s. Laurie Feinswog photo

MYKAWA COLORED SCHOOL

Little is known about the school that taught the Black children of the Mykawa community in the early 1900s aside from vague references in county reports. It was described as a "box structure" in 1907.[90]

Schools N - O

NARROW GAUGE SCHOOL

Residents around the community of Humble petitioned to have County District 28 divided in 1888 with their town remaining in the district while the southern section was split off. The district's school for African American students, which for a time outpaced attendance at the White building, was Narrow Gauge. It drew its name from the Houston East and West Texas Railway, built through the area in 1876, near which the building stood. Attendance hovered around 50 pupils. For a time, the school was also called Pleasant Grove. It was replaced in 1909 by another "Colored School" building by the tracks west of Humble, and that served the district until it was destroyed by fire in 1947 at which time, Humble ISD's Black children were sent to Aldine.[1]

NEIDORFF SCHOOL

The Neidorff School was operating on Grant Road, northwest of Spring-Cypress prior to 1884. For a brief while the school was also known as Christen's after J.P. Christen, an area resident and patron whose family boarded the teachers. A new frame building was constructed prior to 1910, but that building was destroyed by fire. After interim classes being held at a nearby house, another Neidorff School was constructed, including a movable wall that could create two classrooms. It was consolidated with Cypress School in 1936.[2]

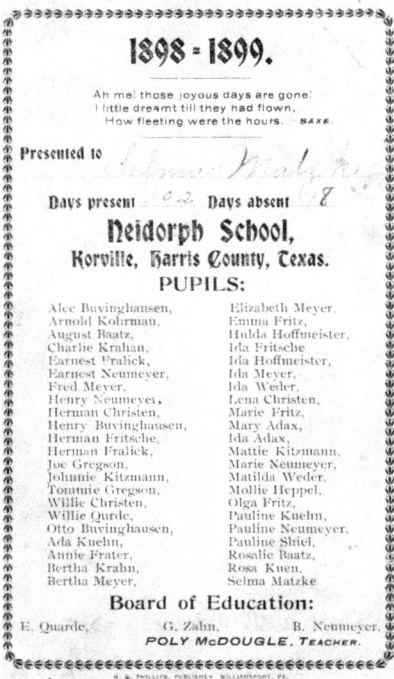

A late 19th Century attendance card from Niedorf shows the heavy Germanness of Northwest Harris County. Cypress Historical Society

NEIDORF COLORED SCHOOL

A Black school at Neidorff in District 7 is mentioned in the county treasurer's ledgers in the early 1890s, but the money set aside for a teacher was left untouched. It is unknown if this school ever operated.[3]

NEWMAN SCHOOL

See Sutton

NORSWORTHY'S SCHOOLHOUSE

A schoolhouse named for W.B. Norsworthy was in operation on the north side of Buffalo Bayou in the area of Clinton prior to December 1875 and is mentioned often through 1892.[4]

NORTH SIDE/END J H S

See Marshall JHS

NORTH GREEN'S BAYOU SCHOOL
The name of North Green's Bayou School shows up in District 16 records for 1894-95.[5]

Free College Education in Houston

"The establishment of our two Junior High Schools will make higher institutions of learning. One reason for this is the presence of the Rice Institute in our midst. Since the establishment of this great institution, it would seem that any boy or girl in Houston who is energetic and ambitious ought surely to be able to obtain a high type of collegiate education. It is possible for a child in Houston to enter a free kindergarten, to pass through the elementary schools and the High Schools supported at public expense, and then to spend four years at Rice Institute without the payment of any tuition fees whatever. Undoubtedly, these facts should prove a great stimulus to educational work in our midst."

Houston City Schools Report 1912-13

Note – Rice Institute/University did not admit Black students until 1963.

NORTH HOUSTON SCHOOL
North Houston School House was the second largest institution in the crowded County District 25 during most of the late 19th century. As early as 1886, there were seven schools in the district, rising to almost a dozen a decade later. North Houston was still listed as a school in the early 1930s.[6]

NOVITIATE, THE
The Convent of the Incarnate World and Our Lady of Perpetual Help, the Novitiate of the Sisters of the Incarnate Word and Blessed Sacrament that opened 1932 on Bissonnet just inside present day Loop 610 was designed to house teaching sisters during the summer and offer instruction to the novices. The following fall, a Catholic grammar school was opened on the first floor and a boarding school added which helped with revenue for the convent. The grammar school was discontinued when St. Vincent's parish school opened in 1942, and the boarding school component a few years later.[7]

OAK ADDITION SCHOOL
Goose Creek ISD's first African American school was started in 1921 after three local women, Mrs. A.J. Johnson, Norah Davis, and Addie Rowls, took matters into their own hands and "rounded up sufficient students" to open a small school on the "old Will Taylor lease." After some time meeting at Mt. Rose Baptist

Church, the district bought property in Oak Addition in Pelly and relocated an old store building there. A second teacher was added in 1926.[8]

OAK FOREST E S

The school at 1401 W. 43rd at the southwest corner of Oak Forest Drive opened in 1949, roughly three years after the first few sections of the housing development of that name was started by builder Frank Sharp and others. The neighborhood eventually grew to 18 sections making it the largest of its kind in America for a brief while, and necessitating construction of two other elementary schools in the 1950s. Oak Forest Elementary was torn to the ground and replaced with a brand new building in 2005.[9]

OAK GROVE SCHOOL

District 2 in the Klein area had two schoolhouses in the mid-1880s, Doughtie's and Oak Grove, the latter of which survived much longer. The Oak Grove School moved twice, but sat roughly near Spring Creek Oaks Clubhouse between Spring Cypress and Louetta Roads. Like many rural schools, it was often dominated by a few families. In 1914, every student but two was named Kleb, Strack, or Eckhardt. By the 1920s, Oak Grove still had a student body in the range of 20 pupils. It was one of the schools consolidated into Rural High School #1 in Klein in 1928.[10]

The 1914 class at Oak Grove. Klein ISD

Corporal Punishment

"Spare the rod and spoil the child" is a phrase coined by English poet Samuel Butler in 1662, but the sentiment is traced by many back to millennia-old biblical proverbs, including attributions to King Solomon.[11]

M.M. Kenney, an engineer and founding member of the Texas State Historical Association, wrote of his frontier Texas schooling in modern-day Austin County during the late 1830s and early 1840s. He described what was almost an eagerness on the part of some teachers, primarily men, to dole out a whipping to maintain focus on the tasks at hand. One teacher even had an entire arsenal of switches in various lengths, strengths, and diameters to be deployed according to the age of the perpetrator and the severity of the offense. On one occasion, when the teacher, an Irish immigrant named Mr. Dyas, attempted to apply the feared "shillelagh" to an almost grown student, the young man jumped out an open window after two blows, not returning to school for a couple of days.[12]

Kenney feared the swats for himself, too. He wrote that they came from "the kind of tree that furnished Indians with arrows and the schoolmaster with switches at the same time. I remember thinking of the feasibility of destroying all that kind of timber growing near the school house."

By the time the 20th century had arrived, and a system of free public schools complete with supervisors had become an accepted part of life, corporal punishment was no longer such an accepted practice. L.L. Pugh, the man in charge of all the public schools in rural Harris County, wrote this instruction for his teachers in 1912: "Use physical force sparingly with children. When administering corporal punishment, let it be done in the presence of another teacher, if there is one in the building. It is needless to say that this form of punishment should be employed only in extreme cases, and when the teachers feel that an improved behavior will result from its use. Do not punish while angry. Punishment should be a corrective agency to the child, and its good effects are lost if there be any spirit of revenge on the part of the teacher, or if the pupil be injured in any way. The use of physical force is a case of unprofessional conduct, and should be avoided as much as possible."[13]

During summer recess of 1925, Houston Superintendent Oberholtzer convened a distinguished committee of educational and juvenile justice leaders and also invited comment from the public. The prevailing sentiment was that the whippings should be allowed to continue, though editorials in both the *Chronicle* and the *Press* spoke against the practice in no uncertain terms. It was pointed out by the *Chronicle* that King Solomon "had 600 or so wives and even more concubines," yet that wisdom was no longer followed, either. The editors felt that if the United States military had abandoned the practice of corporal punishment, the schools could also do better.[14]

The last resort practice was widely used in Houston and Harris County for much of the century, and many a Houston-area boy has stories of a coach's paddle. Gradually, though, the idea of physical punishment dished out at school has lost favor. Today, corporal punishment is outlawed in schools in almost all of Europe, South America, Australia, and several other countries. Poland was the first country to ban it, in 1783. The majority of the United States barred it, as well, though it continues to be allowed in 17 states including in Texas unless a student's parent or guardian requests otherwise.[15]

OAK LAWN SCHOOL

The small Oak Lawn school in the addition of the same name sat between the city limits of Houston and Harrisburg when it showed up prior to 1900. In spite of its lack of size, it was not neglected. The two teachers there in 1904-05 were Kate Deady and Rosa Dullahan, both Houston public school veterans. They handled a combined class load of about 100 pupils. Oak Lawn was closed when Lubbock Elementary opened, not appearing after 1908.[16]

OAKWOOD E S

Goose Creek ISD operated the small Oakwood School for African American students in the late 1930s.

OATES PRAIRIE SCHOOL

With the exception of the county's namesake, perhaps no other family has had their name continuously attached to a Harris County school longer than that of James Wyatt Oates. The North Carolina native was settled in the area where modern day Wallisville Road crosses Hunting Bayou by the mid-to-late 1830s, and the area quickly became known as Oates Prairie. The second generation of the family had a line of houses down the east side of Oates Road, and the Hart, Singleton, and McGee families also populated the neighborhood. It is not proven that the senior Oates started a school, but it is known that his son, James W. Oates, Jr., was offering a school in his home prior to 1876. In 1888, the district split off from Harrisburg to become County District 34 with the White Oates School and the Hart Colored School. A succession of buildings followed, and a second teacher was added in the mid-1920s.

Portions of the first two buildings join together at Oates Prairie ES. Laurie Feinswog photo

In 1929, a lovely two-story brick schoolhouse rose in the 10000 block of Wallisville, just east of Oates Road. For a time, junior high grades were also offered. A second wing was added in 1937, just a year before the district was annexed via election into HISD. During WWII, as industrial workers poured into the area, enrollment ballooned to over 1,000 before new schools at Jacinto City and Green's Bayou brought relief. The name of the school was changed to James Wyatt Oates, Jr. Elementary in 1948, ostensibly to avoid confusion with the local African American school which was then also going by the name Oates Prairie. Roughly a century after the Oates family first started a school for the community's farm and ranch families, direct descendants were still attending.[17]

OUR LADY OF GUADALUPE SCHOOL

The school at Our Lady of Guadalupe opened in a frame building at Marsh and Runnels, a stretch that is on current-day Navigation, in September 1912, only three weeks after the first mass was celebrated there. The story of its place as a cornerstone of Houston's Mexican community, however, is more accurately traced to the arrival of Sister Benitia Vermeerch in 1915. The Sisters of the Divine Providence to whom the church's educational work was entrusted, were focused and willing, but only one of them spoke Spanish, something that was certainly necessary for the refugees who had moved to what would become known as El Segundo Barrio after they fled the revolution that dominated Mexico during and after the downfall of Porfirio Diaz. "La Madre Benita", as she was later known, had lived in Mexico, and understood both the language and the culture of the people who became her charges when she was named school principal.[18]

Enrollment was down to 23 students when Sr. Benitia arrived, and as she made the rounds of the neighborhood, she found many children playing in the muddy alleys who were not attending any school, public or parochial. The immigrants, many of whom worked for the railroads, lived in company-owned houses, sharing one community faucet, and sleeping on cotton sacks spread on the floor. More recent arrivals lived in empty boxcars. The sister contacted local businesses about donating food, clothing, and shoes. The Bender Hotel, undergoing remodeling, gave many of its old rugs. Neighborhood mothers were organized to cook and serve meals, and garden plots were planted on church property. The nuns moved to a new convent on site in 1921, and two years later, when a new church building opened, the two-story frame building was given over completely for the school. By the close of the decade, attendance had risen to over 400 pupils, attending classes at no charge, taught by eight sisters. OLG School continued to be a preferred destination for the city's Mexican American children who were not allowed to attend many other Catholic schools including St. Joseph. Some children walked from that Sixth Ward neighborhood to OLG and back, including on Sunday for Mass, since some Anglo churches would let them in only if they stood behind the last row of pews. A new two-story school building opened in 1948, and a gym, a new convent, and a cafeteria wing followed. Today, Our Lady of Guadalupe School still serves the largely Hispanic community near East End over a century after its founding.[19]

Sister Dolores and the 1930 class at Our Lady of Guadalupe School. Courtesy OLGS

OUR LADY OF PERPETUAL HELP

The sisters of Incarnate Word and Blessed Sacrament operated this private elementary school from 1933 until 1948 when it closed.[20]

OUR MOTHER OF MERCY SCHOOL

This Catholic parish school in Fifth Ward offered classes for Black students beginning in 1930. Teaching students all the way through high school, it was located at 4000 Sumpter and associated with French Town, a Louisiana Creole settlement. Those immigrants to Houston, many fleeing the flood of 1927 in their previous home state, initially tried to attend Our Lady of Guadalupe but were relegated to the back pews and ordered to take confession and communion last, an irony since the Mexican immigrants at Guadalupe had endured similar discrimination at Anglo Catholic churches. The Creoles were mixed race, many were light skinned enough to "pass" for White with employers, preferred not to turn their back on their darker relatives, so the vast majority continued to attend segregated schools and churches. The first church building at Our Mother of Mercy opened in 1929. The students at the school initially paid ten cents a week tuition. The school, staffed originally by the Sisters of the Holy Family, closed in 2009.[21]

Schools P - Q

PARK J H S
See Edison

Houston Schools Gain a Year

On Monday, March 11, 1940, the HISD board voted unanimously to move from eleven years of public school to twelve. Under the new plan, a Houston child would expect six years of elementary school, three years of junior high school and three years of senior high school. An identical arrangement had been proposed as early as 1926, but languished.[1]

It took a bit of time to work out the details, but by spring 1941, it was the law of the district. It applied to students entering high school, not those already there. For those high school pupils with more time before graduation, a non-credit, "directed study hall" was added. Sam Houston principal W.S. Brandenberger said that the plan would be beneficial to current students "by giving them more time to study and to use the library."[2]

PARK PLACE E S

Park Place was a small town "several miles distant from Houston, on the Galveston-Houston Interurban" when a two-story gray brick school with a red tile roof was opened there in the summer of 1915 as part of County District 20. The four-acre campus was on Hastings Street, near the Interurban stop when it opened, described as "one of the finest-equipped county schools in the state." It was definitely overkill for the 32 pupils that showed up for the first term, but the enrollment rose to several hundred by the time it was absorbed into HISD and the

City of Houston in 1927. The school moved into a new building just north of the previous one on Park Place Blvd. in fall of 2002.³

PASADENA SCHOOL

One year after the 1892 development of Pasadena, six of the pioneering families held a meeting about educating their roughly 30 children. It resulted in the men converting Charles Munger's chicken coop near Shaver Street and Little Vince Bayou into a one-room schoolhouse. The first teacher was Munger's 17-year old son. The following year, a one-room school, part of District 20, opened at what is now Wafer and Shaw. An early force in pushing for something better were Swedish immigrants Oscar and Hanna Kruse, who had moved to the area from Montana. They joined others in establishing an independent school district in 1898 with Mr. Kruse as a board officer. The district would remain all-White for decades. The schoolhouse moved to the south side of Broadway between Main and Shaver in 1904, with a lean-to addition and a blanket hung as a divider to create three classroom spaces. School in Pasadena generally started in June or July to accommodate children who needed to work picking strawberries.⁴

Children pose in front of the Pasadena School on the coastal prairie.
Pasadena ISD

In August 1910, a new, two-story brick structure complete with six classrooms, an auditorium, and a bell tower opened next to the frame school. It offered ten grades instead of the previous seven. The verbose Willoughby C. Williams was principal, writing of the school that "Through its portals are entering the stalwart young men and promising girls of maturity who come to share this heritage, the public school." Literary societies encouraged students in debate, and many of the 140 pupils joined singing groups that gathered around the piano in the auditorium. There was even a stable added for student and teacher horses.⁵

After the high school opened in 1924, the brick building became the grammar school, eventually carrying the Kruse name. Also in the 1920s, Mae Smythe became principal and would stay in that capacity for 36 years, joined on the faculty by her sisters Lillian and Sadye.[6]

PASADENA H S

Pasadena High, with its four-year program, was completed at 206 Shaver in 1924, though one student graduated almost a year prior, thanks to summer school credits. The first official class of five PHS grads had their commencement at the Methodist Church auditorium in May 1924. A gymnasium was added to the campus in 1928, only the second in the county outside of Houston. School colors began as green and purple, but the inability to find cloth for the uniforms, coupled with the acquisition of green and white football and band outfits from another cash-strapped district, brought a change in color. Local industries, primarily related to oil and the ship channel, kept PISD afloat during the Depression, and when neighboring districts South Houston and Genoa faced insolvency, they were added to the district with high school students coming to Pasadena. Extra-curricular activities did suffer from hard times. Because too few high school students could afford to buy a horn, membership in the high school band was open to elementary and junior high pupils causing one graduate to joke that he was "one of the few kids that had 10 letters in the PHS band."[7]

PENN CITY SCHOOL

Penn City sat on the north bank of Buffalo Bayou just east of today's Beltway 8. It was promoted by Clarance Waller to be home to dozens of big industrial operations and wharves along with the worker's residences that would accompany them. The two-story brick school in District 16 offered eight grades in the 1910s and was still in existence as late as 1922. Unfortunately, the development largely went nowhere. Today the area that was once Penn City is completely industrial, but only due to later investment, not to Clarance Waller's efforts.[8]

PERRY SCHOOL

The name of Perry school house was listed as the voting place for a trustee election in the number 36 Almeda district in 1899. No further mention was found.[9]

PERSHING J H S

When the municipality of West University Place built its first junior high, they created a shared campus on University Boulevard, west of Edloe. The school opened in 1928 with its nine classrooms, library, and cafeteria at the west end of the property, connected to the existing West U Elementary by a covered walk. Forty seventh, eight, and ninth graders attended that first year under the supervision of Clarence Orman, who was also elementary school principal and the West U ISD superintendent. The junior high building honored the supreme commander of America's WWI army, and the famous general sent the school an autographed photo.

The school reciprocated in 1943 when the "aged warrior" was confined in Walter Reed Hospital, telling him that the students at his namesake institution were buying three jeeps a day during a bond drive. All 1,700 pupils on University Boulevard signed the letter and young Sara Beth Alexander even added a kiss to the page. For a time in the 1940s, Pershing students had the unique position among the city's junior highs of getting to individually choose whether they went on to San Jacinto or Lamar High School. In 1949, Pershing, which had been forced to add seventeen shacks for the student body, moved to a brand new campus on Braes and Bellefontaine, south of Bellaire Boulevard, leaving the old location entirely to the elementary. Clarence Orman moved with them as principal. In 2007, they relocated again to a shiny adjacent complex that offered over 200,000 square feet.[10]

A 1939 class at Pershing JHS. Mike Vance Collection

Staying Healthy in the School

Medical Inspection

Houston and Harris County were prone to infectious diseases from the very start of human habitation. In addition to largely primitive medical knowledge, part of the problem was due to a thriving population of mosquitoes and fleas. The Karankawa Indians who roamed the coastal prairies coated themselves in a rancid mixture of animal fat and mud for protection, leading early colonists to remark on their odiferousness. Yellow Fever epidemics were common. The one in 1839 wiped out 12% of Houston's entire population, prompting the establishment of a city health department the following year.[11]

Diseases that disrupted school activities were slightly different, of course. Even 19th century school officials realized that clean, well-ventilated school rooms were a good idea. By the first years of the 1900s, Houston school officials were conducting annual medical inspections in which a trained nurse or doctor, working with the city health officer, sought to examine every student in the district. In 1908, the schools were sending home forms to parents along with a second form for a physician to fill out following an examination. School officials admitted that it was an uphill battle in some cases. The superintendent's report in 1908 remarked that "the parent himself is in utter ignorance as to the existence of" medical difficulties. He also added that "In more instances than a few, strange as it may seem, the parents are too indifferent to care."[12]

The first examinations that Houston schools routinely conducted were of the students' eyes and ears. A teacher at Rusk School was lauded for her initiative when she "selected some fifteen children from her building who were not making satisfactory progress in their studies and who she had reason to believe were suffering from physical defects. All these children were taken to a specialist, who had generously offered to donate his services in this regard. Out of these 15 children who were not doing satisfactory work, it was found that eight had adenoids, ten had defective eyes, seven had defective hearing, and only one was not in need of some kind of medical attention.[13]

By the next year, a group of local doctors known as the Houston Association of Opticians and Aurists volunteered to check every pupil in Houston city schools using a Snellen eye chart and testing hearing by means of a ticking watch held three feet away from the child's ear. They were looking for symptoms such as inflamed eyelids and tiredness of the eyes at the end of a day's schoolwork. One of the primary eye diseases targeted was the highly contagious bacterial affliction trachoma that was spread by direct contact with other children or even towels and washcloths. The city schools reported 24 cases in 1914. Of those, thirteen were children living in one household.[14]

By the 1909-10 school year, Houston City Public Schools had a full time Medical Supervisor in the form of Wallace Ralston, M.D., a well-respected and published otolaryngologist. He soon started broadening the scope of the system's medical work. Faced with an outbreak of meningitis in 1910, Dr. Ralston bucked local pressure to close the schools, claiming that a classroom was a safer environment, thanks to precautions such as fumigation, than places the students would otherwise congregate such as on the streets or at the moving picture shows.[15]

The list of diseases tracked in the Houston schools includes several of the usual childhood suspects such as measles, mumps, and chicken pox along with fungal and parasitic skin ailments like favus, impetigo, and scabies. Year-to-year numbers show a particularly rough year in 1916 when five year highs in cases of measles (1,073), Whooping cough (60), and scarlet fever (46) were logged. A city ordinance required that students with these infectious diseases be kept home, though there were some parents who objected, saying it was simply part of growing up. Or not, since there were 16 to 38 Houston school children dying of these sicknesses each year just prior to and during WWI.[16]

Diphtheria, a bacterial respiratory infection, was a particularly feared disease, one that has now been largely eradicated in the United States thanks to vaccines. At one time it was the leading killer of children in the country. Students suspected of diphtheria infections, meaning that they had runny nose and coughing, were swabbed and a culture done. They were not allowed back into the classroom until another culture showed them free of the bacteria.[17]

Regular immunization was also responsible for the elimination of smallpox, the first disease for which there was a widely used vaccine, thanks to Edward Jenner in 1796. Houston schools registered nine cases of smallpox in 1914, but by the next year, teachers and principals were involved in seeing that all children and faculty were vaccinated, up from approximately 50% only twelve months earlier. By 1915, there were twenty smallpox cases in all of Houston, and a male student at Colored High School was the only one of school age. In the county schools, there was still enough concern to hire a guard to help prevent the spread of the disease at Tomball and Alief.[18]

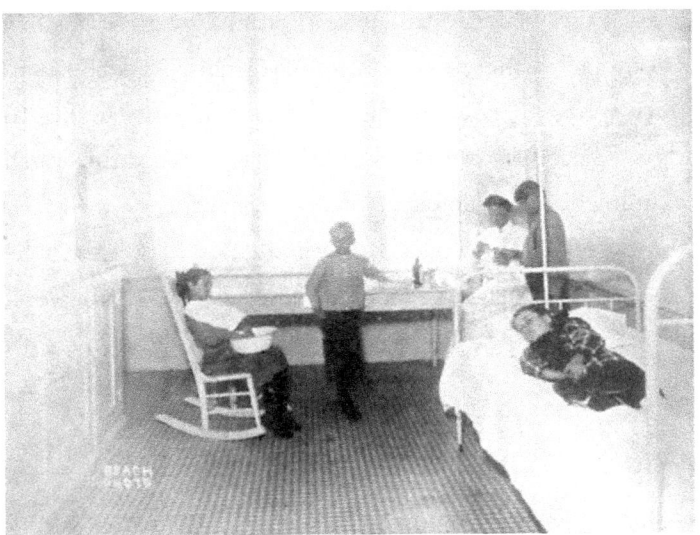

School nurse at Reagan ES tending to students. HISD

Numbers-wise, the biggest outbreak was of Roseola, a strain of the herpes virus that caused a distinctive rash and a potentially high fever. Generally more prevalent in younger children, in 1918 it got out of hand, infecting 2,072 students and 13 faculty members.

It was nothing compared to the pandemic of Spanish Flu that was sweeping the world that same year, of course. Worldwide deaths were between 20 and 40 million; more people than were killed in the world war that was raging at the same time. It was severe enough to temporarily lower the average American life span by 10 years. [19]

In Houston schools, all efforts were taken to ensure a safe environment for the children. Twelve nurses were brought in and cooperation was undertaken with the Army medical staff at Camp Logan. The new man in charge of school medicine and hygiene was Dr. F.W. Slataper who would see to it that the idea of school nurses became a permanent one. The Texas Board of Education issued guidelines for the fall of 1918. Among the suggested rules was that "disinfectant should be scattered over the floor and swept. All woodwork, desks, chairs, tables and doors should be wiped off with a cloth wet with linseed, kerosene and turpentine," and that "Every pupil must have at all times a clean handkerchief, and it must not be laid on top of the desk."[20]

City schools were closed for a period of twelve days in October at the height of the pandemic in Houston, but debate remained as to whether it was the best course of action. The example most commonly used was that there were fewer deaths in New York City schools that had remained open than in Philadelphia schools where they closed. Many doctors contended that "the schools were closed rather as a concession to popular demand than on the basis of scientific judgment."[21]

Over 110 people died from flu in Houston in 1918. One of the victims was Mr. W. Peine, who had been the business representative of the Houston City School Board for twelve years. His loss was felt keenly by the city school system. Of him the superintendent wrote: "It was always his desire to make a dollar go as far as it possibly could, and yet if a dollar was needed for the success of any part of the school work, he made it his distinct business to find that dollar." High praise for a school accountant. Even more telling about Peine's popularity among his fellow employees was this excerpt from a news story: "When (superintendent) P.W. Horn reached the school building at an early hour after sunrise Saturday morning he found an old colored janitor sitting on the broad front steps sobbing bitterly. The man had been with the schools for a period of over 20 years. Between sobs he said, 'I came down to get my orders from Mr. Peine this morning and I found he was dead! What will we all do?'"[22]

Sub-normal students

The new Rusk School in 1910 featured an unfortunately named room for "sub-normal" pupils whose work was ungraded. There were a total of 16 boys and three girls, of whom seven were retained at the end of the school year. It seemed the only way out was for an underlying cause of the student's learning disability to be discovered and corrected. Fortunately for some of these pupils, school officials began to understand the possibilities. "It has been found that a large percentage of backward children are backward through removable causes, "wrote Sybil Campbell, the teacher in charge of the effort. She had enlisted the help of seven local doctors, four general practitioners and three specialists, to give a "thorough physical examination" to each of the students. Recommendations to remedy health concerns were then sent to the parents.[23]

Two of the 1910 cases received special comment. One was an eight-year-old girl who could read but was completely helpless when I came to simple arithmetic. She had "an uncertain hold on numbers to ten." Following a doctor's diagnosis, "She then had an operation for removal of adenoids and tonsils. During the term succeeding operation, her general physical condition improved, but there was no perceptible improvement in her grip on numbers, and it seemed useless to worry her longer with the subject. Suddenly, in the following term— her fifth in the room—number sense developed, and in that one term she covered arithmetic work through the course prescribed for Low and High First and Low Second. In rapid addition, she outran anyone in the room, even those whose number sense is normal. She will be transferred to grade next fall."[24]

The other case that Miss Campbell found noteworthy was that of a 14-year-old boy who, with the exception of some small spelling prowess, was at a level "about what one would expect from a seven-year-old at the end of the first six weeks in school." The youngster was "exceedingly nervous." His diagnosed illness was St. Vitus Dance, now known as Sydenham's Chorea, a condition of rapid facial jerks that was often a side-effect of rheumatic fever. On top of that his father had turned him into "an excessive chewer of tobacco" after being advised by "a physician back in the piney woods to provide him with plenty of tobacco to allay nervousness. He appeared to be under nourished, and was always ravenously hungry."

A Houston physician cut off the tobacco and gave the boy milk and cream throughout the day as well as directing his home diet. "The improvement, mental, moral and physical, was so marked as to be noticed even by his fellow pupils," Miss Campbell reported. "There is a large prospect that he will develop into a normal boy, a thing which would have seemed incredible six months ago."

Health in African American Schools

Health care in Houston's African American schools lagged behind that for White students who had seen a major jump in attention to health in the years just prior to WWI. Before 1925, the only major step taken for Black children was the requirement of a smallpox vaccination. In that year, "Dr. C. H. Pemberton was appointed as part-time physician for the Negro schools."[25]

By the start of the school year in 1929, HISD employed sixteen White and four Black nurses, and district-wide, there were thirteen physicians who were "doing daily part-time work in the schools." Overall, the district's supervising doctor described it as a "system of inspection and not of treatment." School nurses and doctors were not allowed to diagnose nor prescribe for any of the city's pupils.[26]

The superintendent who hired Dr. Pemberton was E.E. Oberholtzer who was relatively new on the job at the time. And it was Oberholtzer who later created a "Negro Branch of the Department of Hygiene of the Houston Public Schools, under the supervision of Dr. A. C. Hutcheson, a White doctor."[27]

Prairie View A&M master's candidate Moselle Anderson wrote her thesis in 1947 on the state of health services in HISD's segregated Black schools, and offered this description: "The school health staff, which consists of a medical director, a number of part-time physicians, a supervisor of nurses, and a dental hygienist carry on a variety of health activities. Among the activities carried on are: health counseling with students and parents in the school and in the home, communicable disease control, first aid, physical examinations, follow-up work concerned with the correction of defects, special work with handicapped children, advice and assistance to the teaching staff, and sanitary inspection of school plants."[28]

When Anderson wrote her thesis shortly after the end of WWII, she noted that most major diseases had been virtually eliminated from the Houston schools both Black and White. Diphtheria remained a major concern, as did several lesser infectious diseases. One malady which she singled out was tonsillitis, and she blamed many of those cases on another Houston bugaboo - standing water through which children had to wade to and from school. "Good streets," she wrote. "Which can be properly drained after flooding rains, would have a tendency to bring this number of tonsillitic sufferers down in the elementary school child."

Drinking Fountains

"A little over a year ago, the Board authorized the installation of two drinking fountains at the Taylor School. They were found to be an excellent remedy for the drinking cup nuisance. Principals and teachers from a number of other city schools inspected them. It soon developed that they all wanted the fountains, but we were again confronted with that question of money.

"The need and efficiency was no longer questioned. Six other buildings were equipped during the year, and orders have been placed for seven more. It is likely that with the opening of the next term every school in the city having sewerage connections will be so provided.

"These fountains consist of an enameled trough, about six feet in length, having four large nickel bulbs in the center, from which the water flows at a sufficient height to enable a child to drink without touching either his hands or mouth to the bulb. It is, in fact, just what the name implies—a sanitary drinking fountain.

"The water furnished through these fountains is pure artesian, and comes from wells ranging in depth from 1,000 feet to 1,400 feet. Its temperature is always pleasing.

"The cost of each fountain, with all connections, will approximate $100.00."

Houston City Schools Report 1909-10

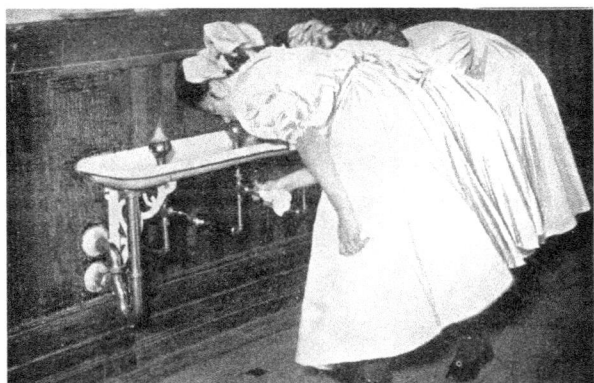

The new drinking fountains in use. HISD

Immunization

Smallpox was the first disease for which a vaccine was widely developed, used, and accepted, so it is not surprising that it was the first immunization required for a child to attend school. The forward thinking W.G. Hanner, superintendent of County District 25 required vaccinations for all pupils as early as 1912. Houston's city schools began pushing for every student to receive the shot in 1915. Only half of the pupils from the previous year had been vaccinated. Not long after, the smallpox immunization was not just a suggestion but a requirement. No vaccination, no school. There were legal challenges, and one after another, the courts ruled for the schools.[29]

One of those lawsuits held up the Bellaire School as having "the most healthy children in the county," noting that it was a district that did not require vaccinations, yet had no smallpox. The lie was put to that in 1925 when the Bellaire School had to be closed and disinfected for a day after it was discovered that a West University boy who attended the school had been to class in spite of being infected with smallpox. There was another case "beyond Bellaire" involving a child who was a student elsewhere. The *Press* reported that many Bellaire parents hurried to Houston to have their children immunized.[30]

In January 1934, with smallpox vaccinations made legally mandatory, the Houston district turned its sights to diphtheria. School health boss Dr. Allen Hutcheson, less than one year into the job, announced a voluntary program that included subsidies for families who could not afford the full cost of immunizations that ran between $5 and $10. The plan was to have 60,000 children between six months and twelve years take the Schick test to determine susceptibility to the disease. Roughly a sixth of that number reported for the free tests, and 3,000 of them showed positive. Hutcheson reiterated his call for all children to be vaccinated.[31]

At the start of the school year 1946-47, a mandatory immunization program for diphtheria was required of all six-year olds enrolling in school for the first time. Since only 22% of the new students had previously gotten their shots, vaccinations were offered at the school for only fifteen cents.[32]

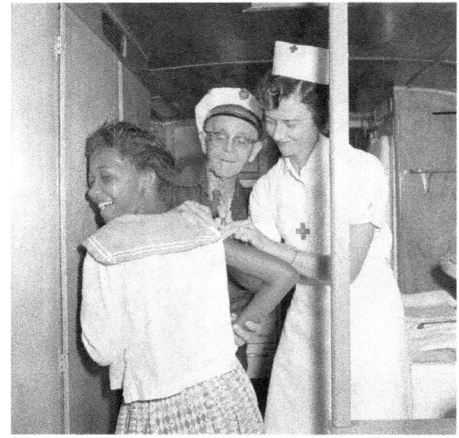

A Langston ES student braves her polio shot in the early 1950s. HHRC

PINEY POINT SCHOOL

Piney Point takes its name from a southerly turn in Buffalo Bayou, a peninsula of the piney woods that extended south onto the prairie and to the San Felipe Road at a time when the only timber to be found was along the watercourses. The African American school bearing this name predated the White one, with the latter appearing in County District 23 before 1891. It operated as a one-room rural school until at least WWI.[33]

PINEY POINT COLORED SCHOOL

With Emancipation, thousands of African Americans who had been enslaved on plantations in the nearby counties and states left to begin their freedom closer to the City of Houston. The population in rural Harris County swelled with Black farmers, sharecroppers, and wood choppers, and one of the earliest settlements was at Piney Point. The community was loosely centered around the Pilgrim Rest Missionary Baptist Church, and the first classes operated within the same building near the modern intersection of Jeanetta and Westheimer.

Eventually Adam Rasmus donated a lot for a separate school building that housed grades one through six. It shows up in County District 23 before 1886 with young Henry Turpin, a Haitian-born "mulatto" as the teacher, a position he held there for at least a decade. By the 1920s, Piney Point had 40 to 50 students crowded into one or two rooms. Children from Piney Point who wanted more schooling went to Booker T. Washington in Fourth Ward since that was the closest high school for African Americans. During the 1930s, they travelled there in a converted Phenix Dairy truck. A sleek new Howard Barnstone-designed Piney Point Elementary opened on Fondren and Pagewood in March 1963 with longtime teacher Frankie Anderson as principal. With a budget of only $11 per square foot, it was another case of a post-war HISD majority-Black school getting the least money but ending up with the best design. By 2017, that modernist structure had been virtually encased by subsequent additions.[34]

PITCHMAN SCHOOL

See Winkler

PLATTE SCHOOL

Platte School is one of the rare survivors from the Harris County school system that still remains today. It opened in District 4 on Richmond Road, today's Bissonnet, prior to 1910, getting its name from a member of the German-immigrant Platte family who served as a generous trustee. By 1912, there were two teachers in a single-story brick school that offered two classrooms, a library of 200 books, and a small auditorium. Like most rural schools, money was tight, and patrons held concerts, suppers, or dances to augment funds. A masked Christmas ball at Platte in 1911 raised $19 that was used to buy a "complete set of carpenters' tools" with which the boy students built "many articles needed in the school room." Platte was taken into the expanding HISD before 1930. Today the building lives on as the Bissonnet Kirby Animal Hospital.[35]

Platte School long before it was saved as a veterinary hospital. HHRC

> **1882 Houston School Policy on weapons**
>
> The City of Houston Public Schools had a definitive policy on weapons. The Pupils were prohibited "from carrying pistols, knives, slung shot or other deadly weapons to school."
>
> Longtime *Houston Post* writer and physician Dr. S.O. Young defined slung shot as a black jack, not a sling shot.

PLEASANT ARK SCHOOL

Pleasant Ark was an African American school in the busy County District 25. In the middle-1880s, it sat on the south side of the T& N.O. tracks in Fifth Ward near present day Panell or Capron Streets and likely taught children of Black railroad workers. The school was still operating in 1915.[36]

PLEASANT HILL SCHOOL

The *Houston Post* reported in 1962 that "the old Pleasant Hill site" was among nine tracts to be sold on February 15. Little else about the school had shown up HISD in records.

POE E S

Edgar Allen Poe Elementary at 5100 Hazard will forever be known foremost for the horrific playground bombing perpetrated by Paul Orgeron on September 15, 1959 that left six people dead and nineteen wounded. Those killed included teacher Jeannie Katherine Kolter, custodian James Arlie Montgomery, two seven-year old boys, the bomber, and his own son. However, prior to that awful day, Poe was one of the more pastoral schools in the city. It had gone on the drawing board as the Chevy Chase Addition School as early as 1926 and opened its doors in spring of 1929. It was one of six elementaries that opened that year with almost identical floor plans designed by Harry D. Payne. Located at the corner of North Boulevard and Hazard, it initially had only 89 students and three completed classrooms, but the enrollment was so overwhelming the following fall that another teacher had to be added on the second day of the semester and another teacher two weeks after that. By the mid-1930s, rooms, both permanent and temporary had been added, and a total of 13 teachers oversaw 450 pupils. Today, Poe is again part of a quiet, tree-lined neighborhood, offering its students a fine arts magnet program.[37]

Kindergarten classroom at Poe ES circa 1930. HISD

Dancing in Houston Schools

The school board met in regular session (last night) at the High School. Dr. Urwitz brought up the matter of dancing in the schools when receptions were in vogue, and it was voted to prohibit this practice for those who attend the receptions. Mr. Watkins was the only member who voted against the motion, he stating that he didn't think dancing at the alumni reception was harmful.

Houston Post 14 June 1904

PORT HOUSTON E S

The Port Houston School in County District 20 opened in a small building sometime between 1909 and 1913 with one teacher handling the first five grades. In 1915, with the deepwater port in operation, District 20 and the City of Houston combined to construct a new building at McCarty and Singleton on sixteen lots donated by the Turning Basin Development Company. Pupils came from both within and outside the city limits. By 1922, with only eleven students, it was combined with Houston Harbor. When WWII-related development in the area increased, the building was reopened, though it was the subject of complaints, particularly the charge that since it lacked a cafeteria, children were forced to buy their lunches in "beer joints." By the 1950s, a newer building at 1800 McCarty let the campus survive, and even thrive with a now abandoned international shipping magnet program. Port Houston Elementary faced closure again in 2014, but neighborhood activism prevailed, and it remains in operation as of 2025.[38]

POST OAK SCHOOL

See Grady School

PRAIRIE HILL SCHOOL

Prairie Hill was a single-room schoolhouse in District 1 in far northwest Harris County. It operated from at least the early 1890s through the WWI years. The school also served as a community meeting place, hosting an annual spring festival that included picnics and target shooting for prizes.[39]

PRAIRIE (VIEW) SCHOOL

Prairie View School opened in September 1894 in a 40' x 20' building that contractor N.C. Jensen built on Clark Street just north of Morris for a cost of $570, fifteen dollars over budget. Attendance averaged 65 pupils for the two teachers in 1913, just before a new building was planned. It operated for White students in District 25 until sometime after 1915.[40]

PRATT SCHOOL

Mapmaker's misspelling. See Platte

PRIDAY SCHOOL

Miss Ada Priday, the daughter of English-born parents, operated a private school for fifteen years, starting about 1910. It was first at the family home at the west end of Quitman until her mother's death, and then, starting in 1917, she held her classes in the home of her older brother, a machinist, at 100 Manfred Avenue.[41]

PRIVATE SCHOOLS, LATER

The number of short-lived private schools that Houston saw between the late 1800s and the end of WWII was high. Some of these small academies rented space for the endeavors, but most were operated out of the teacher's own home. The majority listed here lasted for only a year or two before disappearing from the city directories. No list can be completely encyclopedic, but these teachers who offered private instruction for White pupils included: Clayton Prewett, Annie Bass, Charles Hill, Adelaide Gribble, Mrs. E.C. Wooldridge, Etta Simmons, Gertrude Davis, Jennie Gentry, Kate Pereir, Leila Hutchinson, Lizzie Hutchins, M.E. Watson, Mallei Miller, Nellie Barnett, Notie Howard, Mary Nutini, Mamie Chadwick, Charles Younger, Ada Moore, Cecilia Shoylin, Cecile Forshey, Clara Bochow, Celia Scott, Julia King, Louisa Ebert, Lara Oldham, Mrs. M.H.V. Wynns, Mamie Elsbury, Myrtle Fleet, Mrs. M.P. Kirksey, Mary Krahl, Mrs. T.J. Atwood, Mary Smith, William D. Hughes, and S.I. Bell. Some listings such as Hurley, Bradley, Sunniland, Roseboom, and Cushman Schools did not include first names for the teachers. At least two 1890s-era private schools were attempted for African American students, as well. Those were run by Thomas Mitchell on Conti between Chestnut and Chapman and by Media M. Flake for a single year at 1911 Prairie.[42]

PROSSO PREPARATORY SCHOOL

James Perkins Richardson founded the Prosso School, an elite preparatory institution that also included a lower grammar school component, at McGowen and Brazos in 1913. It was the Houston iteration of a Prosso School he had founded in Kansas City in 1900. Locally, the faculty hovered around eight to ten members for a student body that ranged from 30 to 80. Tuition was $300 a year, so not surprising were the notable surnames among the students: Baker, Carter, Sharp, Hogg, Cleveland, Mistrot, and young Howard Hughes. Richardson had studied at Kansas, Oberlin, and Yale. Also during that time, he taught language at Galveston's Ball High and reportedly started that school's first football team. Houston's Prosso School later moved to a large frame building on Main between Anita and Rosalie that held six classrooms and a study hall, a structure that was later home to a theater company. Dr. Richardson demanded recitations from every student every day, strictly forbade any smoking, and sent report cards home each Friday. The results were that almost all of the pupils went on to graduate college. When Richardson died in April 1922, his wife, Hannah, and son tried to keep the operation going, but Prosso School, alma mater of many of the city's upper crust, closed in 1925.[43]

PUBLIC SCHOOL FOR NON ENGLISH SPEAKING PUPILS

This school at 2502 Navigation was listed in only one city directory: 1930-31. The address is very near the original Ninfa's Restaurant.[44]

Dr. Samuel Clark Red

Samuel Clark Red was a legacy physician. His father, George Clark Red, had moved from South Carolina in 1845, months before Texas officially entered the Union. Despite any assumptions associated with his place of birth, Dr. G.C. Red refused to serve the Confederacy citing his opposition to secession and slavery. Branded a traitor, he was exonerated in court and continued practicing medicine. S.C. Red's uncle, David Finney Stuart, was a well-known doctor and part owner of the Houston Infirmary in the 1870s. His mother and one of his sisters were teachers.[45]

Given his background, it is not surprising that Samuel, a native of Gay Hill, Texas, valued education. After two previous college stops, Red entered the University of Texas in 1883 when it opened, and received his B.A. two years later, the first such degree bestowed by the school. Armed with that diploma, he then attained a graduate degree from Jefferson Medical College in Philadelphia before settling in Houston where he established a general practice that ran for 52 years.[46]

Red was a founder of the Harris County Medical Society and served as president of the state association for a time, a post previously held by his uncle. He is credited by some as establishing the first ambulance service in Houston, though evidence suggests otherwise. He is also "said to have been the... first in Houston to use the X-Ray, perform an appendectomy, to repair a hernia, and to use diphtheria antitoxin."

He was also an author, penning a biography of fellow doctor Ashbel Smith in 1929 and a brief history of First Presbyterian Church where he was a member. His second wife, George Plunkett Red, wrote a history entitled *The Medicine Man in Texas* that recorded copious amounts of information about the early doctors.[47]

Dr. Red's first wife, Katherine, whom he met during medical school, had died in 1900 after bearing him four children. Wife number two had four more. The family lived for decades at 817 Caroline near Rusk, just across the street from the Houston High School.[48]

For almost two decades at the start of the 20th century, Samuel Clark Red served on the Houston school board, much of the time as board president. His second child Hattie Lel, was a teacher in the district. By all accounts, he took his duties seriously.

Dr. S.C. Red

A 1902 photo, taken not long before his appointment to the board, shows him to be a thin man with deep set eyes, a receding hairline, and a bushy moustache.

Dr. S.C. Red died in Houston on February 25, 1940.

QUEEN OF PEACE SCHOOL

Queen of Peace School opened for 105 students with four classrooms, a library, and an office at 2320 Oakcliff in southeast Houston in September 1947. The Dominican Sisters originally staffed the school, and oversaw expansions in 1949 and 1955. It still operates for grades one through eight.[49]

Schools R

RAMIER'S SCHOOL
See Brays Bayou

RAMSEY SCHOOL
Like many rural schools in North Harris County, the Ramsey School was a one-room building that sat on property loaned to the neighborhood by the family whose name was on the building. It sat on the east side of Ramsey Road, just south of where it intersects with North Ramsey Loop. Oft times having only between five and ten students, it was closed and merged into Crosby School in 1924.[1]

REAGAN ES
See Brackenridge

REAGAN H S
The 1924 fire at what had become Heights Junior High School threw schools in the neighborhood into complete disarray. The school board's solution was to turn the new high school into a junior high and replace it with an even grander high school on East 13th St. at Arlington. Lengthy negotiations, cries of homeowners overcharging, and complaints from the public were overcome, and more than 26 residences were acquired and relocated or demolished for the project. The man whose name was chosen to grace the new Heights High was Horace Mann, a Massachusetts politician and lawyer who was best known for being the nation's most energetic advocate of universal public education, but local Confederate veterans groups and their descendants went ballistic. Outraged that a major Houston school would honor a "Republican" Yankee reformer, they demanded and received a change. The mollifying replacement name was that of John H. Reagan who had been both

Postmaster General and Treasury Secretary for the Confederacy. After the Civil War, Reagan had a long career serving Texas in the U.S. Congress before becoming the first chairman of the Texas Railroad Commission.[2]

The newly completed Reagan HS. HISD

The new Reagan High School opened in 1926 with students marching in a parade from their old school on 20th Street to the new one a few blocks south. It was a John Staub-designed structure with an imposing fortress-like Gothic entrance, and it was soon followed by an addition with 29 more classrooms, an auditorium, and a shop. The principal and faculty also moved. S.P. Waltrip was the head of school, a man who had known John H. Reagan personally. Waltrip had headed the school districts in Harrisburg, Brunner, and then Houston Heights. When that town was annexed into Houston, Waltrip stayed on as principal, remaining in the job until his untimely death after complications from gallstone surgery in 1932.[3]

The school grew quickly. Enrollment topped 2,350 by the time the school was a decade old. That same year, the Reagan band was rated the tops in the city, as was the school orchestra. Perhaps most famous of them all were the Reagan Red Coats drill team and their drum and bugle corps. In 1937, the Red Coats even got sponsored for a trip to perform in Mexico City. The sports teams had their moments: a runner-up spot in the state football championship in 1950 and consolation game winner in boys basketball in 1930 and 1938. Most years, the Bulldogs were happy just to beat Lamar, the rich kids' school that became their biggest rival.[4]

Houston vs. Dallas High School All-Star Football Game

Houston's first city rivalry in business, athletics, and elsewhere was undeniably with Galveston. As the 20th century developed, and as Galveston's population began to lag far beyond other Texas metropolises, a new bogeyman appeared for the Bayou City. It was that hated upstart far away in the semi-arid north - Dallas.

The earliest games between the cities were on the baseball diamond, first with semi-professional teams in the 1870s, and starting in 1888, with Texas League ball clubs. Eventually football followed, not between billion-dollar NFL franchises, but in the form of high school all-star squads. The year 1932, at the nadir of the Depression, was a case in point. Houston and Dallas played a home and home series that year. In the Bayou City, the venue was West End Park, and in Big D, it was Fair Grounds Stadium, a brand new 40,000-plus seat concrete behemoth that would soon become known as the Cotton Bowl.[5]

Sportswriter Bill McClanahan of the *Dallas Morning News* opened his game story thusly: "The Black and White-striped jerseyed grid warriors representing the Dallas high schools were forced to turn to the air to gain a 19-to-12 decision over the Houston all-stars Monday afternoon at Fair Park in a battle for sweet charity. Three thousand fans saw the contest. Gate receipts amounted to $800, school officials declared following the tilt."[6]

Houston coaches Arnold Krichamer, Ed Duggan, and Walter Hodges employed a novel rotation for their squad in the Dallas game during an era when players were expected to go on both defense and offense. In the first and third quarters, the team consisted of all-stars who primarily represented Sam Houston and San Jacinto Highs, and in the second and fourth periods, the team "was composed of the players from the John Reagan School." The Reagan Bulldogs' biggest star, 200-pound Marion Asbell, was out with the flu and missed the trip north.[7]

Though the crowd was no doubt dwarfed by the cavernous stadium, the players "tackled, ran, blocked, and passed as if the championship of the entire world depended." Dallas dominated the first three quarters of a mostly defensive struggle, though Houston drove inside the ten twice in the second quarter "only to be halted by a fighting line."

Dallas got "air minded" in the second half. On the day they completed 13 of 21 pass attempts. Houston's aerial production was a scant four of eight with two interceptions. It was a recipe that led to Houston being scoreless and trailing by two touchdowns entering the final period.

Writer McClanahan told what happened next: "... in the last period, when the visiting coaches decided to break into the Reagan School combination, inserting a carrot topped youngster by the name of Cecil Isbell, the Houstonians started going places and doing things."[8]

Dallas scored early, but then the south Texas boys got on the board. "Houston's two touchdowns followed with breath-taking rapidity," the *News* reported. "The visitors recovered a Dallas fumble on the locals' 25-yard line and almost before anyone realized what had taken place, Reed and Royall had worked the ball up to the 8-yard line in short power plunges through the line. A penalty placed the ball on the 3-yard stripe and Royall carried to the Dallas two-inch line. Royall smashed the line for the touchdown."[9]

After a quick and unproductive possession for Dallas, "the Houston lads decided to try the tactics used by the locals and turned to their air, a pass, Isbell to Hallmark, and the resulting run was good for 43 yards and a first down on the Dallas 16-yard line, from which point Isbell carried it over for the touchdown."

Houston's first national football hero - Cecil Isbell - with the Green Bay Packers. Courtesy Green Bay Packers

In the end, the Houston rally fell short, producing only a long trip back home. For young Sam Houston underclassman Cecil Isbell, however, it was a notice served. After graduation, he became a football star at Purdue and then the seventh overall draft pick by the Green Bay Packers in 1938. During his brief five years with the Pack, throwing to Hall-of-Famer Don Hutson, Isbell set multiple NFL passing records including becoming the first man to ever pass for over 2,000 yards in an NFL season and completing a TD pass in 23 consecutive games. That last mark stood until Johnny Unitas eclipsed it in 1957.[10]

RECREATION ACRES

Klein ISD opened Recreation Acres Elementary School with four classrooms at 5908 Chippewa in 1949 to serve elementary students in the southern part of the district.[11]

RED BLUFF SCHOOL

Isaac's School in the Red Bluff area on Galveston Bay predated the school reorganizations of 1876. The reference was to the Samuel and Martha Isaac's family farm on the Seabrook – La Porte Road, near today's Bay Area Blvd. In the late-1880s and early-1890s, the name of this school fluctuated between Isaac's and Red Bluff School. Bay View School also appears in County District 13 during these years, but was sold in 1892. Three years later, Isaac's and Middle Bayou were the only schools listed in the district, but in June 1896, Commissioners Court allows the district to sell "old schoolhouse No. 2." The district remained with the Red Bluff name a year later, though the voting place was the school in Seabrook.[12]

RESURRECTION SCHOOL

Catholics in the Denver Harbor area, primarily Polish when the parish opened in 1920, supported a parish school that was staffed by the Sisters of St. Mary of Namur when it opened in 1937. Originally six classrooms, it grew to 16 by the time the Dominican Sisters took over the teaching in 1994. The school still operates at 916 Majestic.[13]

RICEVILLE SCHOOL

The Riceville community, named after southwest Harris County landowner Leonard Rice, was a Freedom colony and farming community along Brays Bayou near modern day Gessner Road. In 1889, the Riceville Mount Olive Baptist Church opened in the neighborhood, and there was a school in County District 23 by that time, moving to District 22 by 1892. Henry Turpin was the teacher during some of those years, splitting his time with other Black schools in the district. The school name changed to Brays Bayou Colored in the 1920s or 30s, also changing from county to HISD control. Those continuing past the elementary grades went all the way to Third Ward. The school closed in 1967 with the children being bussed to mostly Black Sunnyside, and the stretch of Riceville School Road south of Brays Bayou was eventually renamed South Gessner. City of Houston services including water and sewer did not come to the community until the 1980s.[14]

RIVER OAKS E S

River Oaks was one of six late-1920s HISD elementaries designed by official district architect Harry D. Payne, all of which combined nearly identical floor plans and different exteriors. In the case of the six-room school that opened at the southwest corner of San Felipe and Kirby in the fall of 1929, it was French Colonial. Architect Payne commented years later that "the weathervane we designed, the Goose Girl flapping her apron and the two ganders standing by, was to suggest a familiar story. It would make the school building a cordial and friendly place." The neighborhood it served was barely more than half a decade old.

Classroom at River Oaks ES. HISD

From the start, Principal Eva Margaret Davis' campus was a school for the privileged that in many ways more closely resembled the private schools that some of the neighborhood children attended. River Oaks' own Ima Hogg and the first PTA president, Agnese Carter Nelms, raised money to stock the library and give each teacher $10 a month for extra supplies. The River Oaks Garden Club and a landscape architect from the famed Kansas City firm of Hare & Hare interpreted the grounds. When River Oaks Elementary integrated at the start of the 1970s, it was through the addition of a Gifted and Talented program, later renamed Vanguard, that took over the school in its entirety in 1986. A decade later, after activism from neighborhood parents, River Oaks again began admitting area students. In 2017, ROE was listed by HISD as an "International Baccalaureate World School" [15]

RIVER OAKS PRIVATE SCHOOL

Hugh Potter, one of the developers of River Oaks, kept a brochure about this apparently short-lived school that opened in a "new building" on River Oaks Boulevard at the corner of Westheimer Road in September 1927. There were nine teachers for kindergarten through sixth grade. For monthly tuition between $11.00 and $12.50, children followed the public school curriculum plus violin, dance, French, and group music "together with advantages which other schools are not providing."[16]

ROBERTS E S

Two-time Texas governor, state Supreme Court justice and law professor Oran Milo Roberts was honored by an HISD campus in 1936, and the school at 6000 Greenbriar was enlarged in the years following WWII. Miss Helene Wilson was the first principal, overseeing children from the new and expanding southern neighborhoods of the city. Today it is an IB program. Interestingly, Oran Roberts is one of the few senior Confederate officers whose name remained on an HISD school in the willy-nilly renaming purge of 2016 in spite of the fact that in post-Civil War years he called for a "White man's government." That stands in sharp contrast to poet, scholar and musician Sidney Lanier whose name was removed though his rebel military service was as a private who later chastised the old Confederacy.[17]

ROBERTS SCHOOL
See Memorial ES

ROGERS, W. E S
Will Rogers Elementary School, named after the "cowboy philosopher", comedian, and political observer who was popular in the early 20th century, was opened in 1950 at 3101 Weslayan. It was demolished in late 2006, less than a year after it closed.[18]

Roosevelt ES. Laurie Feinswog photo

ROOSEVELT E S
Theodore Roosevelt's name was removed from one planned Houston school earlier in the decade after an outcry from Confederate organizations, but in October 1929, the bully President and Hero of San Juan Hill finally got his campus. It had been called Textile Mill School when it was on the drawing board after a factory located close to the East Montgomery Road, today's Fulton, location. The ten-acre campus sported a pretty yellow stucco building nestled among pine trees and set back from the highway. It initially taught only the first three grades in its two rooms with principal Zelpha Shumate taking second and third grades. Roosevelt had expanded to a full elementary by the time it was the brief focus of statewide attention when then-principal Mrs. W.T. Archer sent a first grade girl home for wearing a sun dress to school.[19]

ROSE HILL SCHOOL

Though the Rose Hill area began with Anglo American settlers, by the 1840s there were many newly arrived German immigrants in the cotton farming community. All seven of the cotton gins operating by the 1880s were owned by families with German surnames. Though the school was not one of those registered for public funding in 1876, it was in operation two years later. It is possible that the area residents were simply slow to take advantage of the tax money since by 1882, the district was given permission to sell the schoolhouse and land adjoining William Kobs' place with proceeds put into the district fund. The district in the early 20th century was described as having one "beautiful building with good facilities, good outbuildings" and support through private donations as well as the tax money. When the building on the Cypress-Rose Hill Road near FM 2920 was replaced, the old school was given to the Rose Hill Colored School. White Rose Hill consolidated with Cypress in 1933 necessitating the addition of a teacher there, but was de-annexed in 1940 due to a court case over the boundary between Cy-Fair ISD and Tomball ISD.[20]

A 1924 class at Rose Hill. Edna Brautigam Treseler

ROSE HILL COLORED SCHOOL

The Rose Hill Colored School was in County District 5. Among the first teachers there, dating back to 1886, was Buck Grimes who went on to a distinguished career in Houston schools. At some point, the African American students in this community were given the old building previously used by the White school in the district.[21]

Compulsory Attendance

In 1915, Houston schools superintendent Paul Horn included this in his annual report: "Your Superintendent would again call the attention of the School Board and the community to the fact, that the recent session of our state legislature passed a law for compulsory education to take effect in September, 1916. Heretofore Texas has been one of the few states in the Union having no form of compulsory education. The law recently passed is by no means as strong as similar laws in many other states, but it is at least a step in the right direction. It is to be hoped that it will be extended and made stronger from time to time. However, even in its present, form, if it is adequately enforced, it will mean a very large addition to the public school attendance in Houston and in other cities of the state. It will be necessary for our cities during the coming year to take such precautions as may be necessary by way of providing school room for the large increase which we hope and confidently expect will be brought into our schools by the operation of the new law."[22]

Texas had indeed come late to the party. Massachusetts was the first state to introduce compulsory school attendance back in 1852. Since abolishing the requirement a half-century earlier, the Texas legislature created their first such law in 1915, the same year similar statutes passed in Alabama, Florida, and South Carolina. Only two of the forty-eight states lagged behind: Georgia (1916) and Mississippi (1918).[23]

When the first school year of compulsory attendance was finished, however, Houston school officials were left scratching their heads. They gauged that on average, attendance increased about 10% a year, yet with school allegedly mandatory for all children within the law's age range, there was only a jump of 4% in enrollment.

Superintendent Horn looked first to the law itself. "To begin with, the law only included children up to fourteen years of age," he wrote. "And it was so loosely drawn, with so many exemptions, as hardly to be capable of rigid enforcement. The most that can be said for the law as it now stands is that it is a step in the right direction."[24]

Furthermore, the budget contained not a dollar for truant officers to enforce the new law. A worker in the Houston Foundation added policing the attendance law to his duties, and for the African American schools, Horn considered the district "fortunate in obtaining the services of a volunteer colored worker, who, for his interest in the cause, gave a considerable amount of his time to this work. Between the two, probably 600 children were placed in school who would not otherwise have been in school."

By 1918, the school board had hired two officers, one White and one Black, to enforce the rules. It was not enough. How to handle the battle against truancy was a bone of contention several decades later.[25]

ROSS E S

Dudley School, off of Clark Street north of the city limits, was part of County District 25 when it opened prior to 1913. By WWI, there were three teachers in a "brick house" that catered to seven grades. The name was to be changed in the middle-1920s after the campus had been taken into HISD, and the first idea floated was to honor Lawrence Jensen, a local man who had been killed in action during the late war. That plan was rejected by the school board, however, and the name of Betsy Ross, purported seamstress for George Washington's first American flag, was adopted instead. Jensen was honored at the school with the planting of a tree in his honor, a tradition that the student body continued to recognize a different person each year for a time, and it was Jensen's name that went on much of Clark Street when it, too, got a new moniker some years later. Betsy Ross got a new school building in the 1950s at the same location on Bay Street, and it was in that building that four African American students were part of HISD's initial integration in 1960, one of only three schools which can make that claim. Coincidentally, two of the four pioneering pupils had the surname Ross.[26]

ROTH SCHOOL

This small school in the Spring area was near Spring Steubner Road, likely where today's Rothwood leads north to a baseball park.[27]

RURAL HIGH SCHOOL NO. 1

See Klein HS

RURAL HIGH SCHOOL NO. 5

See Cy-Fair HS

RUSK E S

The lineage of Rusk School is one of the most storied in the City of Houston. It began life as Second Ward School at 247 Commerce near the Union Depot of the day. In 1877, two teachers had 74 pupils in grades one and two. Third grade was added soon after. Second Ward got a new T-shaped, multi-story, six-room school at the southwest corner of Hamilton and Commerce in September 1885. The enrollment soon grew to the largest in the city at over 300 students, and it topped 500 first through seventh graders by 1902. Also that year, the name of Texas patriot and politician Thomas Rusk was attached to the school. Many of the top personnel in the school system taught at or led Hamilton Street School, as it was previously called, including Henry Cline, Mary Kleiber, W.W. Barnett, Mamie Bastian, and W.W. Higgins. By 1907, however, the neighborhood around Rusk School was changing. The number of children and teachers was down. Business and industrial property was starting to replace residential. Lubbock School had siphoned off some of the students, and prostitution was moving into the neighborhood. A flurry of meetings and angry letters to the editor decried the alleged gauntlet of "nasty women" and dens of vice that students were forced to traverse on their way to and from school.[28]

On the plus side, the Settlement House had established itself at Rusk and was doing much to help the Eastern European Jewish immigrants and other underprivileged in the Second Ward. They had also established a kindergarten that was meeting with great support from Houston school officials. There were 67 children enrolled in the program in 1908-09. Free showers were available at Settlement House, as well. The school building, though, was drawing great criticism. Officials wanted "fire-proof" brick construction for the White schools. After the 25-year-old Rusk was consumed by fire in 1909, Superintendent Horn openly wrote in his annual report "fortunately it burned last year, and without the loss of any life."[29]

The 1933 faculty at Rusk ES. HISD

The new Rusk opened in May 1913 on a triangle of land at 1701 Maple, slightly north of the old school, on a bend in Buffalo Bayou. The little parcel was not far north of today's Houston Astros ballpark. It boasted three stories, modern heating and ventilation, sixteen regular class rooms, an auditorium that held 500 people, manual training rooms, domestic science rooms, library, club room, and dispensary. At a cost of "practically $85,000.00", it was the most expensive and most trumpeted elementary school in the system. The building's amenities were praised right down to the color scheme. Its opening coincided with the influx of Mexican immigrants into the immediate neighborhood, and the ethnicity of the student body at both Rusk and the Settlement House soon changed. The school had proudly proclaimed that it was "Houston's Melting Pot", containing 25 nationalities. Many in the city began referring to Rusk as the "Mexican School", and some historians even infer that it was a segregated facility, but it was not. The enrollment continued to include 15 to 20% non-Hispanic Whites. By 1939, there were over 600 Mexican-descended pupils at Jones and De Zavala, too. Dow had over 1,200.[30]

Social services at Rusk continued at the new 1913 building, and even expanded. Many in the community came to rely greatly on the school and the Settlement workers. The school dispensary offered nine free clinic sessions a week including for adults, pediatrics, pre-natal care, and even dental work. The manual training classes made items such as rugs that were sent home to families who needed them. The school also continued its specialized programs for deaf and "defective" students. Part-time classes were offered children who had to labor as newsboys, messengers, or factory helpers. Another top benefit was that the school auditorium became the community center with Mexican clubs putting on plays, night school students hosting entertainments, and movies being shown. It even hosted fundraisers in which the Mexican consul raised money for the destitute in Mexico. Eventually, Houston's showplace school became tired and worn, and Rusk was replaced with a new structure at 2805 Garrow in 1959, and that in turn was replaced by a new building in the early 21st century.[31]

Diversity and Immigrants

The Houston Metropolitan Area is now home to about 1.5 million foreign-born residents. The city has not had a majority ethnicity in many years. Though Whites were indeed a majority in the Bayou City at the dawn of the 20th century, it was not nearly as Anglo-American as many people might believe. A large number of those Whites were European-born. In the decade following the Civil War, African Americans, with their newfound freedoms, moved from farms to the city, reaching roughly 40% of Houston's population. Though most were born into slavery, a significant number had been enslaved in Africa and brought to Texas legally or illegally. And as the percentage of Black Houstonians declined, a new wave of immigration from Mexico ramped up in response to the violent turmoil of the Mexican Revolution that began around 1910.[32]

The efforts to deal with this diversity in city schools can be traced to the night school that was established by the school board about 1905. They were soon operating at the high school, Sherman Elementary in Fifth Ward and Rusk School which sat alongside Buffalo Bayou, just a few blocks northeast of downtown.[33]

The tone of School Superintendent Paul Horn was positively giddy with pride as he described the successful English language courses being offered in the night school during the 1906-07 school year He wrote of observing two young adults "studying out of the same book, a brother and sister, fresh from Mexico, who could scarcely speak a word of any other language than the Spanish. On the seat behind the boy was a nicely dressed, big moustached gentleman, who must just recently have come from France, for he could speak no other language than French. In the room were some newly arrived Austrians, a Syrian or two, a Japanese and a miscellaneous assortment of other foreigners. The work of helping these foreign speaking people to learn the English language and to become good American citizens was one of which any public school system might justly be proud. I only wish we had more such people who would give us the opportunity to help them."[34]

An Americanization class at the high school's night school program. HISD

J.B. Wolfe was the principal of the night school program, and he was also enthusiastic. "We consider the teaching of English to foreigners to be a work of the very greatest importance," Wolfe wrote in 1910. "The fact that they receive free instruction from sympathetic teachers does much to make them love their adopted country and become good citizens of the same. The earnest application of these foreigners to the study of English has been one of the most encouraging features of the night school."[35]

The fact that these students were adults didn't deter Superintendent Horn, either. "I do not believe that there should be any age limit for attendance at the night school," Horn declared. "If a Russian 50 years old comes to our city we must receive him, whether we will or not. The sooner he can learn to speak English and to be an American citizen, the better for him and for us. I do not know any better place for him to do this than in the public schools."

The mention of Russians was not random. At the Rusk School campus in 1908-09, the night school handled an enrollment of 127. Seventy-four of those were Jewish immigrants, primarily from Russia. At least some had been imprisoned "because of their sympathy with the revolutionary party." Superintendent Horn wrote of one who had "escaped from Siberia where he had been exiled, because of his connection with a socialist newspaper." Overall, Horn was impressed with them, adding that "Most of them had considerable education in their native tongue, and they were anxious to learn our language and customs and to become American citizens. The quicker these people are assimilated into our body politic the better for us and for them. They are ready and anxious to seize the opportunity to become intelligent citizens. I believe our own good demands that we give them this opportunity."[36]

Some of the foreign learning demands went the other direction, as well. It was a few years later when some Houstonians began trying to learn Spanish. In 1912, Horn reported that "a number of young men and women working in the day time requested that they be given instruction in Spanish at night, an instructor was furnished, and the results were good." It turned out that the "number" of people making the request might have been as low as six, for that was the amount of students who took that course. Just two years later, however, the demand for learning Spanish had increased to the point that 250 students were taking the class at night.[37]

In the years between WWI and the Great Depression, the specific arena of dealing with growing diversity and turning newly-arrived immigrants into Americans continued to be a reason for bragging. The newly formed American Legion post in town became involved in the patriotic welcome that the school district offered. Paul Horn, still superintendent, had this to say in 1921: "The hundreds of non-English speaking adults gathered into our night schools during the past year have profited by the presentation of the American language, of the American speech, of the American Flag and American ideals. Much more ought to be done along this line next year."[38]

RYAN J H S
See Yates HS

RYAN SCHOOL
Ryan Addition School appears in city directories from 1923, perhaps with a mistaken address, but it is listed at 4212 Hardy by 1926. In the early 1940s, there was only one teacher. Also spelled as Ryon School, it was closed by HISD in 2007. The district voted to list the property for sale in late 2024.[39]

Schools Sacred Heart — Southland

SACRED HEART SCHOOL, CROSBY

This parish school opened on Runneberg in 1949, just east of where the Crosby High School sat. That high school site is now the Crosby Kindergarten Center.[1]

The determined 1946 class at Sacred Heart poses on the front steps. Dominican Sisters

SACRED HEART SCHOOL, HOUSTON

Sacred Heart Parish opened a two-room school staffed by the Dominican Sisters in 1897, one year after the parish formed as the fourth in Houston. It shared a block with the original wooden church. The first director of the school, Father Thomas Keaney, died during the 1900 hurricane. He had great interest in using the public school curriculum, and used the same text books found in Houston schools at the time. The school operated in the wooden church after the 1911 Ollie Lorehn-designed church opened, then, in 1922, a new school building rose on the part of the property fronting the northwest corner of San Jacinto and Pierce. With a dwindling residential population in the area, Sacred Heart School closed in 1967.[2]

SAENGERBUND SCHOOL

Professor Carl Zeus taught music, art, and design at the same rooms "over 31 Main" when the Houston Saengerbund advertised an English and German School in 1887. Given that the group was a singing society, it is likely that all classes focused on music related topics.[3]

SALEM SCHOOL

Salem School was a Black school that operated in District 31 in the far northwest part of the county in the 1880s and 90s. In many years, it shared teachers with Rose Hill Colored.[4]

SALEM LUTHERAN SCHOOL

German settlers began coming to Harris County in large numbers in the 1840s, and the majority of them settled in the northern half of the county. Families including Theiss, Winkler, and Sherer founded the Salem Lutheran Church near Rose Hill, and by about 1853 had opened a small school with the reverends as teachers. Classes were taught in a mixture of English and German until WWII, at which time it was still a one-room schoolhouse. After a few decades of combined operation with Zion Lutheran School, Salem went out on its own again in 1982. Today, the Tomball school is still in operation with over 650 students from Pre-K to eighth grade.[5]

SANDERSON E S

See Trinity Gardens

SAN FELIPE SCHOOL

The San Felipe School, also known as San Felipe Street School, was operating on the south side of San Felipe Road at Bagby Street in 1887. That fall, some of the students were moved to the new Washington Street School, later renamed Dow, but the following year it still had 92 students in two rooms. By 1890, San Felipe was listed as a Black school, still two rooms, but with 150 pupils. That number jumped to 189, all first graders, the following year, when overcrowding in Fourth Ward among African American students was epidemic. San Felipe School is off the list of institutions in 1894, and the new Colored High School is at that corner, a lot that had been owned by the city schools for at least a decade.[6]

SAN JACINTO E S, BAYTOWN

San Jacinto Elementary at 2615 Virginia in Baytown went up about the same time as many other GCCISD schools. By the end of the 1930s, the building had eight classrooms plus a cafeteria and a library.[7]

SAN JACINTO E S, DEER PARK

San Jacinto Elementary on Ivy Street in Deer Park opened in 1930. Today it is the Wholers Administration Building. A newer San Jacinto campus is located at 1302 E. 13th Street.[8]

SAN JACINTO H S

By 1910, Houston school official were enamored with the new concept of junior high schools, and the showcase they created was South End Junior High on Holman at San Jacinto. Construction took longer than its sister North Side JHS, and, already located in the most fashionable area of town, South End got the best amenities, as well. Not everything was in place when the official opening ceremonies were held on September 29, 1914, but soon there were top flight athletic fields including "a six-lap cinder running track, a 120-yard straightaway, two baseball diamonds, one Rugby and two soccer football fields, and a grand stand" and clay tennis courts out front. There was also an outdoor theatre. From the beginning, South End had the largest enrollment in the district, topping 900 pupils in seventh through ninth grades that first semester, and by the early 1920s, two wings were added. The result was an open U shape facing Holman. The left front wing was the auditorium with manual training rooms in the basement, and the right one held the swimming pool in the basement, a gymnasium on the first floor, and domestic science rooms on the second.[9]

When the flurry of bond money came to HISD in the 1920s, new junior high schools rose all over town, but what the booming south end of town needed was another high school. South End was elevated from junior to senior high, and the San Jacinto Bears were born. One doubtful story was that the name was chosen so athletic uniforms emblazoned with an S could still be used. It was Houston third White high school, following Central and Heights. The Bears quickly attained sports prowess, taking the city championship in basketball in 1928 and the state title in track one year later. By 1933, it had captured its first district football title, and the Gauchos drill team soon took their place among the pantheon of the city's competitive girls' precision marchers.[10]

Temporary buildings housing the University of Houston at the San Jacinto HS campus. UH Special Collections

The San Jacinto campus saw many programs over the years, serving from 1927 as the home of HISD's Houston Junior College that later became the University of Houston, holding the Houston Technical Institute from 1962 to 1981, and housing HSPVA for the program's first decade of operation that began in 1971. Amidst those bold experiments, the final graduating class of San Jacinto High came in 1970. Along the way, the halls of San Jac saw many of the city's most famous including Walter Cronkite, Denton Cooley, Roy Hofheinz, Kathy Whitmire, and Howard Hughes. Houston Community College bought the old South End/San Jac campus in 1981, and today it serves as HCC's Central College complete with memorials to the educational institution that came before.[11]

SAN JACINTO SCHOOL

The town of San Jacinto was once a thriving concern, situated roughly where the southern landing for the Lynchburg Ferry is today. The site now lies underwater courtesy of hurricane tidal surges, dredging, subsidence, and Ship Channel widening. Among the first school trustees was the son of Texas revolutionary Lorenzo de Zavala whose family homestead was on the north side of the bayou. The town was platted in 1837 by Nathaniel Lynch whose namesake town was just across the river. It, and Lynchburg, quickly filled a vacuum that had been caused by Santa Anna's burning of Harrisburg prior to the Battle of San Jacinto. Soon there were shipyards, a sawmill, stores, and upwards of 100 residents. By 1860, with the shipyards booming, San Jacinto's population surpassed 500, likely about its peak. In addition to the physical challenges, the coming of a railroad between Houston and Galveston drastically lessened the need for area shipping.[12]

SAN JACINTO COLORED SCHOOL

San Jacinto also held a small school for African American children in District 14, one of only three Black county schools that were registered with the new school law of 1876. Like its White district counterpart, it operated at least until around the turn of the century when the town itself largely began to disappear. The Black residents of the town worked in the small industries in the area or were fishermen. Some of them were likely employed in these same industrial jobs as slaves before gaining their freedom.[13]

Progressive Era County Schools

The Texas of the Progressive Era between 1900 and 1920 was predominantly rural. Cotton was the largest economic engine, and Texas produced more of it than any other state in the Union. Lumber, cattle, railroads, and oil were the industries. Fewer than one-fifth of the state's residents lived in towns of 10,000 or more in 1900, but Harris County was an exception. Though the city of Houston was not yet the largest metropolis in the state, it was plenty big enough to exert a major influence on the surrounding communities.[14]

The county school population was roughly a quarter of that found in the city limits of Houston and Houston Heights, but the leaders were determined to move those institutions toward modernity. The County Superintendent was L.L. Pugh, and he was overseen by a five member board. In 1910, those five men were W. G. Smiley of Houston, J. S. Deady of Harrisburg, R. L. Robinson of Spring, Dr. L. C. Hanna of Lynchburg, and Dr. E. E. Grant of Cypress.[15]

The view of the future expressed by Superintendent Pugh could not have been more rosy: "From its topography and location, Harris County cannot fail to have a great future. Its soil, fertile beyond the expectation and conception of the settlers from the North and East, or from foreign lands, is cultivated with remarkable skill and care by the native settlers, as well as by the foreign born, who prosper upon a few acres each. Its county paved roads are becoming more and more a delight to the traveler. Electric lines are traversing a good portion of the county. The terminals of great railroad systems are turning their faces toward us where ship and car can meet. A rapidly increasing number of diversified manufacturing industries are beginning to crowd the water front; the completion of the great ship channel converting the old Buffalo Bayou into a stream for ocean vessels will increase the shipping with amazing strides in the next few years. The extensive vacant holdings will soon be covered by the happy homes of thousands. The cowboy days are gone forever. The small farmer and truckman has taken his place. Prosperous and full of hope, conscious of power, equipped with soil and climate, and good schools, they look forward with confidence, eager to take their part in history, and over us all flies the glorious American flag."

There was indeed growth in the county school system. Between 1909 and 1914, there sprung up 25 brick buildings and 22 frame ones. The county had only five brick school buildings prior to that five year period. Eight of the new structures were either wholly or partly devoted to some form of high school work. The school year of 1913-14 closed with 52 school districts in the county with 129 buildings total, 98 for White children and 31 for Black. They valued that real estate at over $558,000.[16]

Teaching in those buildings were 215 individuals, about 85% of them women. How much those teachers earned, and even how long their school term lasted, depended on whether they taught in a one-teacher, two-teacher, or one of few multi-teacher schools. The bigger the school, the longer the term and higher the pay. Teachers who found themselves on their own averaged only $55 a month, while their peers at the multi-teacher schools could expect an average of seventy dollars. Terms at the White schools ran from seven months, one week to eight months, three weeks. African American schools in the county averaged a term of only six months, three weeks.[17]

True to the name applied to the time period, Superintendent Pugh expected more. His instructions were pointed: "Go to your school elections in April of each year and vote for those citizens as trustees whose slogan shall be for better school, better equipment, better paid teacher, and more homelike environment," he urged county citizens. "Go to your bond and tax elections and vote for both the bond and the tax, and let your slogan be to keep up with the march of progress, as many of the rural communities of this county are doing... If you do not follow the ... suggestions, then do not complain to the County Superintendent, and other authorities of the bad condition or your school and surroundings."[18]

SATSUMA SCHOOL

The community of Satsuma, also known at times as both Ashford and Thompson Switch, was home to a school in County District 6, south of Cypress, from at least 1909 to 1914, the same years the community had a post office.[19]

SCHULTZ SCHOOL

In the 1910s, Schultz School was on McDuffy Road, now Aldine-Westfield. It might be another name for Spring School or a short-lived schoolhouse of its own. Little else has been found.[20]

SEABROOK SCHOOL

The schoolhouse at Seabrook is mentioned as early as 1897 when it was a voting place in District 13, seemingly taking over for Red Bluff as the lead school. It is a town that allegedly got its name from the son of real estate developer John Sydnor. In 1905, the citizens there petitioned the county to sell their old building in favor of a new one. It was likely a necessity since five years later there were 64 students in eight grades occupying a two-story frame school with a "large library." They soon added two more grades to become a high school second class. The town was becoming more sophisticated, holding an election in 1912 on whether hogs, sheep, and goats should be allowed to run at large in the city limits. The population of the town remained steady, even declining, through the 1930s, but that did not deter the opening of a new concrete and tile school building in September 1930. It brought electric lights and flush toilets, albeit ones located outside the school building itself. That school served Seabrook until 1948 at which time the district, which had become independent only three years earlier, became part of the new Clear Creek ISD. A new elementary building opened in 1949, and the 1930 structure was demolished with a city hall going up on the property.[21]

The 1930 Seabrook School caught fire during demolition. Genevieve Curry Dickerson

SECOND WARD COLORED SCHOOL

See Langston

SECOND WARD SCHOOL

See Rusk ES

SECOND WARD FREE SCHOOL

The *Telegraph* for May 12, 1860 stated that the Second Ward Free School, financed by public subscription, was opened with 108 children attending and that the teacher, the Rev. W.E. Compton, "will furnish books when required and the tuition is entirely free, and this arrangement is permanent."[22]

SETTEGAST SCHOOL

This was a small school in a mostly rural community of the same name in County District 48 in northeast Houston that served African American children. The city annexed the area which sat near Hall's Bayou and the Beaumont, Sour Lake and Western rail line in the late-1940s. Today, it is in the North Forest ISD area. In the 1950s, the principal was B.C. Elmore who later had a segregated Black high school named in his honor. It was recognized by the state's Black teachers association for top achievement multiple times under his tenure.[23]

SEWELL SCHOOL

The one-room Sewell School was built in 1917 on the House-Hahl Road, about a half mile south of present day Highway 290. Mrs. R. D. Crews, librarian at Cy-Fair in 1964, wrote that in 1926, Winkler had few students and was in poor condition, so students were moved to Sewell. In 1929, Sewell students began to be sent to Cypress by car. Lumber salvaged from the school was used to build an addition to the Cypress School a few years later.[24]

SHELDON SCHOOL

Sheldon's county school district 32 was created in May 1887 with James Harrington being the lead trustee in the effort. The first building mentioned specifically in county records was a "box structure" that by 1910 was in great need of exterior paint. That school burned around 1915 and was replaced by a two-room frame building that stood on land now occupied by the Future Farmers of America Budling in the community. Beaumont Road in east Harris County was widened and designated as U.S. Highway 90 in 1929, an event that coincided with the demolition of the two-room school in Sheldon. Its replacement was a four-room building complete with auditorium that earned the name Alamo School because of the Spanish style façade. Though more modern than the frame school it replaced, the Alamo had wood stoves and no restrooms, running water, or electricity. Enrollment was about 100 students spread across grades one through eight. High school pupils were initially transported to Crosby in a surplus Army truck. Sheldon's Alamo School closed in 1957.[25]

SHELDON COLORED SCHOOL

Sheldon operated a small school for African Americans in County District 32 as early as 1891. Described as a "box structure" in 1907, it was always small, still enrolling only 35 pupils by 1938.[26]

SHERMAN E S

White children in the Fifth Ward were crowded into the Elysian Street School at the start of the 1890s. It then saw a student population increase of roughly 25% in a single year thanks largely to the development of the Cascara addition north of the giant railroad facilities where the majority of Fifth Warders worked. Relief came on November 13, 1893 with the opening of a six-room, three-story school on a donated lot in, and named for, that same neighborhood. It faced Lorraine between McKee and Terry, all unpaved streets. Classrooms were on the top two floors, and pupils ate and played on the ground level, called the basement. That low-ceilinged space also housed the janitor's living quarters.[27]

Sherman School, originally Cascara. HISD

Principal J.E. Niday soon gave way to J.L. McReynolds, an educator who stayed on the northside, at Cascara and then North Side Junior High, for decades. In addition to the five grade teachers, the early staff had a supervisor of music and a German teacher who passed through. The school's name was changed in 1906 to honor Sidney Sherman, an officer at the Battle of San Jacinto and a Harrisburg railroad entrepreneur. As the city and the nearby railroad yards continued to grow, the new school became over-crowded. Additional classes were held in nearby stores and residences, and ground floor basement rooms were added. Eventually two annex buildings were rented, first at Freeman and Pinckney then on Montgomery Avenue, until the new Lamar School relieved the trouble. Other problems facing Sherman at the start of the 20th century were a spike in neighborhood crime and a diphtheria epidemic that closed the school for over a week while each room was carefully fumigated. Wings were added to the building along with shacks in the yard so that by 1921, there were 36 rooms for 1,000 students.[28]

A major fire damaged the oldest part of the structure in 1957, though the staff and students soldiered on. When the building was razed and a new Sherman ES built next door in 1967, it was the second oldest school in the city system. Sherman was demolished again in 2012 and replaced with modern construction, including a rounded portion at the front entrance reminiscent of the distinctive turreted Cascara School.[29]

Rented Annexes and Temporary Buildings

Many a resident of Houston or another growing Harris County community remembers temporary classrooms buildings known as the shacks. With burgeoning population rates, these pre-fab structures began showing up in the early 1920s. Before that, the policy of Houston schools was to relieve overcrowding by renting all or part of a neighboring building. These included offices, former factories, and even vacant private homes.

The school district reports of the first decades of the 20th century are filled with happy news of new schools opening and eliminating the need for additional rented space. One of several examples was in 1908 when Travis and Lamar elementaries for White students and Luckie for Black added 26 new classroom and "enabled us to discontinue several undesirable rented annexes."[30]

New pupils just kept coming, however. In the 1918-19 scholastic year, the city was paying a total of $184.00 a month for annex space at Austin, Lamar, Douglass, Cooley, Luckie, Langston, and Crawford grade schools and at Heights and Colored High Schools. Rent at Heights High and Lamar Elementary ran $30.00 or more. At the opposite end was the additional space provided for Crawford at a mere five dollars a month.[31]

Much like a modern highway system, the city could not seem to build itself out of overcrowding. The next solution was to begin using temporary buildings, our shacks. Senior staff took a lesson from other urban school districts around the country.[32]

"If experience in this subject is of any value, it should teach us that the time is not likely soon to come when the city will have all the permanent school buildings it needs," the 1920 report read. "To erect temporary buildings at a place where greatly needed, as for instance at the West End school, and then in a year or two to erect permanent building and destroy the temporary ones, would seem to involve a wicked waste of the public's money. However, if when these permanent buildings are erected, it is possible to move the others to some other place, there will be no waste in money."[33]

SHILOH SCHOOL
See Harper

SHIRAR SCHOOL
Mrs. Gertrude Nitze Shirar, a graduate of Newcomb College in New Orleans, operated a school for elementary and a few junior high-age students first at 1910 Baldwin beginning in 1919 and later moving to 207 Pierce. She made special dispensation for students with physical handicaps and continued her academy into the late 1930s.[34]

SIKES SCHOOL
See Jefferson

SINGLETON SCHOOL
The Singleton family name has been connected to education in North Harris County almost from the beginning. A schoolhouse near the Singleton community was a poll location in July 1850, with S. Singleton as the election judge. Whether there is a direct throughline to the later school is not clear, and the school in question may be the same as Dunman's. The 20th century Singleton School, named for Humble area resident Reed Singleton, was a wooden building located off Atascocita Road near where Wilson Road dead ends. It opened about 1903 after the earlier school on Joe Dunman's land in District 35 had closed following Dunman's death. During the 1917-18 school year, a brick structure replaced the wooden one. Though enrollment reached the neighborhood of 30 pupils in the first decade of the 20th century, by 1926 only nine children of the first three grades attended. Humble ISD closed the school at the end of the term. Remnants of the buildings stood for many years, but today a landfill occupies the site.[35]

A 1917 photo of Singleton School. Humble Museum

SIXTH WARD COLORED SCHOOL

African American children from first through low fourth grades attended this small school at the corner of State and Trinity for about a decade before the school was merged into the First Ward Colored School in 1908. The two-room facility held over 100 pupils during several terms.[36]

SMILEY, WILLIAM SCHOOL

Ohio native William G. Smiley moved to Texas to teach at Eagle Lake in 1891 and four years later was principal at Houston's Elysian School. Smiley moved to Houston High a few years later, becoming principal there in 1901 and staying until WWI when he was elected superintendent of Harris County Schools, a post he held until 1938. Some time prior to his retirement, the school at the Dyersdale community, northeast of Houston was renamed in his honor. The later Smiley High School, opened across the street in 1953, was named for his wife, Mary Brantley Smiley, who also served as a longtime member of the county school board. The older Smiley buildings continued to be used for some time. Smily High School merged with Forest Brook in 2008 and was renamed North Forest High.[37]

Smiley School on bookmobile day. HCPL

Teacher Immorality

"TALES OF IMMORALITY OF SCHOOL TEACHERS SHOCKING"

- By Carter Wesley, *Informer*, Saturday, June 7, 1947

HOUSTON - This might appropriately be styled the story of truth forever on the scaffold, and wrong forever on the throne. But inasmuch as it affects our school children, one might prefer to oversimplify it by saying it is a story of corruption or immorality on the part of our school teachers in the presence of and against students.

Within five days this writer has had three harrowing tales told of immorality in the schools in the city of Houston. One is of a reported incident in a high school in which a woman teacher and a man teacher are reported to have been discovered, in broad daylight, undressed, and in embrace in the school building. Another is of a principal of one of our largest schools who has made it a habit to chase young students, and to condone the chasing of young girl students by other teachers in the school. The third is of a county school teacher who has been misappropriating school funds and chasing the school teachers and the school girls.

The thing which makes one boil is the fact that the people who would oppose such conduct are for the most part being pilloried and discredited, while these offenders are being protected and continued in office. It can probably be said with certitude that parents would prefer to have honest, moral, kindly teachers (rather than) brilliant, corrupt, lewd teachers over their children. But for some unknown reason, those whom the people know to be guilty succeed in winning over in their corruption and intimidating the people who would complain.

It is to be wondered whether or not this licentiousness would go on if there were Negro supervisors, with backing from the school board, checking these schools regularly. On this question of moral conduct in the schools, before the children, and with the children, there should be no compromise of any kind.

SMITH, ASHBEL E S

The second bond issue of GCISD in 1927 provided funds for the construction of a new elementary school on Murrill Street in Baytown. The 12-room building was named for Ashbel Smith, a man known as both the "father of Texas medicine" and "the father of the University of Texas." The multi-talented Smith also represented the Republic of Texas to Britain and France and served as the final Secretary of State for the nation. His plantation home, Evergreen, occupied an area along Cedar Bayou that later became part of the Goose Creek Oil Field. The school honoring him thrived, for a time hosting a small branch of the Harris County Library. In 1996, the original building and subsequent additions were replaced with a modern structure.[38]

SMITH, E. O. J H S

Ernest Ollington Smith held as strong a pedigree in Houston's African American education community as anyone. A graduate of Fisk College, Smith served as principal at Hollywood, Booker T. Washington Elementary, Bruce, and Harper before taking the reins as the first principal at Wheatley High when that school opened in the former McGowen Elementary building in 1927. In addition, he served the segregated Black institutions of the YMCA, Pilgrim Congregational Church, Masonic Lodge, and Longshoreman's Union where he had worked to augment his early teacher's salary. It was Smith who spearheaded the fundraising that bought a parcel of land to hold the Colored Carnegie Library, the first in the state to serve his race exclusive of a college campus.

At the helm of Wheatley, he oversaw one of the largest Black high schools in Texas, stressing extracurricular activities in particular. When the high school moved to a new home in 1950, five years after Professor Smith's death, the old McGowen/Wheatley at 1701 Bringhurst near the intersection of Gregg and Lyons was renamed E.O. Smith Junior High, remaining a fixture in Fifth Ward. The iconic building, which remained an architectural work of art, later became the Carter Career Center, but that was not enough to save it. Despite protests first for the loss of the middle school and then a passionate fight to save the century old building that had once been the heart of Fifth Ward's Black community, HISD would have none of it, and ran bulldozers into the school just before Labor Day 2014. Even a brief court fight could not stop the destruction, and the oldest African American school building in Houston came tumbling down, a high-profile victim of the rampant neglect of our built environmental history.[39]

SMITH, JOHN SCHOOL

The John Smith School opened in 1910 at the rural street corner of Westheimer and Reynolds Road, later to renamed Kirby Drive, as part of County District 4. The city was encroaching to the southwest, and by 1912, Miss Willie Sadler, the principal, reported 52 students in six grades and the addition of a second teacher. The school lasted barely over a decade before closing. In May 1925, leading city booster Will Hogg purchased the land and building from the school district for $4,000, hiring John Staub to remodel the old building and making it the Forum of Civics, an organization dedicated to the "betterment and beautification of Houston." Among other accomplishments, using Hogg's money, the Forum planted crepe myrtles and live oaks across a wide swath of the city. The Hogg family bequeathed the property to the University of Texas in 1939, and three years later, the old school was purchased by the River Oaks Garden Club, still carrying Hogg's stipulation that it be used for educational purposes. Today, the gardens around the old John Smith School are open to the public, a valuable green space in the urban grid.[40]

John Smith School shared a design with several others in the county.
HHRC

SMOKYVILLE SCHOOL

The Smokyville White school operated in the late 19th century in District 26 northwest of Houston.[41]

SMOKYVILLE COLORED SCHOOL

The Black population of the Smokyville or Smokeyville community appears to have been higher than the White. The *Texas School Journal* reported it as a colored school community in 1888, and the teacher a few years later was paid $2.50 more than his White counterpart.[42]

The outdoor theatre at South End JHS. HISD

SOUTH END J H S

See San Jacinto HS

SOUTH HOUSTON SCHOOL

The town of South Houston, about eight miles from Houston on the GH & H railroad, had a school prior to 1910. The Western Land Company that developed the community built a "magnificent frame building" and deeded it to the county for use in the new District 44. That same year, the developers paid to have the first ever powered flight in Texas on its property. Enrollment at South Houston was 124 students under the tutelage of four teachers in 1910. It was soon offering two years of high school, and the new campus sported Bermuda grass and shade trees. Crops were planted, and a boys' corn club was formed. Corn clubs were the forerunners to 4-H and the FFA. The Depression in the early 1930s left the district unable to pay teacher salaries, however, and in 1935, South Houston joined the Pasadena ISD. Coming into the district as principal was Pearl Hall who stayed at the school until 1953.[43]

South Houston School. HHRC

Gardening and Agriculture

Between 1850, the first United States Census in which Texas was enumerated, and 1930, Houston's population increased by at least 61% every decade. Twice it more than doubled in ten years' time. Many of the new residents of Houston came from small towns within an hour's drive on today's modern highways, and some of those were from smaller communities in Harris County. It was a national trend. Nationwide, about 40% of America's townships lost population between 1880 and 1890 as people chose to seek higher paying industrial jobs in the big city.[44]

County schools superintendent L.L. Pugh was of the opinion that part of the problem was that his schools were doing too good a job expanding the child's horizons and pointing them cityward. As odd as it might sound to teach agriculture in rural schools where a majority of students lived on farms, Pugh was all for the idea. As he wrote in 1913, the premise was "not to try to make farmers out of the boys but to stop unmaking them… It is the duty of the school to teach the child to understand the life about him and put himself in touch with the professions of his father."[45]

The opportunities were greater in the country than in the city according to this line of thinking. Teaching the elementary principles of agriculture would interest the boys and girls in country life and instruct the neighborhood farmers through their children. "Give the boy a lesson on the planting of corn or cotton, or the production of milk," Pugh wrote. "And you have opened a new field of interest for him; let the girl tell how she cooks and washes dishes at home, and she will look on these duties in a new light.

Gardens, such as this one at the Kinkaid School on Richmond Ave., were popular at both public and private campuses. Kinkaid School

The biggest part of this plan was to have both fall and spring gardens at the county schools. The national and state Departments of Agriculture were listed as resources, as was the Agricultural and Mechanical College at Bryan. Harris County had also hired a county agent, and among his work was organizing boys' corn and cotton clubs, several sponsored by a teacher in one of the county schools. The U.S.D.A. shipped thousands of packets of field and flower seed to the county school children for planting at home and at school. In District 25 on the north edge of Houston, the trustees used not only the government seed but wrangled donations of ten dozen rose bushes from Kerr Florist of Houston and 75 one-year-old camphor gum trees from Alvin Nursery.[46]

The county school doing the most to promote agriculture and gardening was easily South Houston, located in an area already thriving with various fruit orchards. Principal Roy Glasgow reported that 48 students in grades four through nine were actively studying agriculture every day. The ninth graders had a laboratory where they learned about seed structure and performed experiments to determine proper planting depth. South Houston School was even growing certain products in marketable quantities: two acres of strawberries and an acre of cantaloupes were located adjacent to the school yard.[47]

SOUTH HOUSTON SCHOOL, HOUSTON
This was likely the same school as Newman though referenced as South Houston in the late-1800s.[48]

SOUTH HOUSTON COLORED SCHOOL, HOUSTON
The South Houston Colored School was listed in District 24 with other Black schools Glen Cove and Brays Bayou Colored and White school Newman from the late-1880s until 1893 when the tax money was transferred to the others. A note of Emancipation is penciled next to the entry that year.[49]

A class at Southland School. HCPL

SOUTHLAND E S
When Southland School was built just after the beginning of 1915, it was described as being "in the middle of a barren prairie south of the city of Houston." In fact, Allegheny Street in front of the school was not paved north to Dixie Drive until after the building opened. The neighborhood children prospered in their new prairie digs not far from the Pierce Junction oil fields. In May 1924, the school won top prize from the Harris County Public Library system for collecting wildflowers. They were awarded five nature guides for the school library, and two individual students received copies of a wild flower guidebook and cash prizes of five dollars each. Southland left the county schools in July 1927 when District 24 was annexed into HISD with five teachers and 110 students. A decade later, the school held 176 pupils and was comprised of four "classrooms and an auditorium. In the overground basement there are 2 play-rooms and a cafeteria." The new Southland opened in October 1949 with a Tampa Street address. In 1980, Southland was renamed to honor Ruby Lockhart Thompson, a woman with

46 years as an HISD teacher and administrator. A new Thompson on Tierwester replaced the 1949 Southland School.[50]

SOUTHLAND COLORED SCHOOL

City directories from 1926 and the next few years list Southland Colored School at the same location, Allegheny between Mobile and Natchez, as Southland School, the institution for White students. It is unclear if there was a separate small building adjacent to the larger White school or a directory error. Miss Eliza Lewis is listed as teacher there, and she also appears as a teacher at nearby Sunnyside School for African Americans a few years earlier. Teachers at the smaller county schools often moved around, but records other than the directories make clear that there was indeed a Southland Black school in operation despite the lack of a directory listing. Mrs. W.H. Parker, who was involved with the White school, notes in a memoir that Sunnyside was in the same District 24 in 1926 with 16 students in a single room.[51]

Schools Southmayd – Sykes

SOUTHMAYD E S

The Gloverdale and Pecan Park subdivisions southeast of downtown, homes for growing East End and Ship Channel industrial workers, were just getting started when HISD opened Joanna Kent Southmayd Elementary in the fall of 1936. The location at the southeast corner of Japonica and Evergreen was so isolated that Superintendent Oberholtzer had to go before City Council to request that they grade streets to the school, an action which caused Mayor Oscar Holcombe to blurt: "Do you mean to say that you built this school where people couldn't get to it?" Joanna Southmayd herself was a pre-Texas Revolution-era teacher near Harrisburg. She had come to Mexican Texas from New England with her missionary husband, Daniel Starr Southmayd. While preaching at a church in Concord, Massachusetts in the late 1820s, the Southmayds lived in the Thoreau family boardinghouse with young Henry David Thoreau.[1]

SOUTH MAID/MAYDE SCHOOL

South Mayde or South Maid School was a small frame building in District 41 near Katy, operating in the first decade or two of the 20th century. The school drew its name from South Mayde Creek which in turn seems to be a corruption of the Southmayd name. John Allan Southmayd, a relative by marriage, perhaps brother-in-law, of Joanna Kent Southmayd, owned land in the neighborhood in the 1840s. An early photo of the student body shows only 14 pupils, mostly barefoot and most members of one of the three Beckendorff families in the neighborhood.[2]

SOUTHMORE E S

See MacGregor

SOUTHWELL SCHOOL

Spring Colored School in County District 4 was in operation prior to 1886. By 1907, the building, hosting children for a five-month term, was described as being in poor condition. In the years prior to WWII, as longtime principal W. M. Southwell was nearing the end of his 20-plus year run at the wood frame school, there were over 80 students between grades one and seven for two teachers. After his retirement in 1945, the school was named in honor of Southwell. The elementary schools in Spring ISD were finally integrated in 1966. The last location of Southwell School is reflected in a park of that name on Nelson Street not far southwest of the modern intersection of the Grand Parkway and Hardy Toll Road. The community center at the site is named for Benjamin F. Clark, who along with his wife, taught at Southwell beginning in 1950.[3]

Operating the Rural Schools

County School Disadvantages

"The most imperative rural school problems, viz.: the equalizing of school opportunity in the open county with the educational advantages afforded City children, has been, and continues to be, our major concern and is receiving our utmost endeavor. The steps involved in the accomplishment of this purpose are first, the securing of funds for teachers' salaries. Among the many factors in the school process, the teacher ranks first, for 'As is the teacher, so is the school.' However, to compete with the City and its many seeming advantages, the difficulty in securing rural teachers with ideals, standards and qualifications is manifestly a matter of higher salaries for our rural schools, and to meet this requirement, the tax rate in the various Districts is being increased as rapidly as the school sentiment in the community matures. This is evidenced by the fact that during the current year the tax rate has been increased in eight School Districts of Harris County. The second step in the furtherance of educational opportunity in our rural schools involves more and better school buildings and equipment. This, supplemented by the practice of grouping smaller schools into larger units, embraces the main factors in the movement now in operation in this County, for the improvement of our rural school system."

W. G. Smiley, County Superintendent

Harris County Auditor's Report 1928

Boys and wagons at a northwest Harris County schoolhouse. Cypress Historical Society

Hints for Young County Teachers

1. The fewer rules the better.

2. Plan each day's work and work each day's plan.

3. Interest is the first essential of the learning process.

4. Teach the child how to study by studying with him, not for him.

5. Develop the child's faith in himself. False humility is degrading.

6. Attend the meetings of all institutes and of the State Teachers' Associations.

7. In discipline, strive for the order of machinery at work, not for the stillness of the cemetery.

8. Absolute honesty with pupils commands respect. If you make a mistake, acknowledge it willingly and completely.

9. Good light in the school room will save many eyes and prevent interest from going out at the door.

10. Enthusiasm is catching like the measles, but it is never so dangerous.

11. Organize your school for social service, and first set your school house and grounds in fine order.

12. Help ambitious poor boys and poor girls to get a chance.

13. Parents are interested in the doings of their children. Organize in rural communities boys agricultural clubs and girls home clubs to bring the school and the home closer together.

14. Teach the children to care for their teeth. A pure mouth never offends.

15. Have some good songs, and teach your children to sing them with spirit and vigor; music takes the shortest path to the soul.

16. The big things of life are very near to us all. True, noble service in behalf of children is one of the biggest,

17. The schools are for the home and the State. Do something that will serve the home and elevate the State.

18. Headaches and inattention often result from defective vision. Can your pupils see well? Find out.

19. Learn something new each day. You will find it but ten feet away.

20. Pure drinking water will save the lives of many children. What right have we to poison them with infected water?

21. Have the floors of your school room dampened with saw dust or water before sweeping. The dust of the school room is both disagreeable and dangerous.

22. It is possible for you to make a State-wide reputation where you are. The world on the other side of the fence is very much like it is here.

THE RECITATION

5. Let the pupils do the reciting. Most teachers talk too much.

13. Encourage the timid or backward pupil by asking him simple questions, that he may answer without difficulty at first.

Harris County School Report 1913

Transporting rural children to school was sometimes less than comfortable. The common school districts generally reimbursed wagon drivers.
HHRC

Consolidation

"Unite the small schools of fifteen, twenty and thirty pupils, with scarcely two boys or two girls of the same age and size to play and chum together, and you will have infused into the school a new spirit and a new life that can only come with the enthusiasm engendered when there are brought together, with a group of almost every age and size, a hundred or so boys and girls.

"Pick up the school register, and if you can put two and two together, you can read there the sad story of the lack of interest in the country schools. Consolidation is not a cure for all the evils, yet experience has shown us it is the most effective remedy yet offered.

"Games and companionship will draw the children together. Shut these two things out of a child's life and, at the first chance, he will drop out to be thrown in contact with the live, red-blooded boys and girls of his own age in the throbbing world on the outside. Bring a large number of boys and girls together bubbling over with life, the backwardness, the petty jealousies, prevalent so often in the lonely and melancholy one-room school, will be worn away and endearing companionships will be formed by the games played where everyone must play his part with respect for the wishes and rights of his companions.

"Lead your boys and girls to play with their whole heart and soul, losing their petty selves in the game as they are united in joy and interest in their playmates, and you have gone a long way in making them good American citizens, and go with vim and energy into the great game of life.

"Happy companionship, spirited games and recitations, trained teachers for each special grade under the daily sympathetic guidance of an able principal, a homelike school building with all the best of teaching tools in the way of equipment and apparatus—the strong and powerful forces are these coming with consolidated school to give life more abundantly to boys and girls of the farm. With it all will come a still greater life-giving force—an enriched course of study—-subjects that will give the power necessary for grappling successfully with new tasks, and the new problems of the farm that the rising generation will be called upon to solve. Consolidation is in the air, and the farmer boys and girls are rapidly coming to their own. It is being tried and used successfully in twenty-five States."

Harris County Schools Report 1912

Visits from the County Supervisor

The distance to the schools is another factor of no mean importance in my work. Having to reach the schools by railroad, livery rig, on foot and your auto. I had no especially dependable means of travel. Had it not been for your kind assistance with your auto, I should not have been able to have reached nearly so many schools as I did.

The general lack of co-operation between parents and teachers I found of much moment in determining the retarding influences to the progress of our schools, especially in the lower grades. I feel that the teachers ought to know personally and be on a friendly footing with each parent of every pupil under her care; and that the parents ought to be stimulated to the interest in the school that will cause them to work in complete harmony with the teacher and board.

During the year I made 190 visits. Every school in the county, with the exception of the following, was reached at least once during its term: Rose Hill, Georgi, Port Houston, New School, Middle Bayou, La Porte,

Chaneyville. The schools visited more than once are as follows: Berry (4), Platte, Addicks (2), Post Oak (2), Aldine (2). Smith, Seabrook (2), Bellaire (2), Tomball (2), Harlow, Crosby (2), Newman (4), South Houston, Big Cypress (2), Webster (2), Hillebrandt, Willow Spring (2), Harrisburg, Sunset Heights, Pasadena, Humble (2), Fullerton, Janowski (2), Prairie View, Hohl (2), Little York (2). From the above you will see that the schools farthest away were visited least often.

The work done on these supervising visits varied according to the conditions. Most often, I took note of the apparent conditions, found some particular in which the teacher needed help, and then took charge of the class and conducted the lessons. Usually, I asked the teacher to note certain phases of the work and, after dismissal, talked with her and explained the principle. In this way I had many a confidential chat with the teachers, which enabled me to know best what to suggest for her and which gave me a better insight into conditions as they are. I would like to mention here that seldom did I leave a teacher after one of these visits who, I felt, failed to try to co-operate with me.

One feature of work in which I took part and which I enjoyed greatly, was the aid I could give in athletics and games. There has been quite an interest taken in baseball and basketball this year, and I think that playgrounds, games and athletic sports should be encouraged to the fullest extent. I truly believe that their development value is as great, if they are properly conducted, as any other

I beg to remain most truly yours,

Margaret King McShaffry,

Primary Supervisor

The Country Boy's Creed

I believe that the country which God made is more beautiful than the city which man made; that life out-of-doors and in touch with the earth is the natural life of man. I believe that work is work wherever we find it, but that work with nature is more inspiring than work with the most intricate machinery. I believe that the dignity of labor depends not on what you do, but on how you do it; that opportunity comes to a boy on the farm as often as to a boy in the city; that life is larger, freer and happier on the farm than in the town; that my success depends, not upon my location, but upon myself—not, upon my dreams, but upon what I actually do, not upon luck, but upon pluck. I believe in working when you work and in playing when you play, and in giving and demanding a square deal in every act of life.

County Schools Report 1913

SOUTH SHAVER E S

This elementary was one of those born of the post-WWII industrial growth in Pasadena, opening in 1949.[4]

SPRING SCHOOL

The community of Spring was platted by the Houston & Great Northern Railroad in 1873, just prior to a merger that would create the International & G.N. R.R., on land that had previously been used for farming. From an early date, there was a strong German immigrant presence, like most of northwest Harris County, and when citizens registered their existing school under the new 1876 state law, Saxony-born Carl Wunsche was one of the trustees. German surnames remained prevalent for years. In the first decade of the 20th century the town gained a roundhouse and railroad shops and an accompanying increase in population. There were 63 pupils in a turn of the century building on Oak Street in what is today Old Town Spring, and more children in a small school south of town. In 1907, the schools were combined into a larger building located just east of the railroad tracks, by today's Aldine-Westfield and Spring School Road. At least two men who attended that school recalled that it was partitioned with a four foot high wall with White students and teacher on one side and Blacks on the other, though that would have been unusual at the time. The two classes were not allowed to talk or play together.[5]

Frank Schlueter added his birds and airplane embellishment to this photo at Spring School. Klein ISD

Many published histories list that 1907 merger as the start of the Spring Independent School District, but in fact, it remained District 4 administered by Harris County for some time afterward. By 1914, two years of high school classes had been added, and growth encouraged the townspeople to vote bonds for a new two-story, eight-room brick school that included an auditorium. The large frame building was moved to the African American neighborhood. The bullish economic outlook was misplaced, and shortly, the closure of the railroad roundhouse and the loss of saloons and hotels brought a decline in population in the 1920s. In 1935, Spring School was combined with Harrell to the north of today's FM 1960, and Spring ISD was born in earnest. The addition of science and foreign language classes along with 11th grade allowed Spring graduates to go directly to college, if they so desired.[6]

SPRING COLORED SCHOOL
See Southwell

SPRING BRANCH SCHOOL
The Spring Branch community was another of the dozens of German immigrant communities north of Buffalo Bayou. The families of Karl Kolb and Jacob Schroeder arrived in the area in the 1830s, and by 1848, with the number of families at seven, a congregation was organized and a cemetery begun. Yellow fever took a particularly hard toll in 1854, but that same year, a log building was erected and christened St. Peter Church. School classes were also likely held in that structure. It was included in the county's school program that same year under the new state law. In 1856, a separate log building was erected for a neighborhood school with the minister as master. By 1861, Spring Branch was enumerated in the school census to qualify for government funds. The small school house behind the church served as a county school, in addition to a voting place and community building, in what was District 27 by the early-1880s. At the end of that decade, a red, one-room building opened near Long Point and Campbell where Spring Branch Elementary sits today. That location continued to serve as schoolgrounds in the community for decades. By the late 1920s, a small store operated behind it providing students access to snacks and lunch.[7]

Spring Branch School. Ruth Hillendahl Plumb

SPRING BRANCH COLORED
See Lily White

SPRING BRANCH H S

Spring Branch School at Campbell and Long Point continued to grow along with the community, and additional grades were added until the first high school class was graduated in 1949 from the campus it shared with the elementary school. A few years afterward, a new high school building was opened at what would soon become 9000 Westview, operating as the sole high school in Spring Branch ISD until Memorial HS opened in 1962. One of the most publicized early stories from the new suburban school was the haircut feud that took place in October 1953 when rival gangs of Bears students divided along lines that backed either crew cuts or the ducktail haircuts favored by the "bopsters". Twenty-one teen boys were arrested, found with an arsenal that included "a nail-studded baseball bat," brass knuckles, "a .38-caliber revolver, an air pistol, a pair of shears, a trench knife, a Japanese dagger with a folding blade, a metal lug wrench, a piece of electrical conduit pipe, a length of chain," and 21 pocket knives. There were 21 arrests, multiple students were placed on probation, and a local judge lectured parents to assume more responsibility for the children's behavior. Spring Branch High closed in 1985 as the district contracted, leaving behind two generations of saddened alumni, but the campus survives as a charter school.[8]

Summer School

The concept of a summer school program began as a trial during the hottest part of 1911. Classes were offered on a tuition basis at the White high school and at Fannin and Jones elementary schools. The city schools were "co-operating also with the summer school at the Young Men's Christian Association." The following summer, the experiment has been expanded to five Houston campuses.[9]

Early thoughts were a mixture of enthusiasm and reticence. "That the right kind of vacation school would be quite helpful cannot be doubted. On the other hand, the wisdom of the policy of having vacation schools for regular school work during such summer weather as we have in South Texas is yet to be proven."[10]

By 1914, the city district was also opening the new swimming pool at South End Junior High for a nominal fee. The classroom side of things during the summer was backed with a train of thought that remains familiar to the present day. Superintendent Horn wrote: "These schools meet alike the needs of the bright, pupil, who with a little work in the summer, will be enabled to do the work of a grade higher than that which he would have otherwise entered: and of that other pupil who has gotten behind with his work and needs extra help on some subject, or subjects in order that he may not have to do over again his work therein. It is sincerely to be hoped that before very long the financial situation in our school system will be such as to make it possible for us to maintain our schools in the summer on the same free basis as during the rest of the year."[11]

SPRING CREEK SCHOOL

This was a pre-existing school listed under the 1876 public school law. No exact location was determined.[12]

The old St. Agnes building sat empty for a time, then only the large front steps remained in an open lot for years after demolition. HHRC

ST. AGNES ACADEMY

Mother Pauline Gannon and the Dominican Sisters opened the four-story convent and school in February 1906 at 3901 Fannin between Truxillo and Cleburne in the South End. The girls at the school learned a regular course of study from the sisters with a special emphasis on music, art, and language. About 100 girls were enrolled in grades one through twelve by 1907, enjoying "the wide halls, swept by the south breeze, and the attractive reception rooms, embellished with beautiful pictures… Throughout the halls palms and shrubs contributed floral adornment and in the reception rooms were quantities of cut flowers." It did take a few years before paved streets and a streetcar reached that far south in the city. The nuns of that time sent hot coffee to the conductor and motorman, and in return, they got free passage on the cars. In 1939, the boarding option at St. Agnes was discontinued, making it solely a day school. It switched to high school grades only in 1954. Changing demographics caught up with the neighborhood in 1963 when the school relocated to the new suburban neighborhood of Sharpstown. For at least two decades, the vacant lot and high steps remained as reminders of the grand structure. Always a limited enrollment, in the century plus of operation, St. Agnes Academy claims over 10,000 graduates.[13]

ST. ANNE SCHOOL

St. Anne Catholic Church, known today for the Spanish mission style beauty at Westheimer and Shepherd, opened a parish school for first through eighth grade in 1930. The original church had opened in 1924 in a four-room farmhouse at Westheimer and McDuffie, both of which were dirt roads at the time. The school was later placed to the north of the current picturesque church which was opened in 1940,. Today the school continues to offer education to elementary and middle school-age children.[14]

The iconic St. Anne Church with the school at right. Wikimedia Commons

ST. CHRISTOPHER SCHOOL

The Sisters of the Incarnate Word and the Blessed Sacrament founded a small school at the corner of Moline and Broadway for St. Christopher Parish in 1924, giving the duties over to the Dominican Sisters five years later.

A new church building rose in 1939, and the school moved to its current location at Park Place and Meridian a decade later when the Gulf Freeway took much of the church property. Additions to the school came primarily in the 1950s.[15]

ST. EUPHRASIA SCHOOL
See Convent of the Good Shepherd

ST. JOHN LUTHERAN SCHOOL
See Winkler's

Parochial School Snapshot in 1939

Religious schools have existed in Houston since the early days, but it was the Catholic and Lutheran denominations that dominated the field for over 100 years. When St. Christopher Parish in Park Place opened a new building in 1939, the *Chronicle* commented on the parochial school scene in the Bayou City: "The enrollment at 19 Catholic schools for White children in the fall was 4,113, and the enrollment at two Negro Catholic parochial schools was 477. At seven Lutheran schools the enrollment was 516, and at two Seventh Day Adventist schools, the enrollment totaled 55. Kinkaid School, a private school which includes both elementary and high school grades, enrolled 225."[16]

ST. JOHN'S SCHOOL
Many modern Americans know of St. John's School as the setting for the film Rushmore, shot there by alumnus Wes Anderson, or as the private school that famously rejected the application of George W. Bush. Its roots, however, are firmly grounded in the staid propriety of River Oaks. It opened its doors in September of 1946, and the list of founders' names included several of the wealthiest and most influential Houstonians going, including the Cullens, Farishes, Garwoods, Blaffers, and R.E. "Bob" Smith to name but a few. Though the connection has long since ended, the school at Westheimer and Claremont was at first affiliated with the adjacent St. John the Divine Episcopal Church, and Reverend Thomas Sumners was one of those involved in the hiring of the first headmaster, Alan Lake Chidsey, who would remain for the first 20 years.[17]

The mascot at St. John's was originally the Crusaders, but that was dropped quickly to separate them from the religious connotations. It was replaced with the Rebels and a Confederate-costumed mascot. That lasted until

1990 when the name was retained but the symbology was pointed toward the American Revolution. Finally, in 2004, the Board of Trustees unanimously voted to change the nickname to the Mavericks. Though the faculty was in support, there were many cries of protest from both students and alumni.

St. John's opened with 344 students on six acres of property and a program and creed that stressed academics, leadership and "moral and spiritual values." It was co-educational from the start, serving 13 grade levels. Today the campus covers 28 acres of very valuable Inner Loop real estate and has a student body of around 1,200. The prestige of the expensive school has never wavered, and one description of that was given by a woman who is easily among the most famous alums. Political columnist Molly Ivins reflected on her youth at St. John's and her notable height with the self-deprecating comment that she felt herself to be "a Clydesdale among thoroughbreds."[18]

ST. JOSEPH SCHOOL

Sisters from Incarnate Word Academy downtown started a school when St. Joseph Parish was organized in October 1879. It was located at Clay and Lubbock in Fourth Ward North which was later designated Sixth Ward, and it originally served "young ladies and small boys." The sisters commuted to and forth by mule carts and were said to have become expert at imitating the recalcitrant animals and occasionally helping push the carts out of the mud. In 1893, the parish took over operation of the school. Following major damage from the 1900 storm, the new Romanesque Church opened in 1902 and the school was placed behind and to the west of it. Enrollment topped 450 immediately after WWII, but the students were all of European descent since Mexican-American children, even those who lived in the immediate vicinity, were not admitted for the first several decades of operation.[19]

ST. JOSEPH SCHOOL, BAYTOWN

The Incarnate Word and Blessed Sacrament Sisters opened this school in Baytown in 1948. The parish itself dates back to 1924. The school still operates for students through eighth grade.[20]

ST. MARY OF THE PURIFICATION SCHOOL

This small school at 3006 Rosedale was opened in 1930 and closed in 1967. It made blessed history in 1960 when it became the first parish school in the Galveston-Houston Archdiocese to comply with Bishop Wendelin Nold's desegregation directive. Many years later, the parish reopened the school and operates a Montessori school through fifth grade today.[21]

ST. MARY'S SEMINARY, LA PORTE

This Basilian seminary opened on the shoreline at Sylvan Beach in 1901 in a large, grand building that had originally been built in the late 1800s as a luxury resort hotel. The seminary included a high school course for the young men. That was discontinued in 1940, and in 1954 the bayside was abandoned and those studying for the priesthood were relocated to Houston's Memorial Drive.[22]

ST. NICHOLAS SCHOOL

The Catholic diocese opened a parish school for African American children in 1887 at Chenevert and Lamar, east of downtown. By 1890, enrollment topped 100 pupils. The White sisters of Incarnate Word commented that the students showed great "intellectual and moral growth," including several who warranted private lessons on piano and violin. The school spawned a parish church shortly thereafter. The 1924 church building that still welcomes parishioners at 2508 Clay today marks the location where the congregation moved. A new convent and school building was opened in August 1931. The high school at St. Nicholas ceased operations in 1967 due to declining enrollment, and the parish elementary followed suit four years later.[23]

ST. PATRICK SCHOOL

In early 1880, a number of Irish Catholics in Fifth Ward successfully prevailed upon the diocese to open a church on the north side of Buffalo Bayou. Sisters from Incarnate Word walked to and from the small school that opened that September. It would be a star-crossed existence. The school, growing quickly to two buildings, was destroyed by fire in May 1890 and again in May 1892. The new 1893 building, along with the church and rectory were all completely destroyed in the enormous Fifth Ward fire of February 20, 1912, still Houston's largest conflagration by area. Reopened that fall, St. Patrick School closed in 1939 because the neighborhood had transitioned from residential to industrial. That first closure lasted only two years, and the school reopened "to take care of the Mexican children of that section of the city." The small school at Conti and Maury finally closed permanently in 1963.[24]

ST. PAUL'S LUTHERAN SCHOOL

St. Paul's Lutheran School was at 605 Majestic in Fifth Ward in the 1930s, a block from Lyons and Lathrop. It appears to be a vacant lot at time of writing. No further information for such a church was found.[25]

ST. PETER THE APOSTLE SCHOOL

Dominican Sisters opened a three-room school in 1942. The archdiocese had received the 21 acres of donated farmland on which the church complex sits sixteen years prior. Today a modern school building serves the parish at 6220 La Sallette.[26]

ST. PIUS V, PASADENA

This parish school in Pasadena was opened by the Sisters of Divine Providence in 1947. The school, now operated by the parish, is at 812 South Main Street in Pasadena, serves students through eighth grade.[27]

ST. ROSE OF LIMA

St. Rose of Lima School on Brinkman in the Garden Oaks neighborhood opened its parish school in 1948. It still flourishes today with a lengthy waiting list.[28]

ST. STEPHEN SCHOOL

St. Stephen School at 1910 Center, also called San Esteban, opened in 1932 as part of a mission program to cater to the needs of Hispanic Catholics in Sixth Ward. The church remains, but the school closed in 1948.[29]

ST. THERESA SCHOOL

Four Sisters of the Incarnate Word opened St. Theresa School on September 29, 1947 for over 200 pupils with rooms unfinished and equipment such as desks and blackboards not yet delivered. It was a large school with eight classrooms, library, office, and cafeteria, though the first eighth grade graduating class the following May was 16 students. The school near Memorial Park still utilizes the original buildings.[30]

ST. THOMAS AQUINAS

For Houston's most established Catholic boys' school, the earliest years for St. Thomas High School were rather nomadic. It was established with the grand moniker of St. Thomas College by three Basilian fathers in 1900 at an unused, two-story 1860s monastery building that was part of the old Catholic compound at Franklin and Caroline. The great storm that September forced the priests and 44 boys to relocate to the Masonic Building on Main near Capitol. In 1903, school head Fr. Roche led them to a site on the south side of Hadley between Austin at La Branch, all graveled roads. The school building, with gas lights and wood stove heat, faced Austin Street, but the campus occupied the entire block in the form of playing fields. Tuition was twelve dollars a month, though many boys worked after school to offset the cost. By 1939 there were 438 students, and the campus needed a new home.[31]

*St. Thomas HS boys, including one sporting a large band-aid, in 1945.
St. Thomas HS*

Fr. T.P. O'Rourke, the principal at the time, had previously secured 32 acres of, what was for Houston, "gently rolling" land at the northeast corner of Shepherd and Buffalo Bayou. The school opened there in September 1940, enjoying two new school buildings designed by Maurice J. Sullivan and a stadium. The Cordova shell-stone-faced educational building held 17 classrooms, four science labs, commercial and typing rooms, a library, cafeteria, and chapel. The other building was a two-story monastery to house the priests/teachers. That building held 25 bedrooms, community space, and two chapels. St. Thomas had always placed a great emphasis on sports, and the stadium on the eastern edge of campus actually pre-dated the school buildings. Its capacity was increased from 2,000 to 3,000 in 1939 and a year later lights were added for night games. The Eagles faithful have been rewarded with over 100 parochial school athletics titles since 1900.[32]

In the 2010s, St. Thomas, feeling cramped on the original 32 acres, acquired more land to the north from HISD after George Washington Junior High closed. Like its female contemporary, St. Agnes, St. Thomas High School has surpassed the 10,000 alumni mark.

ST. VINCENT SCHOOL

The history of Catholics in Houston starts at the intersection of Franklin and Caroline. It was the site of the first Catholic church in Houston and a variety of educational activities that went with it. The first parochial school was established there perhaps as early as 1842, but was certainly operating by January 1847. It existed for over 40 years, but perhaps with some gaps included. It was definitely thriving in the mid-1850s when "A Protestant" wrote a letter to the editor complimenting the Catholics who have 1/8 of the population but were educating "about one fourth of the youth of our city." By 1869, there was a School of the Convent of St. Vincent for 50 girls, and a year later, the St. Vincent School reopened with 49 boys between seven and thirteen. When the new Annunciation Church opened a few blocks away in 1873, the seat of Catholicism in Houston shifted there. St. Vincent served a German Catholic population for a while, under the name German Catholic School.[33]

ST VINCENT DE PAUL SCHOOL

In 1940, a new parish dedicated to St. Vincent de Paul was established on Bellaire Boulevard near West University, splitting off from St. Anne. A school followed two years later, staffed by four sisters from the Incarnate Word order. The parish school, though opening in temporary buildings, was large from the outset with 180 pupils the first year. The first permanent building was constructed behind the church in 1948 and still remains. More land was acquired along Buffalo Speedway, and the school, from pre-K through eighth grade, has expanded further over the years.[34]

STAPLES SCHOOL

Staples School opened in the mid-1890s at the southeast corner of Bleker and Liberty Road as a small one-room building taught by Miss Beulah Rone. In 1897, the 35' x 200' lot, the building, and all the furniture were valued at $1650. It was part of County District 25 that covered the area north of Houston. As the city expanded, the school was annexed by 1903. That year and the next there were roughly 75 students from first to fifth grades with almost a third of them residing outside the city limits. Paul Horn, the generous superintendent of Houston schools wrote: "Many of these live three and a half miles from the nearest school in the country. The Staples building is not crowded, and it would not be to our advantage if these children were excluded. Many of them, if excluded by us, would be deprived of school privileges altogether." The school was closed by the city not long afterward.[35]

STEUBNER SCHOOL

Young Adolf N. Steubner came from Hanover in Germany prior to 1880 and established a store on the north edge of Harris County. Soon a small community of that name sat at the top of Steubner-Airline Road. The county established School District 31 in 1885, and a one-room schoolhouse called Steubner opened. It remained in operation until around the turn of the century when the nearby towns of Hufsmith and Tomball became the area's population centers.[36]

STEVENSON E S

Cottage Grove started as an independent community west of Houston about 1909 with lots priced from $500 to $100 and terms as generous as fifty cents down. Within a few years, a young population had moved in, and a school was needed. Cottage Grove High School, serving up through seventh grade, opened its doors in February 1915 as part of the Brunner ISD. In August, it served as a shelter for the Taylor family whose nearby home was destroyed by the big hurricane. Cottage Grove was briefly its own ISD before becoming part of Houston. The seven-room building was done in the single story patio style, and HISD remodeled it in 1927 and renamed it for author Robert Louis Stevenson. A year later, Stevenson was the location of a special health program designed to increase the weight of students. With over half the school population underweight, those students were given milk and graham crackers and a rest period every school day for six weeks resulting in most being brought up to normal and some moving into the overweight category. After nearly a century of service, Stevenson Elementary at 5410 Cornish was slated for closure in 2012 even though new townhomes were sprouting across the neighborhood. HISD sold the property to developers.[37]

Stevenson ES. HISD

Houston Teachers Association

Teachers have no doubt suffered indignities since the first class bell rang. In Harris County, they were often forced to bunk with local families in lieu of a portion of their pay. They were subjected to angry parents and indifferent children and made to reapply for their jobs at the close of every single school year. Then there was the issue of pay.

In 1909, the City of Houston granted teachers a five dollar raise. That increased maximum pay for a White classroom teacher from 80 to 85 dollars and for the African American teachers from 55 to 60 dollars a month. For those lucky enough to be classified as school principal, salary maxed out at $1,600 a year. Superintendent Horn excoriated the board to do better.[38]

Two years later, Horn again reported that salaries had gone up five dollars a month across the board. He reminded the school board that "It is undeniable that the amount of money paid to the teachers of a school system has a direct connection with the quality of the instruction furnished. The money which a community pays in salaries to its teachers it really pays to itself."[39]

By November 1918, World War I was over, but the teachers' battle for fair wages was not. Horn was still arguing for the classroom teachers with ever increasing vehemence.

"While it is interesting to notice that within the fourteen years salaries have in some instances almost doubled," he wrote. "We cannot refuse to recognize that this same increase is far less than that given to workers along many other lines, and far less that the increase in the cost of living."[40]

This time he spelled out examples upon which the board could reflect: "Not long ago a master plumber stated that by working overtime a number of his men were making as much as $90.00 a week. There is not a teacher in the Houston school system who is making that much... In June, 1918, a young woman with two years of college training entered an office in the city of Houston as a stenographer. For the first two months she worked with no salary at all. At the beginning of the third month she was put on the payroll at $75.00 a month. In June, 1919, she received an offer at $115.00 a month, or $1,380 a year. If she had entered teaching instead of stenography, she would not at the end of the first year have been making more than half that amount."[41]

As far as the teachers were concerned, the time for pleading their cases as individuals was over. Though the history of unions in Houston dates to the printers in the first year of the city's founding, and by the start of the 20th century, there were dozens of extremely strong unionized work forces in town, the teachers had not joined them. That was in spite of the fact that the largest teachers' union in the nation was already over half a century old. African American teachers in Texas had organized an association of their own back in 1884.[42]

By the summer of 1919, though, the Bayou City had not one, but two teachers' organizations: the Teachers' Council and the Teacher's Association. The first welcomed principals and supervisors. The latter did not.[43]

Superintendent Horn was philosophical and a bit guarded. He noted that such organizations "are here with us, and here to stay. It is not a matter that is local in our city, but it is a nationwide, movement." After acknowledging that "an organized body of teachers can be a factor for good in a community," he felt the need to add a post-war warning of potential danger that was perfectly reflective of both the viewpoint of one who is economically well off and the Red Scare mentality of 1919: "It some times happens, too, that when there is not money enough to go around, the result is to a certain extent, an arrayal of class against class. This is always an unmixed evil. Anything which tends to set class against class works to the injury of all classes. In the American army, founded on principles of democracy, the soldiers respected their officers and obeyed them. The characteristics of the Bolsheviki was that the men shot their officers. This is perhaps the crucial distinction between democracy and bolshevism. Any educational doctrine which would tend to array grade school teachers, high school teachers, principals, supervisors, or superintendents, in hostile camps, is not democratic, but bolshevist."[44]

By the start of 1919, school teachers had unionized in Denison, Austin, and Galveston, and there were steps being taken in both Dallas and San Antonio. In early April, L.V. Lampson, the national organizer for the teachers union, was in Houston, urging over 200 members of the recently formed Houston Teachers Association to officially join the national union. They did exactly that later in the month when they voted to affiliate with the American Federation of Teachers and the American Federation of Labor.[45]

By 1920, the Houston Teachers' Association was no longer an experiment. For his part, the city school superintendent was breathing easier after "the actual test of a year's trial" He had dealt with union representatives for over twelve months and "in every instance it has touched it for good and not for harm." [46]

The early goals of the Houston Teachers Association was to increase salaries and expand sick leave for their members, but the organization also began making charitable contributions including one of $100 annually to the Museum of Art to continue the free class for gifted children. With Mamie Bastian as the union president, the group formed committees on course of study, press, legislation, efficiency, civic activities, grievances, and compensation.

Having a single voice brought only limited power, something demonstrated more than adequately during the Great Depression. With government budgets in Houston and everywhere else cut due to lower tax revenue and bad municipal investments, all employees felt the pain. That included HISD teachers who took an across the board pay cut in 1932. Almost immediately, the HTA began lobbying for a restoration, but the school board was entrenched "until better times return," even when pay hikes were approved in other Texas cities. A final indignity came in 1935 when, after teacher pay was finally brought back to pre-Crash levels, a local taxpayer group filed a lawsuit claiming the board could not grant the raise.[47]

Another issue for teachers was reasonable retirement pay. Statewide, teachers associations, both those already AFL-affiliated and not, had banded together to lobby for a teachers' retirement fund in Texas starting in 1916. Traction was a long time coming, however. It was 1935, amid a national union movement, before enough legislators felt the pressure to send an amendment to the voters. The Teacher Retirement System of Texas officially went into effect on July 1, 1937 with 38,000 members, but it took another four years before an additional amendment was passed mandating the state to match teacher contributions.[48]

STEWART, ELLEN McCARTER SCHOOL

The director, Ellen McCarter Stewart and her mother, Mrs. W. W. McCarter, began teaching kindergarten and "pre-primary" children in 1920 at 2007 Lamar Avenue. They moved frequently before ending up in a two-story house at 3403 Yupon that was loaned by W.S. Myers who owned Myers-Spalti Furniture. By that time, it enrolled 80 students through fifth grade.[49]

STOCKDICK SCHOOL

This white, one-room building sat at the corner of Stockdick School Road and Peek Road. Beginning about 1914, it served families northeast of Katy. True to the modern intersection where the school once sat, two of the early school trustees were W. C. Stockdick and A. J. Peek. Stockdick School consolidated with Katy ISD in 1931.[50]

SUNNY SIDE PLACE SCHOOL

The Holmes Brothers put 1,200 lots on the market in 1915, and the Sunnyside community sprouted south of the road that bore their name. It was the first new addition offered for African Americans south of the Houston city limits. Three years after their first sales, the Holmeses donated nine lots east of Scott Street to the county for use as a school. The first year, only 18 students attended. Tina Whidby began teaching there in 1924, over a decade before she would get her college degree, and continued in the role through at least WWII. It was Whidby who wrote a wonderful vignette of the neighborhood at the end of the 1930s. By then there were 92 families made up of common laborers, "18 cooks, 2 teachers, 2 preachers, truck farmers and businessmen. There were also cows, horses, hogs and mules living there." The school entered HISD in 1927, and until 1935 when bus service finally came to Sunnyside, students wishing to go past fifth grade "rode on horseback, some in wagons and many walked from Sunnyside to Jack Yates School, so determined were they to complete their high school work." By the late 1930s, there were 33 students who had finished at Sunnyside and were at Yates." Sunny Side School was renamed to honor Ethel Mosely Young, a longtime teacher at the school, in the early 1990s.[51]

An early faculty at Sunset Heights School. HHRC

SUNSET HEIGHTS E S

In late February 2012, Lovett Homes, in spite of many overtures from the preservationist community, razed the two-and-a-half story, pink brick school building at 27th and Harvard rather than utilize the unique structure. When it was turned to rubble and a few bricks were scavenged by nearby history lovers, the Sunset Heights School was almost exactly a century old. County District 25 had spent about $20,000 for the school to replace an earlier frame building that served the small neighborhood northeast of the established Houston Heights and at the terminus of a trolley line. Louise Waters, principal when the new four-room brick building opened, heartily sang its praises. By 1918, there were eight classrooms, and by 1920, 12 classrooms and over 520 students spread over temporary shacks. Commanding the entire block, there was still room for school vegetable gardens that drew special praise and ample recreation areas. In 1926, by then under the control of HISD, Alamo Elementary was built adjacently, along 27th, but the old Sunset Heights School continued to serve as classroom space.

Harris County drew on national recommendations in 1911 to arrive at the plan for the Romanesque design of the brick building, and they replicated the structure in a dozen locations around the county in the following three or four year span. By the time that Sunset Heights School met its fate, it and Alamo had been relegated to a storage space, and its once beautiful grounds were a parking lot for district maintenance vehicles. When it was demolished, it was the last remaining example of that vaunted design that had been trumpeted as ideal for the health and learning of Houston area students.[52]

SUSIE BOOKER SCHOOL

This was a private kindergarten for African American children in Independence Heights that operated for many years. It was at 3310 Courtlandt.[53]

SUTTON, WILLIAM S E S

County District 24 had a school operating south of the city limits toward Brays Bayou at least as early as 1884, and it was sometimes referred to as South Houston School House. By 1891, voting for the school district was held at the home of Charles E. Newman whose family also boarded the school's teachers during the week. Located on the south side of Chocolate Bayou Road, today's Blodgett, and five blocks east of Dowling, Newman School added a second teacher sometime prior to 1910. By that time, a new two-room building had been constructed. As the district with one White school, Newman, and two Black schools sat poised to be incorporated into the city, the reports were positive. In 1912, Principal Sarah Hill noted that no school in the county had "a larger cistern of pure water than Newman, or more wide-awake, intelligent children." A year later, her replacement W.C. Williams offered a more high-flown and overwritten description of a country school "securely nestling in the pines, slightly removed from the whir of industries of busy Houston." In 1914, they were added to the Houston public schools, slightly relocated to a six-acre campus on Holman Avenue extension, and installed in a four-room building.[54]

Sutton ES building. HHRC

In the late 1920s, thanks to HISD's flurry of bond issues, the Newman property was returned to the family, and a new school opened at 3300 Rosedale in November 1929 under the name William Seneca Sutton Elementary, honoring an educator who once led the Houston schools and later the University of Texas. The new structure, referenced initially as Feldman Court, had six classrooms and a lunchroom. Mr. A. Feldman who was developing the surrounding addition, also set up a trust worth $1,750 to endow the school library. After serving the area for decades first as Newman and then as Sutton, the name was moved to a new campus in the Sharpstown area in 1958, and it continues there today. The Sutton campus was then renamed to honor longtime African American teacher George B. M. Turner with a segregated school.[55]

SYKES SCHOOL
See Jefferson

Schools T - V

TAYLOR SCHOOL

The Houston public schools built five very similar tall, wood frame elementary schools for White students in the mid-1880s. Edward W. Taylor School at Milam and Clay was one of the earliest, opening in 1884 for students up to sixth grade. Principal Eloise Szabo oversaw a faculty of six. By 1905, adjacent land was acquired and an annex built to bring the capacity to 447 students in 11 classrooms. Just five years later, a new building was being called for, with recommendations to double its size. Even so, the Mothers Club of 1910 was giving their children every extravagance - two good pianos, a "talking machine," "a stereopticon outfit of the best make," a staffed, complete kitchen, and rooms for manual training and domestic science. A new location was identified only a few years later, and a brick, one-story Taylor School opened on Louisiana between Bell and Leeland in September 1916. True to desires, there were 22 classrooms and desks for 541 pupils. That would prove to be the high water mark, however. Junior high schools siphoned off sixth and seventh graders, and the "once nice residential section began to be commercialized, business sprang up and people moved away." In 1929, the Taylor location was converted to the district vocational school, and just a few years after that, the HISD administrative offices were moved there. The final use was as home to "troubled" children before the assets of Taylor School were transferred to San Jacinto High.[1]

An artist's rendering of the new Taylor ES that graced Louisiana St. HISD

School Cadets

The forerunners of the Reserve Officers Training Corps date back to 1819 at Norwich Academy in Vermont, and Land Grant college campuses authorized under the 1862 Morrill Act were required to maintain some sort of military component. The real explosion of the idea, though, dates to the years just prior to United States involvement in WWI. The Junior ROTC program sprung from the National Defense Act of 1916. That authorized the military to loan equipment and training officers to qualifying high schools, but military drill at non-military public schools had been around before that.[2]

Houston High School started a company of School Cadets in February 1908 and built on the program over the next few years, extending it into the more prominent grade schools. U.S. Army Captain Wagner, in Houston to inspect National Guard troops in 1913, made a stop to inspect the Cadet Corps at Fannin School and told Commandant C.H. Druse that he would report to the War Department that Fannin was the very "first cadet corps in a grammar school in the United States."[3]

Druse had organized the Fannin School corps in November 1911, and it was so popular that there were immediately two companies formed. By comparison, the high school didn't get its second company of cadets until March 1913. In fact, even by that date, the two companies at Fannin had more boys than those at the High School. Austin, Taylor, and Sherman Elementary Schools also had companies of around 30 boys, all outpacing the high school.

Though it is easy to imagine that high school age boys had more things to occupy their time than the grade school lot, Druse believed that the lack of enthusiasm was related to the lack of an armory, a feature that existed at Fannin. The High School, Austin, and Fannin boys all had .40 rifles at their disposal, though practice was not necessarily performed even once a year. Furthermore, any boy whose parents wished him to opt out of shooting was readily assigned to other duties.[4]

Cadets from Fannin ES march in Sam Houston Park. HISD

Becoming a member of the corps of cadets meant meeting size and age requirements. Specifically, that was 15 years old and 5'4" at the high school and 12 years old and five feet tall in the grade schools. Exceptions to that rule were a minimum of 13 years old at Fannin and a height of only 4'11" at Austin. Boys paid dues of ten cents a month at Austin and Fannin and fifty cents a year at the high school. Activities included drills at least once a week and up to four hikes per school year, some of which exceeded 25 miles. Commandant Druse trumpeted that as valuable exercise.

Perhaps the biggest benefit for the cadet corps boys was a summer camping trip to grounds at Sylvan Beach in La Porte. The camping gear was loaned to them for the occasion by the State Department.

TEXTILE MILLS SCHOOL
See Roosevelt ES

THIRD WARD COLORED SCHOOL
See Douglass ES

THIRD WARD SCHOOL
See Longfellow

THOMPSON E S
See Southland

THOMPSON VOCATIONAL OR THOMPSON SCHOOL
See Brunner

THURBUR SCHOOL
Professor W. J. Thurbur opened a school on the second floor of Dibble's Building near Main and Franklin in 1844, one of several such private operations in the city. He also announced a night class conducted "for the young men who must make their living during the day hours." A 20th century newspaper writer claimed that Thurber's innovation was "the first night school in Texas, and one of the first three west of the Mississippi."[5]

Tom Ball School. A riff on a design shared by several around the county. HHRC

TOM BALL SCHOOL
The Trinity & Brazos Valley railroad stop known as Peck was barely a year old before it was renamed Tom Ball in 1907 to honor one of the line's executives. There were already notable railroad facilities and a cattle pen by the time the first school was erected in 1908, but the term was brief since it was the only district in Harris County that voted against creating a school tax. That was corrected shortly thereafter when land was donated and a $6,000 bond passed to construct a two-story brick schoolhouse. By 1916, there were 62 students, and the town had added electricity and telephone service, as well. The discovery of a major oil field in the early 1930s brought not only greater prosperity but a tripling of population. In 1935, a new buff brick school replaced the old one on Cherry Street, serving grades one through eleven. Tomball, now spelled as one word, became an ISD

just two years later and, over the next 17 years, absorbed the schools at Decker Prairie, Bauer, Kohrville, and Rosedale.[6]

TOMBALL H S

In 1938, only one year after becoming an ISD, the growing oil & gas town of Tomball opened a red brick high school and accompanying gymnasium in the 700 block of Main Street. The building was destroyed by fire in 1961, and pupils attended classes at area church halls until a new one was constructed on the same site. Tomball HS moved to the new campus on Quinn Road in 1974.[7]

TRAVIS E S

The front part of Travis Elementary School at 3311 Beauchamp in Woodland Heights is one of the city's oldest extant school buildings, but it traces its origin back much further to September 1899 when trustees of County District 25 organized Beauchamp Springs School, perhaps in an old saloon building, and placed Miss Ethel Whisand in charge at a high salary of $40 a month. The community of the same name, with its cool artesian springs, perhaps as many as four of them, and higher elevation north of Houston had been remarked upon by locals and visitors alike since the 1830s. Thomas Beauchamp marketed his site as a parklike spot for recreation and a source of prime drinking water. The later school there also briefly used the name of McCasland School at the turn of the century, but by 1905, it was back to Beauchamp Springs.[8]

Campfire Girls at Travis ES. HISD

The running of a streetcar line and the creation of an amusement park by the streetcar company increased the amount of development in the area which had been taken in by the city. From 36 students in 1905, Beauchamp Springs grew to an enrollment of 72 the following year, and a third school room was added to the frame building at a cost of $470. It had grown enough to warrant a new school. William Wilson Realty, developers of Woodland Heights, donated land and the city provided the eight-room building that opened in 1909, renamed in honor of Alamo commander William Barret Travis. The Mothers Club was active enough to garner first prize in a citywide PTA contest for most beautiful school grounds. They received a fountain. A four-room annex came in 1915 followed by one more room and the overhaul of the janitor's residence. By 1922, there were also four temporary buildings in the schoolyard. Travis was still not done growing. A second brick building added 11 more rooms, and there have been subsequent renovations in 1980 and in the early 2000s.[9]

Tooth Brush Drills

In December 1913, the *Post* reported on "three hundred clean-mouthed and clean-toothed children" at Reagan Elementary on the near Northside. The students had been taking part in a daily tooth brush drill held at the school each day at noon. The drills consisted of the youngsters "brushing their teeth to the rhythmic time of music made by the Victrola," which had been furnished by the Mothers' Club.[10]

The idea was the brainchild of school principal Helen Holley. The Dental Association of Harris County pitched in by furnishing tooth brushes and tooth paste. The brushing was to be "strenuous and thorough," conducted "with as much exactness and regard to rules as a military manual arms drill." The drill master took the children, everyone in the first four grades, through sections of the mouth by commands. Brushes were held in exactly the same manner. Molars, bicuspids, and incisors each received close attention, and the drill concluded with a cleaning of the tongue.[11]

Children practice tooth brushing to music. HISD

The idea for the five-minute daily drills had come about when Principal Holley observed that "fully 90 percent of the students had defective teeth and that as a direct result of that condition class work was continually interrupted by children suffering toothache." District hygiene guru Dr. F.J. Slataper prepared a pamphlet that was given to students so that each would take them home and spread "among their neighbors the gospel of dental prophylaxis."

The tooth brush drills were a huge hit. Superintendent Horn crowed that "it may be remarked that a moving picture was taken showing the giving of one of these drills. Enquiries came to the superintendent's office from States as far distant as Rhode Island asking for details concerning the giving of this tooth-brush drill, and stating that the writers had seen it in moving picture shows."[12]

TRINITY GARDENS E S

Trinity Gardens was a two-room African American school opened in the mid-1930s by HISD at 7115 Lockwood in Fifth Ward. By the 1950s, the name had been changed to J.C. Sanderson Elementary. The old building was demolished in 2005 and replaced with a brand new school a year later, consolidating with Easter and Chatham and changing the name to Felix Cook. Jr. Elementary. Cook, a 36-year teacher and administrator with HISD, had attended Sanderson Elementary as a child.[13]

TRINITY LUTHERAN SCHOOL

A group of parishioners dissatisfied with Rev. Caspar Braun formed Trinity Lutheran in 1879 and opened a school the same year. The church faced Louisiana with the school behind. In 1903, faced with a neighborhood that was becoming disreputable, a new school was built at 12 Reisner Street, just south of Washington Avenue. A sanctuary was constructed two years later. Remodeling and addition proved inadequate, and in 1933, a two-and-a-half-story blonde stone school replaced the wooden one. It contained a bowling alley in the basement and a gymnasium on the top floor, subjecting students in classes below to pounding dribbles during P.E. Grade levels were divided two to a teacher. A large new "life center" replaced the old school in the mid-1990s, but ultimately Trinity Lutheran closed their school in May 2017.[14]

Trinity Lutheran School. Courtesy of Ruth Stoerkel

TRINITY LUTHERAN SCHOOL, KLEIN

The Klein community, another of the German settlements of north Harris County, sat in the rough vicinity of today's Kuykendahll and Spring Cypress Roads. To avoid the 15-mile trip to Salem Lutheran Church every Sunday, they built their own church in 1874. The school building may have been extant on the property, and predated the steepled sanctuary, serving neighborhood families for generations. There is still a church school up to grade eight.[15]

TURKEY POINT SCHOOL

A Black school in District 19 near Webster, Turkey Point was on the books from at least 1886 until 1894 when it disappears. Some of the sparse funding had been transferred to Galveston County District 8 in 1890, presumably when there was no teacher for the children in that community.[16]

TWAIN E S

HISD opened a new campus at 3801 Underwood in 1950 and named it for American author Mark Twain. Two years later, Mrs. Ruth Montgomery's class corresponded with Little House on the Prairie author Laura Ingalls Wilder, and that correspondence is preserved.[17]

TWENTY-THIRD AVE SCHOOL

When the Houston Heights was designed in the 1890s, there were two industrial areas, one on the southern edge, and one on the northwest edge of the town. Workers housing near those districts was basic and racially segregated. Schools for the children of the African American workers in those areas did not come right away. For those northwest of the Heights, 23rd Avenue School opened in 1902 on that street just west of Nashua. Miss Mary McKinney was the teacher in what was surely a small one-room structure. Only four years later, the Heights school board paid the Newbanks Brothers to build a 24' x 40' white, two-room schoolhouse with 13 foot ceilings. There were 81 students there by 1918 when Houston annexed Houston Heights and its school system. Twenty-third Avenue School continued in operation for HISD at least into the 1940s. P.H. Holden Elementary School began serving Black students in the area in 1960.[18]

ULRICH SCHOOL

The Ulrich School, situated at the corner of Wolcik and Bohemian Hall Road was a one-room school that operated during the late 1920s and the 1930s. The school building was provided by the Ulrich family who also gave library books and school supplies along with occasional lunches and holiday parties. Students above fifth grade transferred to Barrett in 1940, and all younger children followed in 1947.[19]

UNION HILL SCHOOL

Union Hill was an original school registered under the new law of 1876, and it continued under that name in the northwest part of the county until about 1887. Two years later the only school listed in District 9 was Willow.[20]

UPPER BRAYS BAYOU SCHOOL

Upper Brays Bayou was operating prior to 1876 and is most likely the same as Brays Bayou School for White students that was located in District 22.[21]

UPPER GREEN'S BAYOU

Upper Green's Bayou Colored School was listed in County District 16 in 1893 along with Clinton Colored School. Emma Austin was the teacher at both. It is possibly the same school, but the answer is not known.[22]

UPPER SPRING CREEK SCHOOL

This school was registered under the new law of 1876 with R.A. Jamison as a trustee. An A.R. Jamison, 51 years old, is listed as a school teacher in that census, but no further mention of the school was found.[23]

VOLMER SCHOOL

See White Oak

Schools Waller – Whittier

WALLER SCHOOL

The Waller School started on Penick Street at Cherry in 1887 under the jurisdiction of Waller County, but in August 1894, Harris County Commissioners voted to "cooperate" with the school given that community virtually straddles the county line. Harris County Common School District 37 was created and a small amount of money expended to support their children attending Waller School. An African American Waller school opened in 1898, but it does not appear to have received Harris County money. The combined funds continued to be administered by Waller County, and in the first decade of the 20th century, an ISD was established, and Harris County signed on to the idea in 1912. A two-story school on Cherry opened in 1899, and in 1916, a new campus with 165 students opened on five acres north of the town. The district became Waller Consolidated in 1930 as other rural schools were folded in. High school amenities such as a gymnasium came late in that decade.[1]

WASHINGTON AVENUE SCHOOL

See Dow

WASHINGTON, BOOKER T H S

Secondary education was slow to come for African American students in the South. The best intentioned White school boards did not see a need for the expenditure, and the worst likely viewed limiting education for Blacks as a means of continuing the racial domination that they had recently reasserted after Reconstruction. Among the former slave-holding states, Texas led the way in providing the opportunity of high school to Blacks. By 1916, there were thirty Black public high schools in the Lone Star State, more than three times any other state in the former Confederacy, or even border states such as Kentucky, Maryland, and Delaware. By comparison, Virginia had six Black high schools. Georgia, Louisiana, Mississippi, and North and South Carolina had no four-year public high schools for their African American children that year. In South Carolina and Mississippi, that meant no high schools for a group that made up well over half of the school age population.²

In Houston, the roots of such a high school began as early as 1888 when city school officials began to comment on the disrepair and overcrowding of the Gregory Institute that served African American children in Fourth Ward. The suggestion was made by the board president that a new building "could be erected quite economically on lots belonging to the schools, situated on the San Felipe Road." By fall of 1893, the new $20,000 Colored High School opened on San Felipe, today's W. Dallas, east of Bagby and across Frederick from Antioch Baptist Church. The original Gregory Institute was abandoned. Charles Atherton was the first principal, and he also taught 7th and 8th grades, the highest offered that year. The White high school went to 11th grade, but prior to this opening, no other schools in the city, White or Black, went past 6th. The two-story brick building under Atherton's charge had six rooms the first year, eight a year later and ten by 1895. It achieved that rise by utilizing its basement as did most other crowded Houston schools.³

A 1911 drawing class at Colored HS. HISD

Though it was called a high school and took all African American pupils in town for seventh grade and above, CHS also was responsible for teaching the elementary schoolers in Fourth Ward, still home to the city's largest Black population. It led to fluctuations in attendance including days on which several hundred students had no desks until a new Gregory Elementary opened in 1903. Still, Colored High saw great progress. The first diploma was handed out in 1896. Wright Munger became a railroad porter after graduation. By far the most common single profession for CHS grads was teacher. Annex buildings were rented, then finally added by the city in the block immediately south of the school. A Mothers Club was founded in December 1908, but participation in it rose and fell. In 1918, by then a Parent-Teacher Organization, there were only 29 members. In 1909, head city librarian Julia Ideson opened a library branch in the school, the first public library available for Houston's Black citizens. A new toilet system came in 1912. The radiation heating system went out in a freeze when the building was barely a decade old, and in 1907, Colored High still had no electric lights.[4]

James D. Ryan took over as principal by 1913, and he would oversee growth and changes. By 1920, there were 23 rooms at the school and over 1,000 pupils. Classes included English, History, Science, Mathematics, Latin, Manual Arts, including woodwork and mechanical drafting, and Home Economics, including sewing, cooking, millinery, and home nursing. Auto mechanics was added in 1923. The school worked with businesses to secure students work before and after school. Still the horrible overcrowding was a problem. Some class sizes topped 80. Entreaties were made, and HISD officials began to talk of building another African American High School. Houston's Black schools became a hot topic related to the bond issues of the mid-1920s with civic leaders and the Black press trying to tie support at the polls to expenditures for the underfunded schools. The *Informer's* harsh rhetoric was center stage: "Right here in Houston the rat-trap called a colored high school building would reflect discredit upon Podunk Creek or some other jerk-water settlement."[5]

The changes did indeed come. Jack Yates High School opened in 1926, taking Principal Ryan, and Wheatley quickly followed. William E. Miller became the third principal in school history, and benefitted from expensive rehabilitation. The number of classrooms increased to 32 not including two shops and the combination cafeteria/gymnasium. Chemistry and biology labs got huge upgrades. The addition of new Houston high schools created instant rivalries. The school had started competitive athletics in 1907, playing segregated high schools from towns such as Beaumont, Bryan, Galveston, and Palestine, almost never more than four games a season. Also in the late 1920s, the school's name was changed to honor educator Booker T. Washington. For its first 114 years of existence, Booker T. Washington High had only six principals including Ira B. Bryant who was also a 1924 graduate of the school.[6]

In 1959, the old school which was built in 1892 became Richard G. Lockett Junior High. Lockett, a Houston native and early graduate of Colored High in the same building, had served many years as a teacher in Houston schools and started the sports program at this very school. It was open very briefly after W. J. Moses became the principal on Jan 22, 1962 before it fell victim to the Pierce Elevated portion of I-45. The Booker T. Washington name was moved to a new campus on Yale Street in Independence Heights. In 2017, a new building was constructed at that site.[7]

Industrial Education in Houston Schools

The industrial education movement, as a means of expanding general knowledge as opposed to career training, began as a national movement in the late 1870s. The first regular program along such lines came to Texas at Austin in 1886 thanks to a bequest from a believer in the capital city. Houston followed suit in 1890 with a "small appropriation" that would bring "in a very modest way, manual training instruction for boys in the high school."[8]

National proponents of such manual training lobbied state legislatures, including Texas. In 1899, a state subsidy of $500 was offered to any high school which would provide matching funds, and in 1906, the amount was increased to $2,000.[9]

Like virtually all programs in the area's segregated school systems, industrial education came late to African American students. For his part, Houston School Superintendent Paul Horn kept pleading to include Black students, but kept getting rebuffed by the people with the checkbook. His request in 1908 was to the point: "I am strongly convinced that some form of industrial education, should be afforded to our colored children. We criticise our prevailing system of education of the Negro as tending to unfit him for useful labor, and yet we do not offer him the opportunity to prepare himself for such labor. I believe that if the boys were given the opportunity to learn woodwork, including such practical features as the making of furniture and the bottoming of chairs, and if the girls were taught to cook and sew, it would add greatly to the opportunity of the Negro to do useful work in the world."[10]

Booker T. Washington and other Black leaders of the time were in favor of increased industrial education for their race, contending that it was of the highest practical value, but some pro-intellectual African American leaders, including W.E.B. Du Bois and Paul Lawrence Dunbar, saw it as a ploy by the White elites, both North and South, to limit education for Black citizens that they viewed as subservient. Du Bois pushed for a classical education rich in humanities. The record in Houston and elsewhere, though, shows that industrial education came to White schools first, and that the African American schools wanted it, but were forced to wait for money to be expended on them.[11]

Some of the city's Black schools took matters into their own hands. At Hollywood and Langston Schools, the regular teachers began to offer instruction in classes such as sewing and simple wood working. In May, at the continuing education institute for Black teachers, one speaker was E. L. Blackshear, head of Prairie View A&M University, who spoke eloquently in favor of offering these classes. Several citizens in attendance for the talk took up a subscription, and over $100 was raised to buy industrial education equipment for both boys and girls at Houston's Colored High School. Another teacher organized student musical performances and raised $100 through the sale of tickets at a dime apiece. The school board finally approved the courses beginning in fall of 1908.[12]

The pioneering teachers in bringing these classes to the African American campuses were Mary J. Holden teaching domestic science to the girls and G. H. Miller, who later was succeeded by Robert M. Catchings, handling the manual training classes for boys.

In both the White and Black schools, administrators soon focused on having the students build things that could either be sold, or could save money for the school system. By 1917, the manual training classes were held at the Houston's White and Black high schools, Heights High School, North Side, South End and West End Junior Highs, and at six White elementary schools (Rusk, Taylor, Crockett, Longfellow, Montrose, and Dow) and three Black elementaries (Washington, Douglass, and Luckie). Those well-equipped classrooms were "turning out very nearly every panel door needed, every sash, all wooden locker and cabinet work, library cases, book shelves, dictionary stands, numbers of laboratory cases, manual training work benches, specimen display cabinets, yard benches, lunch tables and counters, screens for doors and windows, tables, various equipment for athletic work, repairing of all kinds of school furniture and equipment, and in addition to what is actually done in shops we are taking care of every kind of repair work upon the forty-four school buildings and their surrounding appurtenances." Among the more interesting outputs of the manual training classes were Houston city street signs.[13]

Both Black and White schools manufactures street signs for their neighborhoods in the 1910s. HISD

The list of equipment was varied and impressive, and included not only industrial machines but mechanical drawing at all levels. Several of the elementary schools had hand or foot powered printing presses and an assortment of type for learning that popular trade. Woodworking was also offered at some elementary schools, and in some cases 4th and 5th graders had access to band saws. Crockett and Longfellow even had dedicated lumber and tool rooms adjacent to the shop.[14]

The junior high facilities at North Side and South End were also used for night school and summer school classes. South End, where the well-lit shop turned out furniture for the auditorium stage and had even equipped one of the school's men's restrooms, offered manual training students four power saws, two planers, three jointers, an automatic mortiser, a belt sander, two trimmers and 12 lathes, most individually motored. North Side had three separate woodworking shops including a pattern shop and a cabinet shop with "machinery belt driven from shafting and counter shafting in pits underneath the floor of the shop."

Furniture manufactured by Houston HS boys and made available for purchase. HISD

Central High School downtown even had machines made by students – lathes, gas engine, drill press, and gas furnace. They had a forge shop with down draft power driven forges. A tool supply room contained a reserve supply of equipment for renewing and equipping new shops in department. Local unions such as the sheet metal workers held classes for apprentices at the high school shops on weekends.[15]

In 1917, with the United States at war, Congress passed the Smith-Hughes Act mandating industrial education on a national level in order to increase the number of skilled trade, home economics, and agricultural workers. Some historians assert that the act and other legislation only served to reinforce economic and racial inequalities, but the Houston school board complied.[16]

The Smith-Hughes classes offered locally were quite varied including courses on Salesmanship, Blueprint Reading, Estimating, Steel Square, Electricity, Sheet Metal Drafting, Shop Mathematics, Trade Millinery, Art Needlework, Dressmaking, Table Service, Cooking, and Elementary Sewing. One of the more popular programs was the retail salesmanship classes "for the benefit of girls already working as saleswomen in the large dry goods stores of the city." Classes were held during work time, and cost the employer not a dime.[17]

There was one lament from T.W. Ray who oversaw the program: "Perhaps the greatest difficulty which has confronted us in this work has been our inability to get competent teachers to conduct these classes. Skilled tradesmen can be found, but they do not know how to teach. On the other hand, trained teachers usually do not know a trade.[18]

Auto shop at South End JHS. HISD

WASHINGTON, BOOKER T E S

There was a First Ward Colored School taught by Mrs. Wren, an African American woman whose own education was limited to "the common branches", as early as 1872 under the Reconstruction-era school laws. About 64 pupils attended in a building immediately north of the H & TC machine shops that year. She was soon replaced by Miss M.F. Brinkley. By 1887, the First Ward Colored School was firmly established at the corner of Bingham and Colorado, and the enrollment was almost double capacity. The school, initially for the first three grades, had gained a classroom and another grade level by 1895. In 1907, under Principal J.N. Dodson, First Ward was consolidated with Sixth Ward Colored School, though no rooms were added. The overcrowding actually forced some children to stay away from school entirely. Within a year after the merger, the school had changed its name to Booker T. Washington. In 1910, a Mothers Club was formed and E. O. Smith became the new principal. Shortly after his arrival a larger patch of ground was purchased across the street to the south, and the sixth and seventh grades were added. The new school consisted of two "old, dilapidated board shacks, two stories each, in very bad condition generally, and badly over-crowded; about 500 students in ten rooms, some of them very small and poorly lighted." [19]

In the late 1920s, after Colored High School was named for Booker T. Washington, the elementary school by that name was changed to honor Richard Brock who was born a Kentucky slave. Upon being brought to Houston, and following Emancipation, Brock owned a Blacksmith shop then went on to become one of the city's first Black alderman in 1870, later donating land for St. Paul's A.M.E. Church and helping establish Olivewood Cemetery. The Brock name was later moved down Bingham Street and applied to the Hawthorne Elementary property. In 1967, a new Brock became the first completely air-conditioned school in HISD.[20]

Booker T. Washington ES in First Ward. HISD

WASHINGTON, GEORGE J H S

In HISD's first big building flurry as an independent school district, four new junior high schools opened in February 1926: Lanier, Jackson, Yates, and George Washington at 4701 Dickson, not far north of Buffalo Bayou on the east side of Shepherd Road. That thoroughfare was still called Brunner Road by some of the old-timers. The campus had a lone rectangular eight-room building originally with a detached auditorium sitting just southeast. W. B Davis was the first principal at the school that was called West End Junior High while it was on the drawing board. The music department gained early praise, and the school boasted a "natural amphitheatre… among the pines, oaks, and evergreens on the banks of Buffalo Bayou." Set in a fast growing part of town, the number of classrooms more than doubled within a few years. The Grey Wolves of GWJHS did not survive changing demographics unscathed, though. In 1980, the fledgling High School for Law Enforcement and Criminal Justice, a partnership between HISD, the Mayor's Office, and HPD, was consolidated on the old Washington JHS campus. Ground was broken on Scott Street for a new modern location for that program in 2016, and the 90-year-old George Washington campus became part of St. Thomas High School.[21]

George Washington JHS. HISD

WASHINGTON ROAD SCHOOL

The Washington Road School for White children in District 25 was open on the south side of Center Street opposite Glenwood Cemetery by 1887. It may have lasted only a few years in the crowded district before the growing area demanded a larger school, or this might have morphed into Chaneyville School.[22]

Penmanship

These suggestion on penmanship are from the 1912 Harris County Schools report, offered by someone who might be considered a taskmaster with too much time on their hands:

"The writing of pupils of Harris County is not nearly so good as it should be. In fact, most of it is unsatisfactory. Only a few schools are actually teaching writing. Writing is one of the subjects prescribed by law to be taught in the schools of Texas. The laws of this State demand that it should be taught. It is more frequently omitted from the daily program than any other subject for... trivial reasons. There is time for everything if we make definite plans.

"Sometimes the teacher uses the writing period as 'a time to rest.' Sometimes the only instruction given is 'make your t's a little taller.' 'You forgot to dot your i's.' 'You do not space your letters properly,' etc. Such instructions amount to nothing. The writing period should be the period of most active teaching of the entire day. In the first place the teacher should be prepared. Some vigorous exercises for the development of speed and movement, should be given. The exercises should be graded so that the pupils may advance from the easy exercises to those that are more complex. When they have acquired some movement, some speed and some control of the hand, some of the more easy letters and combination of letters may be used for practice.

"Do you know how to teach writing? If so, teach it. If not, get a teacher's manual on teaching writing and go to work on it… Fellow teachers, will you not do some serious and strenuous work for the improvement of the writing? Please read this subject over and over, again and again. Let us all join together and secure better results in this great work."

Webster School with its large cistern. HHRC

WEBSTER SCHOOL

Webster, a town named for land developer James W. Webster, had a school in operation much earlier than even the city itself recognizes. Originally known as Websterville, the school was in existence prior to April 1877 when Messrs. Ludgate, Davis, and Thompson petitioned to have their school operate under the new state law. It sat along the Galveston, Houston and Henderson Railroad which had been completed between those first two cities in 1859 and 1860. The school carries the name Websterville, as did the later post office that opened in 1882. In 1887, the Websterville School was moved from its "site on prairie to location near county bridge over Clear Creek provided it doesn't cost the county money." The Gardentown community school, northeast of present Webster, appears in County District 19 in the early 1890s, but is quickly merged with the longer tenured Webster School at the request of its citizens. The old schoolhouse in Gardentown was sold off in 1896. There were about 30 students a decade later, and growth was enough to warrant a two-story frame building "with good equipment and apparatus" by 1910. At that time, Webster was offering two years of high school, increased to full high school in the early 1920s by which time it was also an ISD with 150 total pupils.[23]

WEBSTER COLORED SCHOOL

Extant records do not indicate if this was a direct continuation of Turkey Point School or if there was a gap in educating African American children in District 19. It was operating in the first decade of the 20th century with a school term of only three or four months.[24]

WEBSTER H S

Webster was fielding competitive high school sports teams by the early 1920s, indicating that it was a full-fledged high school operation. Senior Gail Whitcomb, Jr. even won the county oratory contest in 1924. The district spun off a separate high school building at 400 South Walnut Street in 1939. It was an Art Deco beauty by R G Schneider. Thanks to the Humble Oil Tank Farm off Highway 3, the Webster ISD had a solid tax base. It served as the high school for multiple Clear Lake area communities farther east. In 1947-48, Webster, League City, Seabrook, and Kemah districts joined to become Clear Creek Consolidated School District. Webster HS continued to operate until 1957 when it was replaced by Clear Creek High. The lovely 1939 building still serves area students as part of the Clearview Education Center.[25]

The basketball team at Webster HS included several boys from immigrant Japanese rice farming families. HHRC

WEBSTERVILLE SCHOOL

See Webster School.

WESLEY CHARTER E S

A school at 800 Dillard in northwest Houston opened in 1949 named for iconic Houston educator Mabel Wesley.[26]

A 1977 photo of the West End JHS/Ben Milam ES building. Mike Vance Collection

WEST END H S

The town of Brunner and its small school district had just completed a new eleven-room high school building at the northwest corner of Center and Sandman when it became part of Houston at the close of the 1913 school year. Houston public schools got a bargain, the building and grounds were in good condition, with the addition of water fountains being the only recommendation. Principal Stephen P. Waltrip oversaw students in the first two years of high school plus seventh grade for all residents in the former communities of Brunner and Chaneyville. By 1916, the name of West End High School was in use, and one year later, it was West End Junior High. In 1918, as the students enthusiastically bought Liberty Bonds and Thrift Stamps, the school was approaching its limit. Three years later, enrollment topped 500, and four shacks were erected to surround the brick building. In the mid-1920s, the school was "rehabilitated" and a play-lunchroom and two more classrooms were added as it became Ben Milam Elementary. The junior high duties for the west side of town moved to the new George Washington. Milam served the young children in the neighborhood until 2004 when HISD finally stepped away from the campus. Currently the Esperanza School, providing for kindergarten children, sits on the site, still surrounded by the shady oaks planted by the West End High Mothers Club in 1915.[27]

WEST RIVER SCHOOL
See Humble School

West River School in 1909. Humble Museum

WEST UNIVERSITY E S

The recently organized West University ISD opened an elementary school in October 1925. The students had been attending in temporary buildings for over a month. The junior high that shared the same campus in the 3700 block of University Boulevard at Edloe came online shortly afterwards, giving students a home through eighth grade. Only 75 elementary students started the year, but that number quickly rose along with the surrounding homes. Past the junior high, children moved to Houston high schools. The independence in West U was short lived. At the start of 1929, citizens in both Houston and West University began discussion as to whether annexation of the schools was desirable, prompting a "showdown." The ayes had it, and 280 students, 10 teachers and free kindergarten were all brought into HISD. In 1949, a quarter million dollar remodeling job was performed on the school to coincide with Pershing Junior High moving to a new location, leaving West U Elementary in total control of the campus. Students from that time recalled Principal Zelpha Shumate, a woman "shorter than some of the students" who maintained a subtle discipline. It made for an attractive, neighborhood feel, something that has been revived. With over 1,000 pupils, West U was the largest elementary in HISD in 2017, and roughly 96% of the children came from the immediate neighborhood.[28]

A well-dressed West U class in 1934. Mike Vance Collection

Kindergarten Beginnings

Given its German name, it is not surprising that the origins of kindergartens can be traced to that country, as early as 1779. The purpose was to provide care and education for young children whose parents were absent during the day. In several European countries over the next decades, the benefits of starting the child on the road to literacy, morality, and good play habits was touted and refined. The movement was slower to find a place in America with a privately run free kindergarten in New York City in 1870 and the first publicly financed one appearing in St. Louis three years later. Galveston boasted the first in Texas, opened by Johanna Runge in 1892.[29]

In Houston, the first efforts were privately organized, first by individual women then by civic minded groups, and held in homes or rented space. Churches were often utilized. By the end of the 19th century, there were organized Kindergarten Associations lobbying for approval of free kindergarten in public schools for children as young as three all the way up to the minimum mandatory legal school age which was then set at eight.[30]

The Houston Woman's Club opened the first free kindergarten in the city on October 1, 1902 "in a little old store building." A "Houston Free Kindergarten" column appeared in the local papers, spreading the virtues of the operation. The targeted beneficiaries were children of immigrants, mostly Eastern Europeans, many of them Jewish refugees. A year later the women opened a second kindergarten in an abandoned church. Within another year, they were also training kindergarten teachers.[31]

In the African American community, a Daily Bible Class organized at Antioch Baptist Church in 1910 morphed within five years into a Kindergarten Association being run by teachers, the first such effort for Houston Blacks. Other Black churches of various denominations, Protestant and Catholic, followed suit.[32]

The first free kindergarten at one of the Houston public schools opened at the Charlotte Allen campus in the fall of 1906. Even Superintendent Horn admitted that "This was not as a matter of fact the building where a kindergarten was most needed; but it was the building where there was most room available for the purpose. The kindergarten there was a success, and I trust that it may prove an entering wedge, and an object lesson for the future."[33]

Progress was slow. By 1912, the city had appropriated a mere thousand dollars for a kindergarten program with the remaining cost to be picked up by "private individuals and organizations." Horn expressed hope that free kindergarten at public expense would be coming soon, but three years later, it remained confined to 198 pupils at Allen, Rusk, Travis, and Hawthorne. He placed the blame for inaction "partly in finances and partly in the fact that most of our school buildings are so crowded that it has been difficult to find room for the kindergarten."[34]

A year farther down the road, the state legislature finally bowed to pressure from Mothers' Clubs and other civic and church groups. Free public kindergarten became the law of the state, at least for any school in which a certain number of parents petitioned for it. Paul Horn, who had championed the idea in words, was far from pleased, however.

"To carry the letter of this law into full effect in Houston nest year would cost the city $50,000, he wrote. "This law is based upon the theory that the mere wave of the legislative wand can cause money to grow where no money was before. It was undoubtedly intended to aid in the development of kindergarten sentiment, but … One of the very best ways to harm any good movement is to enact an unreasonable law in favor of it."[35]

Of course, like many other programs, free kindergarten was for Whites only. It was not until September 1949 that HISD offered kindergarten to African Americans. For the first two years, a small fee was charged, but that was quickly dropped.[36]

Kindergarten for both races was usually a half day program in HISD with children drawing a morning or an afternoon session, lasting two and a half to three hours. The young students generally sat at tables and had open shelves to access toys, blocks, games, puzzles, and books as well as supervised time with paint, paper, crayons, paste, clay, and perhaps even scissors. Nap time was also part of the program.

As schools began to be built with kindergartens required, special accommodations were often included. Most kindergarten rooms had a separate entrance. Schools such as West University and River Oaks offered a fireplace for its youngest charges. When air-conditioning began to appear at the schools in the early 1960s, it was in the form of window units provided to keep the kindergarten class cool. In many cases during those years, the kindergarten window units were the only air-conditioners in the entire building.

WESTFIELD SCHOOL

Westfield School in the community of the same name was operating prior to 1876 when trustees W.H. Higgs ad H. Moon asked to be accredited under the new law. Higgs would later give his name to other schools in

District 29. The Westfield community revolved around Hermann Tautenhahn's general store that started in 1864 a mile or so farther west, but moved to a better spot near the new railroad a decade later. By 1881, the old schoolhouse and its acre of ground was being sold to pay for a new one. Westfield operated on the south side of Humble-Westfield Road, today's FM 1960, just west of Hardy, until 1932 when it and three other White schools merged to create the modern Aldine ISD. The new school's opening in February 1933 spelled the end of the old Westfield School.[37]

WESTHEIMER SCHOOL

German-immigrant Michael Louis Westheimer's 640-acre farm was located about where Lamar HS is on a shell road colloquially known as the road to Westheimer's place. He built a school there in the 1860s for youngsters in his own household, of which there were sixteen including three orphans taken in, and other neighboring farm children. Westheimer later operated the largest livery stable, moving company, and funeral home in downtown Houston. When he donated right of way for a road to the county in 1895, it was officially named in his honor.[38]

Wharton ES. HISD

WHARTON E S

When the parents of children at William H. Wharton School, 900 W. Gray, fought to have the campus remain open in 2007, they likely did not realize they were following a tradition. When HISD began searching for an elementary school site in the West Dallas area, a neighborhood "becoming thickly populated, several hundred apartments and hundreds of one and two family homes," choosing the property became the most contentious school issue of the year. There were issues of imminent domain, and one faction protested loudly against the W. Dallas location because they considered it too close to "a Negro district." A site on W. Clay that was then a cornfield was floated, but ultimately, the twelve-classroom, yellow and ginger brick school was placed on W. Gray at Columbus. The protesting parents in the late 1920s were possibly unaware that an African American cemetery, dating at least to Emancipation, if not earlier, sat underneath what became the school's crescent drive and front steps. Wharton opened on September 16, 1929 with 459 pupils, climbing to a jammed 600+

a year later. The school was notable for its large blue and white clad rhythm band and for its safety patrol that saw younger children across the busy thoroughfare. As for the parents in 2007, they won out, and HISD divested itself of the Milam Elementary property instead. Wharton's campus underwent extensive renovation in 2016-17.[39]

WHEATLEY H S

For much of Houston's early history, Fifth Ward citizens, north of Buffalo Bayou from the main part of the city, felt like an afterthought. When Yates High School was announced for African American students in Third Ward, it was by no means a given that Fifth Ward Blacks would be getting their own high school at all. It did come to pass, though, and the building named for enslaved poet Phillis Wheatley opened on January 31, 1927 in what had been the White McGowan Elementary on Lyons Avenue. Temporary shacks were constructed around it before a new main building was opened facing Gregg Street. Enrollment grew from 490 at opening to 2,567 in just eight years.[40]

E.O. Smith oversaw a school that strived for high academic standards. By the 1940s, Wheatley students had gone on to virtually every African American college in America. Music became a focus early, and various bands were organized with teachers over the years that included Percy McDavid and Sammy Harris. The bands featured a variety of instruments and ran to 20 members. Some of the international greats of jazz and R&B got their starts as Wheatley Wildcats including Arnett Cobb, Illinois Jacquet, Calvin Owens, Hubert Laws, Joe Sample, Milton Hopkins, Archie Bell, Clarence and Cal Green, and Roy and Grady Gaines.[41]

Principal Smith died while doing yard work in 1945, leaving Houston's Black community and his Wheatley students particularly shocked and saddened. His fellow school administrator Pearle Tallman noted that he always "exhorted his students to go in the way of righteousness and good will." By the time of Smith's death, Wheatley had established a rivalry with Yates High School that would become the Thanksgiving Day Game that outshone any other Bayou City high school rivalry in history.[42]

The original Wheatley HS building that became E.O. Smith JHS. HISD

In 1949, a new Wheatley was constructed at 4900 Market Street to improve crowded conditions, and in spite of the fact that the design came about to cut costs, Karl Kamrath's structure was the best modernist school building in the region. "Clad in salmon colored brick with buff cast stone trim and window turquoise glazed tile between rows of windows," Architectural Digest praised it in 1953 with comparisons to" Dutch architect W. M. Dudok's work of the 1920s, which in turn was derived from Wright." For all of the significance that the Wheatley buildings held in Houston, both met sad and unnecessary ends. With enrollment down below 750, the Kamrath building was slated for demolition with HISD citing "deferred maintenance" as the reason. The 1929 school that had been the pride of Fifth Ward at least got its day in court, but HISD prevailed, and bulldozers took it in 2014, within hours after the judge's short-sighted ruling. The Wheatley name lives on, however, at a shiny, new building on Providence Street that opened in 2006 as its immediate predecessor was torn down.[43]

Music Education

Music was one of the primary windows through which to judge refinement, and to that end, Houstonians set about getting instruction for their children almost as soon as the Allen Brothers set out boundary stakes. Various professors of music advertised private lessons in both instrumental and vocal music. It was a cultural alternative for the upper crust citizens who sent their youngsters back East for a classical education.[44]

The set of Rules and Recommendations of the Public Schools of the City of Houston produced under Mayor James T. D. Wilson in 1877, when the second run at public schools was made, included vocal music as part of the curriculum.

A snapshot of music training from the 1904-05 Houston school year shows vocals were still paramount. The Department of Music was holding regular singing periods in all the White schools. The city plan was for each class at the High School to "receive two singing periods of forty-five minutes each, twice a month", but Music Director Bessie Hughes complained that it was hard to find the time. Fifth, sixth and seventh grades were getting roughly half an hour two or three times a week. This proved particularly inadequate since those grades were supposed to be learning sight reading.[45]

A wonderfully eclectic high school orchestra in 1925. HHRC

Nonetheless, schools were all still putting on music recitals. At the high school in 1905, there were two chorus performances at the mid-winter commencement and two more at the June commencement. The tunes, accompanied by the school orchestra, included Zollner's "Ode to Music" and four parts of "Lucia di Lammermoor" by Donizetti.

When the City Auditorium opened at Louisiana and Texas in 1910, it provided a nice boost for music education. The renewed focus on bringing top artists to town benefitted the students. Business tycoon Jesse Jones invited five thousand Houston school children to see the Russian Symphony Orchestra as his guests. And when the Damrosch Orchestra visited in May of that year, the sponsoring Music Festival Association arranged for city students to attend a matinee for only a dime each. It began a long tradition of area school children being exposed to performances at the Auditorium and at Jones Hall, the building that rose on the same site in the mid-1960s.[46]

Houston got its own resident symphony in 1913, and shortly thereafter, all White students from seventh grade up got to attend a rehearsal of the orchestra. It was viewed as a wonderful opportunity for the young people to be exposed to "the best music well played."[47]

Music in the schools was not neglected even while the United States was enmeshed in WWI. The new Music Department head, Lulu Stevens, reported that violin classes were being held after dismissal and on Saturdays. Music courses in the high school and outside piano classes had become eligible for graduation credit for the first time, and over 800 students took part. Community concerts were held on Sunday afternoons with over a thousand people attending on more than one occasion. Among the performing entities were the Boys' Glee Club, Girls' Glee Club, Girls' Trio, and the Boys' Sextette. There were orchestras that year not only at Central High School but at South End and North Side Junior Highs and at Taylor, Sherman, and Dow Elementaries. Every grade school spent time on music every day, and regular singing assemblies were held.[48]

As Houston added more high schools and junior highs in the latter half of the 1920s, so too did they add more school orchestras and bands. Soon one of the most notable school organizations was the All-City Band. The director of the "First Band", and its junior counterpart, from the 1920s though 40s was Victor Alessandro, Sr. whose Houston-educated son of the same name would go on to fame as conductor with symphony orchestras in Oklahoma City and San Antonio. The younger Alessandro would begin leading a "Baby Band" of toddlers playing instruments, under his father's direction, when he was only four.[49]

Victor Alessandro's Junior Public School Band in 1937. HHRC

The elder Alessandro emigrated with his parents from Sicily, first to New Orleans and then to Waco, finally moving to Houston as a music professor in 1919. Several of his pupils' early advertised performances featured the children of fellow Sicilians, and on his first Columbus Day in town, one of his compositions was featured at the Italian-American celebration. Soon he was director of the Houston Municipal Band, a boys' band, and the HISD bands shortly thereafter. Alessandro and his family lived on Colquitt Street for many years, and his wife, Josephine was an early volunteer with the Alley Theatre. Victor, Sr. died in Houston in 1971.[50]

WHITE SCHOOL

See White's Settlement

WHITE OAK SCHOOL

White Oak, also known as Volmer after one of the area families, was one of many German communities north of Buffalo Bayou prior to the Civil War. The St. John Lutheran Church was established on today's Mangum Road there in the 1860s, and the parishioners likely started a school around the same time. In the late-1880s and early 1890s, the teacher was Frank Neuhaus who was also the parish pastor. In spite of any possible religious connection, the school was part of County District 26, and continued as such decades into the 20th century. The district trustees purchased a new building for the school sometime near the start of the century. One longtime teacher at White Oak School was Katherine Smith, and a nearby elementary bears her name today. The church building was moved to Sam Houston Park where it remains today.[51]

White Oak School and St. John Church on Mangum Road

WHITE OAK COLORED SCHOOL

See George Washington Carver School, Aldine

WHITE SETTLEMENT SCHOOL

White Settlement, named for Rueben White and his relatives who settled between modern day Crosby and Highlands prior to the days of the Republic, was the location of the first school in what eventually became County District 17 and then Crosby ISD. It was well-established prior to 1876 when Robert Blalock, John Farmer, and Fred Jaeger registered it under the new public schools law. As the 20th century dawned, the new communities north and south of White Settlement overtook it, and pupils began going to Elena School, modern-day Highlands, in 1903.[52]

WHITTIER E S

The school named for poet John Greenleaf Whittier opened with six teachers and 225 students in a wooden building at 10511 Lacrosse in 1948. A brick school replaced it after a 1959 fire.[53]

Schools Willow - Z

WILLOW SCHOOL

The little school on Willow Creek pre-dated the 1876 school law. It served a community in District 9 that included a large percentage of French immigrants in the far northwest portion of the county. Lore suggests that it was "was originally a log building on the south side of Willow Creek just west of the John Brill place." The community was located near where the FM 2920 bridge crosses Willow Creek.[1]

WILSON E S

The need for a new school in the Hyde Park/Cherryhurst additions southwest of downtown was discussed by Houston school officials as early as 1919. It opened at 2100 Yupon between Indiana and Maryland, a site that had once held Republic of Texas President Mirabeau Lamar's country home, in December 1924 and was named in honor of President Woodrow Wilson who had died at the beginning of that year. It was a large elementary to meet the needs in the growing upscale suburbs - a two-story brick building with seventeen classrooms and a large playground. A large auditorium was on the second floor at the rear of the building with the kitchen below it. HISD's first Safety Patrol was organized at Woodrow Wilson School in October 1931. The PTA was also notable with over 800 members in the mid-1930s, the largest in the state at that time. Graduates at Wilson included Walter Cronkite and Texas Governor Mark White. In 2005, HISD turned Wilson into the first all-Montessori campus in the district, serving students from K through 8th grade, and a major renovation and addition was in the works for the campus a decade later.[2]

Wilson ES in shady Cherryhurst in the 2010s. Laurie Feinswog photo

Score Cards, Bond Issues and the Reality of Segregation

In the late 1910s, educational administration professors George D. Strayer and N.L. Englehart of Columbia University in New York City began working on a system to codify the condition of public school buildings. They were part of a national movement concerned with securing "more intelligent public interest in the work, aims and methods" of the public schools." Strayer and Englehart also joined with Professor F.W. Hart, of the University of California in Berkeley to design an architectural checklist for new schools being constructed. Though the two professors did dozens of assessments themselves, their score cards, priced at a dime each, sold to school districts, state and local officials and even Chambers of Commerce across America.[3]

Their rating system for existing schools allowed that a maximum of 1000 points could be awarded to a given physical plant, broken into 125 points for the site location, environment and things such as drainage, 165 points for the structure itself, 280 for the building systems such as ventilation, electrical, toilets and lighting, 290 for classrooms and 140 points for special rooms, a category that included science labs, industrial arts facilities and home economics rooms.[4]

HISD superintendent E.E. Oberholtzer was one of the score card customers. He formed a committee comprised "of two school supervisors, one architect, one efficiency engineer, and one doctor. ... After a careful study of the standards given in the score card, the committee visited each building in a body and registered individual scores for each item. The average of the scores of these five committeemen then became the final score for the building." The junior and senior high schools were inspected in October 1924 and the elementary schools eleven months later.[5]

Oberholtzer was not doing the study out of idle curiosity. HISD was a new entity, having taken over control of the school system from the city, and the 1920s was a decade of one bond issue after another. This information was ammunition to make voters say yes. It also served as the greatest quantifier for the inequality that existed between the White and Black school buildings in Houston's segregated system.

That inequality was hardly a secret. The public schools both in the City of Houston and Harris County had always been segregated, and expenditures had always been unequal. Houston Superintendent Horn admitted the fact in his 1907 report when he said that the African American schools were operating under adverse conditions, especially overcrowding, and asked for money for improvements.

By 1910, things were not much better, however. As that school year opened, there were 284 rooms for White children and 68 for Black. That meant an average attendance per room of 36 and 50 respectively. To be fair, Houston was dealing with incredibly rapid growth everywhere, but they were clearly putting their money where the Whites were.

The illustration in 1911 was blatant. City schools had gotten over half a million dollars to spend from a bond issue plus another $59,000 from the sale of four school properties. At the top of their list was replacing Dow, Longfellow, Taylor, and Rusk, four frame elementary buildings for White students, the last of which had recently burned. They were just over 30 years old, dating from a time when Houston was putting down some of its first street paving using blocks of bois d'arc wood.

Of that enormous sum of money, the board expended $75,000 on each of the four replacement schools. New grounds for three of them cost between $15,000 and $40,000 apiece, and a new building at Hawthorne ran sixty grand. Total monies spent on the White schools was $543,000, no doubt all needed. By comparison, First and Fifth Ward Colored Schools got new grounds at the cost of $3,000 each, and the new African American school building for Fifth Ward ran $7,000.[6]

Money sent by the state was uneven, as well. As World War I ended in 1918, Texas was paying out $9.06 per White pupil and $6.90 per Black pupil. Still, after the Houston Sanitary Committee toured local campuses they described "good conditions in the colored schools. In many cases the committee found these old frame school buildings in a cleaner slate than some of the new buildings occupied by White children."[7]

Houston has always grown quickly. Between 1850 and 1950, the city's population increased 250 times over. Overcrowding in all Houston schools by the early 1920s was astounding. Roughly 1,200 elementary students were going to school only half a day because there was no place to put them. Another 3,000 of them were housed in wooden "shacks", a similar number in basements and thirty-eight grade school classes were being held in hallways, cafeterias or rest rooms. Of the district's 507 elementary school rooms, 192 were recommended to be scrapped.[8]

When the Houston Independent School District was formed in 1923, a bond issue was floated that would have constructed multiple new schools for the city's Black and White students alike. It failed. But E.E. Oberholtzer was not to be denied. Armed with the Strayer-Englehart score card data, the district went back to the voters three more times in the decade, getting $3,000,000 in December 1924, $4,000,000 in February 1926, and a third bond issue, also of $4,000,000, passed in May 1928.[9]

Only two schools in the entire city broke the 700 mark to place them as excellent physical plants for education. They were the two new junior highs: South End and North Side. Only two high schools, the new Central and Heights, and four elementary schools, Wilson, Dow, Rusk, and Southmore, fell in the range between six to seven hundred that was considered very good. Crockett, Longfellow, Bowie, Lee, Taylor and Helms felt less than 25 points short. The scores ranged all the way down to Abbot and Thompson which both failed to crack 300. The same was true of Sykes and Janowski in County District 25, the only non-HISD schools evaluated, it seems.[10]

The scores for Houston's Black schools were startlingly low, almost all lower than the worst performing White schools. With 1,000 points constituting a perfect score, only one Black campus in the entire city, Ryan (not to be confused with the current James D. Ryan Middle School), topped 300. Colored High School, the only one for African Americans in the city, posted 240. There were three basic tiers among the grade schools. Chew, Luckie, Blackshear, Bruce, and Eighth Avenue in the Heights, came in around 260 to 270 points. Gregory, Douglass, Harper, Langston, and Washington all managed only 210 points, and Green Pond, Dunbar, and Twenty-Third Avenue were just below that mark. All alone in last place was Independence Heights which scored only 146. Among them, only Colored High was a brick building. In all, 15 of the 16 Black grade schools were in the range identified as subject to condemnation.[11]

When HISD's bond came up for a vote only three months after the Strayer-Englehart scores for high schools, it was backed by the influential Black newspaper the *Houston Informer*. The paper claimed in 1924 that Black schools received only 7% of the school appropriations though Blacks were 25% of the city's population. Black leaders, including *Informer* publisher C.F. Richardson, were promised that more money would be spent on construction of new Black schools this time around, five hundred thousand to be precise. Some Whites in the city argued that the low percentage spent on Black schools reflected the amount of taxes paid by that demographic, to which the *Informer* responded that schools were not determined by who paid the most taxes, but were for "the good of the entire social family".[12]

The city's other major Black newspaper, the *Freeman*, took the other tack. Unlike the *Informer*, the *Freeman* recommended that its readers vote against the bonds, running a headline on Halloween 1925 that read "Colored People Generally Get Lost in the Shuffle. The Future is Judged in the Light of the Past." The editor said he was "disgusted with the soft soap policy" of the school board when it came to keeping promises to Houston's

African American community. He also included the long list of all the repairs, additions and replacements that were being promised.[13]

The overall benefit of the construction bonds to all students, Black and White, was impressive. Between 1924 and 1930, roughly 7,000 seats were added in more than 950 classrooms. That was in addition to 39 play-lunchrooms, 7 auditoriums, 12 gymnasiums, and 9 swimming pools. School-wise, that was twelve new high schools, 36 new elementary schools, and 33 buildings were rehabilitated.[14]

Houston's African Americans saw some concrete gains. Schools such as Douglass, Gregory, Harper, and others were replaced by new brick buildings of the same name. New Black high schools named Jack Yates and Phillis Wheatley were opened with the bond money, though the *Informer* complained not enough was spent on Yates, which was supposed to be a showplace. Though the district remained rigidly segregated and expenditures were still not equal, things drew closer. In all, over the five years covered by the schools bonds, the value of the Houston's Black school campuses increased from $243,498.50 to $888,643.00, and every single one of the schools saw some notable physical improvement.[15]

It was enough to bring statements of pride from the city's Black educational leaders. When Principal Ira B. Bryant wrote *The History of Houston Negro Schools* in 1935, he included this passage in the opening: "Few cities of similar population can boast of three junior-senior high schools, one junior high school, 22 elementary schools and a university branch for Negroes. Many of the Negroes who contributed to the growth of the Houston Schools are men and women who were born slaves or who are only one generation removed from slavery."

WILSON SCHOOL, CROSBY
Wilson was a short-lived one-room school in the Crosby district.[16]

WINKLER'S SCHOOL
The Little Cypress community, also known as the Settlement community, was started by a group of immigrants from Posen, Germany in 1848. By 1853, they had built their first church, called St. John Lutheran, and also established a parochial school. It appears to have remained a church school, possibly taught by the pastor, until about 1886. In that year, Little Cypress received public tax money from County District 7 with Big Cypress

White and colored schools. All of those institutions would soon be part of District 6. The county sent money to the district trustees, $2.75 to be exact, to clean the well at the site and also do repairs to the school building.[17]

Early in that same year, residents in District 7 petitioned Commissioners court to "move schoolhouse to north side of Little Cypress Creek to be closer to center of scholastic population." They even offered $100 for the work. It is unclear if the school was actually moved, but an entry almost exactly three years later denied a petition to move the school building. By that time, the county was paying $50 a month for a teacher, and the school was most definitely a public one.[18]

St. John Lutheran School and parsonage. Cypress Historical Society

In 1890, an area resident named Gottlieb Pittschumann, a name subjected to many different spellings, deeded to District 6 a four-acre tract at Diamond Point, near the intersection of today's Telge and Huffmeister Roads, for use as a school. Seven years later, his building was moved near St. John Lutheran as a new home for the school there, and the four acres reverted to Mr. Pitschumann. The school was definitively known as Winkler's by then, a name that had been listed with "Pitchman's" for several years. Adding to the confusion, Pitschumann's School was also noted with the name Bundick in some records. One more school fit into the Winkler's tree. Prussia-born Henry Hartman's name was on a small District 6 schoolhouse in the Cypress area from at least 1884. The county treasurer noted that the name was changed to Winkler for the 1892-93 school year. The Cypress schools were all part of District 6 by this time, and the Winkler's name, honoring early area resident and benefactor Winkler, was there to stay.[19]

The school remained in operation in that old building on Cypress Church Road, just west of Cypress Rosehill Road, until 1926 when the condition was deemed bad enough, the lowest ratings in the county, to transfer all the pupils to Sewell. Three years after that, the children began going to the school at Cypress, where lumber from both Winkler and Sewell was used for an addition. The surviving entity of all this history, the Cy-Fair ISD, sold the Winkler School tract near the old St. John Church site in 1959.[20]

WOODCREST SCHOOL

Woodcrest was a tiny African American school named for the addition in which it sat at 5216 Feagan. Building value in the 1930s was barely a thousand dollars, but it occupied a large parcel of land. The school was renamed for Pearl Harbor hero and Texas native Doris Miller shortly after WWII. During those post-war years, the campus still had a glorified outhouse that was accessed by a stone walkway. The amenities were a study in improvisation born of HISD-induced poverty. Orange crates served as chairs in some classrooms. Apple boxes served as library shelves, and the fire alarm was fashioned from a wheel drum and a long screw. In the 1950s, it was torn down and replaced with a new building, still segregated. That school subsequently turned into HISD's library services, and much work for this book was done by the author at that location.[21]

WOODLAND SCHOOL

See Browning

WOODWARD SCHOOL

The Woodward School, also known as the Moonshine Hill School or simply Hill School, came to be because of the huge oil strike in the Humble area in late 1904. Within weeks, the sleepy sawmill community grew from about 100 families to over 10,000 people, and the activity was centered around the epicenter of the strike at Echols Ridge, a spot about two miles east of Humble that was soon rechristened as Moonshine Hill in honor of the first company to strike black gold there. By 1909, the workers in the area finally got a two-room wooden school building in County District 35 for their children. Principal Fannie Davis wrote of great gains such as a library of "sixty-odd volumes." During the first year in operation, "The boys spent quite a while in clearing up the grounds for a nice ball diamond." For five years, District 35 squabbled with the town of Humble's District 28 over whose territory held Woodward with the courts finally awarding it to District 28. Four years after that, the two districts merged anyway. As oil and gas boomed and busted, so did the community of Moonshine Hill. It was enough growth to warrant a new building, but nothing lasts forever. Woodward School closed in 1932 due to low enrollment.[22]

WOOSTER SCHOOL

The Baytown School is listed as early as May 1888 in District 17 with Lynchburg and Crosby area schools, but funds for the school are transferred to Goose Creek in District 15 indicating the children from that area were attending school there. The county finally established a school district for the community of Wooster, designating it District 38, separated from District 17, in April 1895. Shortly thereafter two Iowa transplants, Quincy Adams Wooster and Junius Brown, began building the schoolhouse out of cypress and pine that grew along Scott's Bay. Just over a year later, the residents there voted 9 to 0 to levy a school tax to support the 20 or so young scholars.[23]

The preserved Wooster School building in Baytown. Mike Vance photo

The one room school was located at Market and First Streets, what is today Bayway and Arbor. Wooster's and Brown's sons and sons-in-law are believed to have done the construction. It became part of the new Goose Creek school system in 1919, and by the 1930s, with the giant oil field having dramatically expanded the area population, David G. Burnet Elementary opened on adjacent property. The old Wooster school was repositioned twice on the original property and used as a classroom, cafeteria, and music room before being retired from active educational duty entirely in 1980. Six years later, the sturdy building was acquired by the Bay Area Heritage Society and moved to 5117 N. Main in Baytown for use as a museum.[24]

WUNSCHE SCHOOL

In the early 1930s, the Wunsche family donated 13 acres of land on Spring-Cypress Road to the local school district with the stipulation that it be named for their German immigrant ancestor, Carl Wunsche. It opened for junior high and high school students at the end of the decade. An addition for elementary students came in 1947 and went in 1958. The school then operated solely as a middle school until 1983. In 2006, the Carl Wunsche name was placed on a brand new high school building on the same piece of property.[25]

The Yates HS building shortly after opening. HISD

YATES H S

The cornerstone laying for Jack Yates High School drew a "mammoth crowd" and a mix of praise and outrage from *Informer* editor C.F. Richardson. The biggest complaint was that longtime African American educator and Gregory School principal William Miller had the temerity to refer to three of Jack Yates' daughter, teachers all, by their first names. Virtually every living member of the Yates family was present to witness the honoring of the Reverend Yates, first pastor at both Antioch and Bethel Baptist Churches and one of the city's earliest Black leaders. The highlight according to many was found in the speech of R. T. Andrews, a "colored businessman and substantial citizen" who publicly told the assembled school board members: "In this great metropolitan municipality we are one of the children. We will take the crumbs - but wish for the slice of bread that is rightfully ours." The school at 2610 Elgin in Third Ward opened on February 8, 1926 for registration of students, and classes for 700 students started a few days later under the watchful eye of nineteen teachers and Principal James D. Ryan who had transferred from Colored High School downtown.[26]

Several additional buildings were added to the campus in the first decade bringing it up to 36 classrooms, a boys and a girls gym, two science labs, five home economics rooms, and a "fine library." Shortly after it opened, the campus also became the location of the Houston Colored Junior College. It operated at night, and by 1930 was teaching 548 pupils. Like its rival Wheatley, Yates had a fine music department including a jazz orchestra that produced Art Foxall, Conrad Johnson, and Jewel Brown. The school also produced scores of teachers who later populated HISD schools.[27]

The longest list of famous alumni at Yates is that of top football and basketball professionals. That success on field and court can be traced back to Coach Pat Patterson, a former Negro League baseball star who coached Yates to state titles in four sports: football, basketball, baseball, and track. More importantly, it was Patterson who organized the Prairie View Interscholastic League in 1940 that allowed African American high schools to compete under a framework similar to that which existed for Whites.

Pat Patterson, a Texas coaching legend at Yates. HHRC

Principal Ryan died in the summer of 1940, and the following year William S. Holland took his place. Holland had been brought to Yates as a coach, then became assistant principal. When he took the reins, there were almost 900 students and 58 teachers. He added dramatics and public speaking to the curriculum his first year. The yearbook from 1941 tells of the many organizations including a Negro History Club and a Lonely Hearts Club along with the gift of a portrait of Rev. Jack Yates by his daughter Pinkie, herself a teaching legend in the city. Principal Holland was hugely popular with his community, and was outspoken about the inequality in HISD due to the continuing segregation. Most believe that his bluntness cost him the chance to move to the new Yates High School campus. Instead, he remained at the old school which was converted to James D. Ryan Junior High. Holland stayed there until his retirement in 1974.

The new Yates was a modern school that was much needed due to overcrowding. It opened at 3703 Sampson between TSU and UH in September 1958 at a cost of $2.5 million. In 1978, it became a communications magnet school. It received a major upgrade and addition in the late-2010s.

Black History as a School Subject

Black History Month started decades prior to the Civil Rights movement, and it began as only a week. Historian Carter G. Woodson was the person behind the idea of an official time for study of African American subjects. He founded the Association for Study of Negro Life and History in 1915, adding the Journal of Negro History a year later. By 1926, he felt that a week should be set aside for Americans to understand "that beautiful history and it is going to inspire us to greater achievements," and an announcement was issued declaring it so.[28]

The mid-February date was set to honor two of the most influential people in the fight for emancipation: Abraham Lincoln, born on the 12th of the month, and Frederick Douglass, born on the 14th.

Others had already been inspired by Woodson's earlier writings to push the subject, including the administration at Prairie View A&M. The college principal, Dr. J.G. Osborne, and history professor M.P. Carmichael combined with associate professor Mrs. M.J. Davis to teach PVAMU students starting in 1924. Mrs. Davis taught the subject there for eight years using Woodson's own *The Negro in Our History* as the textbook. After her time at Prairie View, she took a job in Houston teaching at Douglass Elementary. She and other African American teachers taught Black history as an addition to American History. In other locales, Woodson's textbooks were sometimes hidden under the desk "to escape the wrath of the principal."[29]

The Colored Teachers' State Association annually reported that Negro history Week was being observed in various places around the state. By 1949, the organization was offering a special kit to teachers around the state at the price of two dollars to cover printing. It included "recitations, declamations, a play, programs for each day of the week and sentence sketches of all prominent Negroes."[30]

The study was not confined to African American communities. The national Boy Scouts publication, *Scouting*, ran a reminder for Negro History Week in its January 1943 issue complete with an address to write Carter Woodson's Association in Washington, D.C. for more information and posters.

Fifty years after Woodson's Negro History Week press release, and six years after his death, the Congress of the United States declared February to be Black History Month. Even before his passing, Carter Woodson had called for African American history to become a daily part of American history study.

YOUNG E S
See Sunny Side

YOUNG LADIES DAY AND BOARDING SCHOOL
See Miss Brown's

YOUNG LADIES INSTITUTE
Katherine Bledsoe Aldridge Kidd, known commonly as Kate, was a pillar of the First Presbyterian Church and the "guiding light" behind the first cookbook ever published in Texas, an 1883 project of that congregation. She had come from the antebellum planter class and attending a well-known boarding school at Chappell Hill. After the Civil War, though considered by many to be too young to teach, she opened a school in the old A. G. Allen home at Travis and Rusk. It seemed to be a matter of necessity due to economic hardships. At the time, some of her pupils were even older than she. Patrons such as William Vincent and Charlotte Allen helped her gain a place in the town.[31]

At first, she accepted boys as pupils, but she soon settled on the female students. Briefly, Kidd ran afoul of the Reconstruction government in Houston for refusing to have her school examined and approved by an "illiterate Negro." She married merchant George Kidd in 1872, but continued to teach. By the 1880s, under the name Young Ladies Institute, she had a large school at the southeast corner of Main and Polk, employing as many as a half dozen teachers as her assistants. She later downsized her school, and by the turn of the century was doing little more than tutoring a few pupils in her home on Polk. Kate Kidd died in 1930.[32]

YOUNG LADIES SCHOOLS
There were several other private institutions in 19th century Houston that advertised themselves with the moniker of Young Ladies School. All of these post-Civil War operations set the goal of turning girls into "ladies" through instruction in needlework, music, and piety. These included schools operated by Mrs. W.P. Cunningham on the east side of San Jacinto between Congress and Franklin, Mrs. M.J. Young's operation on the second floor of the old Houston Academy building, and other schools run by Mrs. M.E. Flake, Miss Kate Murphy, Miss Julia Stansfield, and Mrs. A.B. Stiles. The name was even revived around the turn of the century at a 1215 Main Street school run by the three Hargis sisters.[33]

YOUNG LADIES SEMINARY
Professor Horace Clark operated this school which seemed to average in the neighborhood of 40 students. It occupied the second floor of the Houston Academy building at Caroline and Rusk, taking the space in September 1871 when Mary Jane Young gave it up to enter the new public school system. It was also known as Clark's Seminary. Though the price was dear, advertisements listed tuition as $24 in gold per semester, it was

"the only institution in Houston which announced that its intention was to place it upon a college basis as soon as possible." The curriculum included French, German, painting, drawing, and music.

ZEISS SCHOOL

The Zeiss schoolhouse was listed in Waller in the late 1890s, named for influential German immigrant George P. Zeiss. Whether it was different than the regular Waller School or merely a short lived name is unknown. Zeiss moved to Houston and headed both the Turnverein and the German Immigration League.[34]

A Few Final Stories

Etiquette in 1877

Among the rules laid down by the city for the schools that year were these:

- Every pupil is required to attend school punctually and regularly; to be diligent in study, and kind and obliging to school-mates; to refrain from the use of profane or improper language, and to be neat and cleanly in person and attire.

- Each pupil shall be assigned a seat, and it shall be his duty to keep it, together with his books, and everything pertaining to his desk, in perfect order. He shall permit no paper or litter on the floor near his desk.

- All pupils shall go directly to and from school, and shall abstain from all playing or quarreling by the way.

- No pupil known to be affected by any contagious disease, or coming from a house where such disease exists, shall be received or continued in the Public Schools.

- During the regular exercises of school, pupils shall refrain entirely from communications with each other by signs, writing, or speaking, without special permission.[1]

The supply room at Houston High School 1910s. HISD

Night School

The Houston school board approved the idea of a night school in 1904, and by the next year, administrators had made it so. More than 200 pupils took part in the classes that first year, and it continued to grow, though with a few rough patches at the beginning. The primary issue was that some of the teenage students, people who had already left school once, were still less than fully committed to the concept of completing an education.[2]

Much of the attention was paid to the foreign pupils. By the second full year of the night schools, Houston was offering classes for those who wanted to learn to speak, read, and write English and "to be an American citizen the better for him and for us." [3]

Plenty of other opportunities were presented for those already American, however. To be eligible, "the pupils who attended were required, before admission, to bring a certificate showing that they are employed at some form of useful labor during the day time." Houston Superintendent Paul Horn added that "all classes of trades and occupations were represented."[4]

Boys at the night school far outnumbered the girls. Some of the younger boys worked as newsboys during the day, selling papers all over the city. Older boys might have jobs for which they sought a better replacement. J.B. Wolfe, principal of the night school at the High School building downtown, reported the manual training classes and a course in mechanical drawing offered at Sherman in Fifth Ward were extremely sought after. One of the most popular courses for girls was domestic science. A regular curriculum of spelling, reading, writing, arithmetic, grammar, and composition was available at each of the three night school campuses, and downtown also offered classes in bookkeeping, typewriting, and stenography.[5]

Though the minimum age for night school was twelve, the biggest progress was noted in the older students who "generally feel the need of better equipment for life, and make extraordinary sacrifices to attend school." Some of those young men referenced had specific goals in mind. Fifteen, about half of whom were seeking jobs as post office clerks, took specific courses to help them with the civil service examinations. Others were angling for clerk jobs with Southern Pacific, the city's largest employer. Two of the young men even used the night classes to study "the junction points of the railroads of Texas, Oklahoma and Louisiana."[6]

The expenditures appeared to make sense to the school board. In 1909-10, Houston's night schools taught 508 students, 446 of them being boys. The enrollment was roughly split between pupils over and under the age of 17. The cost of teacher and administrator salaries for all of the classwork came to $2,419.00.

The following year, the city schools created a night school for African Americans, and the response was overwhelming. Holding classes at the Bruce School in Fifth Ward under the supervision of E.O. Smith, more than 100 regular students signed up for the initial offering for Blacks. The oldest person attending was a 72 year old man, meaning one born into slavery, who "wanted to learn to read the Bible." No mention was made of his previous bondage, merely that "in his early days he had not had the opportunity of learning to read and write." Nonetheless, the Houston school administrators reported with enthusiasm that after one term, the man had "made such progress as to enable him, with more or less of difficulty, to read the book of his choice and of his affection."[7]

With opportunities for advancement often scarce, Houston's African Americans responded quickly to the chance for adult education. In only the second year of availability, Black night school students at Langston and Bruce outnumbered the White students at four campuses by a total of 852 to 832. Most of the pupils were adults, with several of them over seventy. The oldest that year was another former slave, a woman known as Aunt Susie who was attending the night classes in Fifth Ward to learn to read and write. She was 86.[8]

A year later, a third segregated Black campus was added at Frederick Douglass School in Third Ward. An offer was also made to the city's employers to let the school officials know if there were a "number of his employees (who were) deficient in the needful branches of an English education." Classes could be arranged. The city was committed to "the general policy of trying to make public schools of the greatest help possible to the greatest possible number of people." Notable response came from several of Houston's labor unions, and classes were assembled for union painters, plumbers, and electricians.[9]

Spring of 1914 brought another milestone aside from continued growth, though that was significant with just short of 2,000 total students in the various night schools. For the first time, night school diplomas were handed out. Twenty-two men and women went through formal commencement exercises in the high school assembly room, receiving collegiate-style diplomas that bore the title "The City Evening Schools of Houston".[10]

Three years into the offering of Spanish language classes, roughly 250 people signed up to take them in the evenings after their work. The school report crowed that "This growth is merely another indication of the extent to winch the eyes of our community and of our section of this nation are turning toward Latin-America."[11]

The issue of how to educate minors who were forced to work became a bigger focus. Some employers, including Houston's largest, tried to balance work and education on their own. "There are already in the city of Houston at, least two great institutions which are themselves maintaining part time schools independent of any help from public funds," the district reported in 1920. "One of these is the Southern Pacific Railroad. The apprentices in the shops of this road are required to attend school a certain number of hours each week. The school is in the shops, and the instructor is a mechanic who is employed by the company. The instruction is in such lines as mathematics, iron work and other kinds of work needed by the young men in their daily work." The other employer taking the bull by the horns was one of the largest dry goods stores.[12]

Saturday afternoon classes were added in 1916, and by the start of the following year, administrators were wondering how they could offer night school opportunities to the thousands of soldiers at the new Camp Logan. All of the night school classes still remained free of charge to Houstonians, a perk that continued until 1932 before Depression-era economic conditions required application of tuition at the rate of three dollars for the first class and two for each additional subject.[13]

The Americanization program continued to be offered for decades, as well. In 1924, Judge J.C. Hutcheson, the man who would hear their applications for citizenship, spoke to 42 graduates from around the world, advising them that "taking the oath does not guarantee good citizenship; it is up to the individual to make good." The graduates themselves provided a program including a piano solo and more than a half dozen patriotic readings. Countries of origin included Italy, Greece, Mexico, Russia, Poland, Germany, the United Kingdom, and more, and the students were encouraged to continue taking more classes at the night school.[14]

For almost three decades, the Houston schools committed resources to provide free education to adults in the community and to children who had been forced to leave school to provide a living. Houston school officials were proud of this fact: "The boy of fourteen may be seen working at the Blackboard beside a man of forty years as a 'leveling' influence and as a builder of democracy... The fact that these students are in daylight hours engaged in arduous labor shows that they mean to get something from the night school when they are willing to work two hours after they have done a man's work for the day. It shows that the quality of manhood and grit they have is high class, the kind we need for a greater Houston."[15]

Overall momentum for the night schools continued to grow until two segregated junior colleges were established by HISD in 1927 to meet some of the needs.

Typing class 1920s. HISD

Dr. Ray Karchmer Daily

Bitter battles between moderating voices and the hard right are nothing new in Texas politics, nor is the power of money. Dr. Ray K. Daily's 24 years on the HISD Board saw plenty of contentious issues. A medical doctor, she had served on the city's board of health but had never before sought elective office, and women had been eligible to vote for less than a decade. She was motivated by the seemingly complete power of the Klan over the school board and the city with their hate-filled campaigning against not only African Americans but Catholics and Jews, as well. She first got new Mayor Oscar Holcombe, who shared her opposition to the Kluxers, to appoint Mrs. Maurice Goldman to the school board, then eventually, Dr. Daily decided to run on her own. In her initial campaign in 1928, the progressive Daily stressed the importance of understanding children's needs and mentioned lessons she had gleaned during a conference at the home of noted Viennese psychologist Alfred Adler. She even supported a tax hike if that was the only option to increase teacher pay.[16]

Daily was born in Lithuania, and came to Denison, Texas as a child, and she retained a slight foreign accent throughout her life. She ended up in Houston after getting her medical degree from UT Medical Branch in 1913 at the age of 22, the first Jewish woman ever to earn a degree from that school. Her medical practice was very successful, as was that of her husband, an ear, nose and throat doctor she had met in medical school and with whom she shared offices.[17]

Ray K. Daily. Jewish Women's Archive

Her first political effort was the cause of women's suffrage. Her biggest impact on her city, however, was almost certainly through her school board efforts. She was supported by crusading newspaper editor Marcellus Foster, and remarked that he was the greatest man she ever met. Dr. Ray Daily was a guiding hand in turning HISD's community college into the University of Houston, making the motion at an HISD board meeting in 1934 to set that juggernaut in motion. Within the parameters of the times, she tried to nudge the needle on improvement of Black schools in Houston. It was generally Daily who represented the board at events related to those minority schools including the opening of Wheatley High. By the WWII years, she had found a sometimes board ally in Ima Hogg, working for women's causes and better conditions for children, though Daily also believed that Miss Ima was "taken in" by other board factions and was "not capable of working with a group where there is a lot of difference of opinions." Often times, it seemed Dr. Daily was a lone voice for progressivism in the schools through things such as adult and vocational education.[18]

One fight for which she held the losing hand was her advocacy for accepting federal money to provide free school lunches to children who needed them. The conservatives on the HISD board in 1948 called it "creeping socialism." That was despite the fact that school had often had policies of supplying free lunches using local money. Ultimately, it cost Daily her seat four years later when McCarthyites attacked her over the issue, along with dredging up her Russian Jewish origins yet again. The woman who defeated her at the polls, like all of those who cloaked themselves in false patriotism, was adamantly against integration of the school district, as well. To add to matters, there was a third candidate who drew thousands of votes, but whom Daily believed never even existed since he did not appear at a single campaign event.[19]

Dr. Ray, as she was often known, continued practicing medicine until age 83. She passed away in 1975. Thirty years later, an HISD elementary school was finally named in her honor.

Public Service

It is a matter of pleasure to report that during the past year our schools have undertaken to make some direct return to the city by way of social service for the support they have received from the city... It has nevertheless been the policy of the schools to encourage the children to make such immediate returns as may be in their power by way of social service to the city. In line with this policy, the schools last year co-operated with the other forces of the city in the matter of clean-up week. The little folks were willing and active workers in helping to rid the city of the accumulated waste and debris. The children also co-operated with a local firm of merchants in distributing and setting out some ten thousand shade trees. After the disastrous Fifth ward fire last winter, the Jones School building for White children, and the Bruce building for colored were opened to the fire sufferers for a number of days.

Houston City Schools Report 1911-12

Acknowledgements

This project was a long time coming. For a decade and a half, I envisioned a big, beautiful coffee table book presentation of this material and the photographs, but the budget and distribution for such a book never materialized. I finally came to grips with the notion that this important research was doing no one any good sitting on my computer. So here we are. While the packaging may be a bit more modest, the content is largely the same. As with all books, that means there are so many people who deserve a hearty thanks for helping compile it. So many people helped in ways big and small during this journey.

She is always mentioned at the end of these sections, but I will put her up here. Anne Vance is kind enough to make a proofreading pass on these books, and it is invaluable. Thanks so very much.

When I started this project way back in what now seems the 19th century, my old non-profit, Houston Arts and Media was still in business. That organization has now become Night Heron Media, but it is still working on Texas history projects. From the way back, I'd like to thank all the HAM board members who were also good friends. I'd especially like to mention Laurie Feinswog, who braved insects to accompany me on numerous photo safaris to old school sites, and JR Gonzales, with whom I talked history for hundreds of hours. Those last two had to wonder if this much talked about book of mine would ever see the light of day.

I was also serving on the Harris County Historical Commission at the time, and my fellow commissioners Susan Armstrong, Trevia Wooster Beverly, Shelby Cantrell, Chuck Chandler, Gayle Davies, James H. Ford, Jr., Debra Sloan, Paul Scott, Janet Wagner, and Dan Worrall all helped with important information about far flung school sites and communities. Service on the historical commission is an act of love.

My good friends Sarah Jackson and Annie Golden of the always valuable Harris County Archives were indispensable. So were the staff at the Houston History Research Center, and I want to mention Joanna Collier, Emily Scott, Tim Ronk, and Jennifer Sessa in particular for this project. That entire staff pulled so much material for me over several years. Top of the list at HHRC is Joel Draut, the best photo archivist who ever lived. Prove me wrong. My work on this book spanned three directors of what was then called HMRC - Kemo Curry, Elizabeth

Dickens Sargent, and Laney Dwyer Chavez - and sincere thanks go to each of them. Lisa May of the Archdiocese of Galveston-Houston was likewise most supportive.

Alyssa Honnette and Sarah Conlan who worked with me at a now defunct TV station were enormously helpful. Alyssa did some great digging into old records, and Sarah scanned hundreds of slides. Bonnie Wilson did digging for me in some obscure boxes at the Texas State Library and Archives during times when I could not get to Austin myself. Gayle Fallon at the Houston Federation of Teachers gave her time to visit with me. Public school teachers are the backbone of our society, and teachers unions should forever be praised for fighting to see that their members are rewarded properly, something that has almost never happened. Shame on all who denigrate a teacher.

I visited almost every school district in Harris County, or attempted to, at least. I want to thank Joyce Griffin, Jim Hundemer, Norm Uhl, Georgia McGlasson, and Debbie Hall at Houston Independent School District; Karen Collier at Humble ISD; Matt Lucas at Deer Park ISD; LaNell Allee at Klein ISD; Chuck Davis at La Porte ISD; and Kay McBride at Pasadena ISD.

Many individual historians and researchers provided good information. Virginia Blalock, Virginia Hancock, Betty Chapman, Anne Sloan, Larissa Lindsay, Emily Todd, Dr. William Kellar, Mary Ann Malone, Mark McKee, Marie Neuman Gray, Nancy Stuart, Reggie Browne, Jeff Dunn, Ruth Taube Stroeckel, and the charming Birdia Churchwell are some, and I'm sure I have omitted others. Sincere apologies for that.

Area historical societies, vital caretakers of our past, were particularly helpful, as well. Several organizations provided valuable help including Fred Collins of Harris County Precinct 3 and Kleb Woods, Robert Meaux at the Humble Museum, multiple members of the Bellaire Historical Society, and Jim Sigmund, Jane Krahn Ledbetter, Jay Gavitt, and Joyce Zaboroski Kleb at the Cypress Historical Society.

There was even one long-dead contributor I want to mention. Edwin Bonewitz who corresponded with the various Houston newspapers and the city's head librarian to what was undoubtedly the point of great annoyance. It is easy to imagine those folks seeing the Bonewitz return address and rolling their eyes in anticipation of what he might complain about next. Over the years, though, reading the letters kept by the librarians, I got the idea that they might have become friends. That would be thanks to Mr. Bonewitz's undying love for Houston history and the nitpicking that is necessary to get the story right. One thing that he held most dear was that his grandmother, Frederica, had come from Germany at a tender age and ended up as a private student of Zerviah Noble in that woman's private school more than a decade before the Civil War. Bonewitz detailed the stories he heard and cherished. While he may have been exhausting to some, he was a great posthumous help to this book.

Finally - huge thanks to The Brown Foundation, an invaluable Houston institution which provided financial support for research expenses in this large undertaking.

Endnotes

The Start of HISD

1. *City Report* 1920-21; *Post* 3 March 1899

2. *GDN* 9 August 1920

3. *City Report* 1920-21

4. ibid

5. Keller; HISD report 1924-30;

Early African American Teachers

1. *New Orleans Tribune* 23 July 1864; 22 September 1864; Blasingame, John W.. *Black New Orleans: 1860-1880*. University of Chicago Press, 1973; Anderson, James D.. *The Education of Blacks in the South, 1860-1935*. University of North Carolina Press (Chapel Hill) 1988

2. *Flake's Bulleting* (Galveston) 11 November 1865

3. *Loyal Georgian* 3 February, 10 March 1866; Butchart, Ronald E.. *Freedmen's Education: 1862-1875*. Greenwood Press (Westport, CT) 1980; Anderson.; Winegarten, Ruthe. *Black Texas Women: 150 Years of Trial and Triumph*. University of Texas press (Austin) 1995

4. *Daily Houston Telegraph* 15 October 1871; Hornsby, Alton. *Freedmen's Bureau Schools in Texas*. SHQ 76:387. April 1973; TSLAC 2-9/648. Statements and Reports of Treasurers of County School Boards.

5. United States Census 1880 Harris County, TX

6. Anderson

7. Anderson; Armstrong, Samuel C. *Normal School Work Among the Freedmen*. Normal School Press (Hampton, VA) 1874

8. Anderson; Armstrong

9. https://www.tshaonline.org/handbook/online/articles/kcp06 accessed 10 February 2016;

10. Anderson; Houston City Schools Report 1893-94

11. http://www.fisk.edu/about/history accessed 9 February 2016; http://www2.howard.edu/about/history accessed 9 February2016;

12. Bryant, Ira B.. Jr.. *The Development of the Houston Negro Schools*. ; Houston City Schools Report 1893-94; https://en.wikipedia.org/wiki/Calabar_High_School accessed 21 January 2016; https://www.themico.edu.jm/web/www/home%20founded%201836 accessed 21 January 2016

13. Anderson, Du Bois; Houston Informer 14 June 1919; Sorelle, James Martin. *The Darker Side of Heaven: The Black Community in Houston, Texas, 1917-1945*. Kent State University, 1980

14. *Houston Infor*mer 20 July 1940

15. Sorelle; Johnson, Johnny, Ed. D..*African American leadership from 1876-1954: A Study of an Urban School District*. Texas Southern University, 1993

16. Winegarten

17. Informer; City Reports; Brown, Mrs. Clifford John. *A Comparative Study of the Teachers in the Public Schools of Dallas, Houston and San Antonio*. M.A. Thesis. University of Texas. August 1929

18. ibid

19. *Houston Informer and Texas Freeman* 10 June 1933; *Informer* 17 June 1933; *Detroit Free Press* 24 February 1931;

20. http://teachercases1.weebly.com/the-naacp-thurgood-marshall-and-the-equal-pay-for-black-teachers-cases.html accessed 10 February 2016; Sorelle; HMRC, Yates Collection, Box 4, Folder 20; *San Antonio Register* 19 March 1943; https://tshaonline.org/handbook/online/articles/kat08 accessed 10 February 2016; Pitre, Merline. *In Struggle Against Jim Crow*. Texas A&M Press (College Station) 1999

21. Houston City Schools Report 1905-06; Houston City Schools Report 1909-10

Hygiene

1. *County Report* 1913

2. http://www.salon.com/2007/11/30/dirt_on_clean/ accessed 15 February 2016; http://www.historyconfidential.com/2011/08/history-bathing-in-early-america/ accessed 15 February 2016;

3. https://tshaonline.org/handbook/online/articles/pwsgr accessed 16 February 2016

4. Kirkland, Kate Sayen. *Captain James Baker of Houston 1857-1941*. Texas A&M Press, 2012; Chapman, Betty Trapp. *Houston Women: Invisible Threads in the Tapestry*. Donning Co (Virginia Beach, VA.) 2000; *Houston Business Journal*, Betty Chapman, 28 August 2009

5. McWhorter, Thomas. *Trailblazers in Houston's East End: The Impact of Ripley House and the Settlement Association on Houston's Hispanic Population*. Houston History. Vol. 9:1. Fall 2011. UH Center for Public History

6. Sandy Reiser. Interview with author. 3 September 2006

Schools I - K

1. Archdiocese Archives; Valdez, Sister Mary Paul, *The History of the Missionary Catechists of Divine Providence* (The Missionary Catechists of Divine Providence, 1978); Digital Sanborn Maps 1924

2. Archdiocese Archives; De Leon, Arnoldo. *Ethnicity in the Sunbelt: Mexican Americans in Houston* (College Station: Texas A&M Press, 2001)

3. City directories; http://immanuelhouston.com/about-us/ accessed 9 October 2017; Immanuel Lutheran School staff conversation 14 October 2017

4. Sister Belinda Delaney; Texas Historical Marker File. Incarnate Word Academy. 1973; McHugh, Sister Mary Sebastian. *History of the Order of the Incarnate Word and Blessed Sacrament in Houston, Texas* (M.A. Thesis, University of Houston; 1948)

5. Valdez

6. City Directories;

7. Sanborn digital maps 1890, 1896, 1907, 1924;

8. Delany; Valdez; Oakes & Daniels. *Step by Step*

9. County Reports 1912, 1913, 1914; Map 1914

10. Meaux; HCCM F436. 14 May 1892

11. http://www.jacintocity-tx.gov/history/ accessed 12 November 2016; https://tshaonline.org/handbook/online/articles/hfj01 accessed 12 November 2016

12. HISD websites; City Reports; *Post* 7 February 1926; *Post* 9 February 1926; Pugh

13. *City Report* 1912-13

14. ibid

15. *City Report* 1913-14

16. *City Report* 1914-15

17. Lewis, Kirk. *A Century of Learning. A History of Pasadena School District 1898-1998.*; City Directories

18. U.S. Census Harris County 1880, 1910; USGS Map Houston Heights 1922; https://famhisttranscriptions.wordpress.com/2012/05/24/catherine-pt1/ accessed 7 August 2016;

19. SD 25 Minute book; County Reports; Suburbanite 8 March 1918; HISD reports; *GDN* 9 August 1920

20. Pugh & Dennison; HCCCM E213. 9 June 1885; HCCCM F285. 14 May 1891; GDN 16 July 1896; Suburbanite 8 March 1918; GDN 1 March 1919; City Directories; County Reports; SD 25 Minutes book; HCCCM P440. 19 December 1910

21. Pugh & Dennison; County Reports

22. *Press* 5 July 1925; *Press* 9 July 1925; *Post* 9 July 1925; *Press* 10 July 1925; *Post* 14 July 1925; HISD websites; City Reports; Pugh; City Directories

23. HISD websites; Author's personal experience

24. *GDN* 9 April 1893; City Directories

25. *GDN* 20 December 1883; *GDN* 27 September 1884; *GDN* 16 July 1885; *Post* 7 April 1887; U.S. Census Harris County 1880, 1900; City Directories; *GDN* 18 October 1888; *GDN* 12 August 1889; *GDN* 20 December 1889; Digital Sanborn Maps 1890, 1896

26. *Post* 7 April 1887; Post 19 September 1897; Johnston

27. Post 9 April 1893; City Reports

28. De León, Arnoldo. *Ethnicity in the Sunbelt: Mexican Americans in Houston* Texas A&M Press (College Station) 2001; *Papel Chicano* 6 March 1930; Pugh & Dennison

29. *Post* 4 April 1967

30. Baytown Museum; Henson; Baytown Sun 22 April 1953; Scott

31. *Houston Press* 29 June 2009; HISD websites

32. United States Census, Harris County, TX, 1900; Bryant, Ira B, Jr.. *Development of the Houston Negro Schools*. 1935 (Houston). p 104-107

33. Bryant; *Post* 16 December 1926

34. Bryant; Progressive Music Series. Parker, Horatio; McConathy, Osbourne; Birge, Edward B.; Miessner, W. Otto. 1914. Silver, Burdett & Co. (Boston, New York, Chicago)

35. United States Census, Harris County, TX 1910, 1920, 1940; Texas Death Records 1903-2000

36. LaNell Allee. Klein ISD;

37. Author interview with Virginia Hancock 2007; Young; Dallas Morning News 09 September 1960; Bush, Johnny and Mitchell, Rick. *Whiskey River (Take My Mind)*. UT Press. 2007; *Post* 17 August 1949

38. Rylander, Roberta Wright. *Applauding the Past of Katy, Texas* 1991; Schlipf, Louise. *A Brief History of Katy*. 1931; Barwis, Susan DeVries http://www.katytexas.com/katyhistory.cfm%20accessed%208%20March%202010 accessed 8 May 2010; Post 19 March 1899; HCCCM N080. 11 July 1906; HCCCM O502. 11 February 1909

39. http://www.katyfinder.com/eCommunity/Article/08-04-23/katy_s_black_history.aspx accessed 9 May 2010; Barwis; Adams, Carol 23 April 2008; *Brookshire Times* 29 August 1947; *Brookshire Times* 3 September 1948; *Brookshire Times* 27 May 1949

40. County Reports; Barwis; *Brookshire Times* 29 August 1947; *Brookshire Times* 9 April 1948; *Brookshire Times* 3 September 1948; *Brookshire Times* 15 September 1950

41. Cole; Scott

42. Lavender; Hornsby; Elliott; Baggett, James Alex. Handbook. https://tshaonline.org/handbook/online/articles/fki42%20accessed%2019%20June%202013 ; *Missions and Schools Abroad Among the Freemen.* The American Missionary Vol. 11, no. 1 (1867); *Telegraph* 22 December 18969

43. Hickman

44. Kinkaid films by Houston Arts and Media; United States Census Harris County 1910; Santangelo, Susan. *History of Kinkaid School*; Kinkaid School Historical Marker file. Ulmer, Francita Stuart. Harris County Historical Commission; Digital Sanborn Maps 1924; Hickman

45. *Chronicle* 22 September 1929; Historical marker; Author interview with Carrington Weems HAM N2N 9 August 2006; Author interview with Dr. Denton Cooley. HAM N2N 1 August 2007

46. City Reports; *Washington Post* 2 June 2011; Author interview with Lesta King HAM N2N

47. Gomez, Stephanie. *German Settlers of NW Harris County.* Houston History Magazine. 30 July 2016; Smith, Margaret Mallot; Daniels

48. Heritage of North Harris County; USGS Map 1914; Severance, Diana Lynn, Ph.D.. *History of the Kohrville Community and Kohrville School.*

49. Severance; County Treasurer ledgers;

50. HCCCM E98. 18 June 1884; County Treasurer ledgers; Severance; HCCCM E372. 9 May 1887; Post 15 May 1897; County Reports

51. USGS maps 1914; HCCCM F436. 14 May 1892; Post 15 May 1897; Post 19 March 1899; County Reports; Chronicle 28 May 1957

52. Hickman

53. USGS Map 1914; Cole

Schools L

1. De Leon; *Gaceta Mexicana* 15 September 1928

2. Black, John. *Bayshore Sun.* 29 June 1997; Malone, Ann Uloth and Becker, Dan. *Around La Porte.* Arcadia. 2011

3. Black; Malone and Becker; Bayshore Sun undated 1964; Bayshore Sun 21 September 1945; http://www.lpisd.org/apps/pages/index.jsp?uREC_ID=215189&type=d&pREC_ID=476026 accessed 24 November 2016

4. http://www.ci.la-porte.tx.us/589/History-of-La-Porte%20accessed%2028%20November%202016 ; Malone and Becker; Black; County Reports; County Treasurer ledgers; HCCCM F488. 14 February 1893; GDN 19 September 1911

5. Malone and Becker; Black; County Reports; *Bayshore Sun* undated 1964 article

6. HC school original 1876 ledger

7. GCCISD websites; *Baytown Sun* 12 September 1950; Henson; *Denton Lasso* 25 September 1945; Scott

8. Sloan, Anne. *The History of Mirabeau B. Lamar High School*. Donning Co. (Virginia Beach) 2013;

9. Martin, Betty. *Chronicle* 25 October 2007; *Chronicle* 15 November 2007;

10. *City Report* 1911-12

11. *City Report* 1914-15

12. *Chronicle* 13 January 1930; *Press* 13 January 1930; *Post* 14 January 1930; *Chronicle* 19 September 1930; *Chronicle* 23 June 1933; *Press* 23 June 1933; *Post* 24 June 1933; *Post* 26 June 1933

13. *Chronicle*

14. *Daily Court Review* 28 March 1940;

15. *Port Arthur News* 21 August 1940; *Daily Court Review* 15 July 1941; *Post* 25, 26 September 1941;

16. https://en.wikipedia.org/wiki/Robertson_Stadium accessed 5 April 2016; *Post* 19 September 1942; *GDN* 13 November 1942;

17. *Daily Cougar* 20 March 1996

18. Fonville; Pugh; City Reports; Digital Sanborn maps 1924; Chronicle 28 August 1967

19. Author interview with Orie Clark at Burbank ES 29 June 2007; United States Census Harris County 1920, 1930; *Chronicle* 27 March 2003;

20. City directories

21. *Houston Age* 1 October 1877; City Reports; United States Census Harris County 1880; *GDN* 20 December 1883; *GDN* 27 September 1884; *Post* 19 September 1897; *Red Book of Houston*; United States Census Harris County 1900, 1920; *Chronicle* 29 May 2008

22. Bryant; *Washington Post* 7 June 2008; City reports; HISD websites; *Post* 7 December 1962;

23. HISD websites; Post 7 February 1926; Lomax, John Nova. *Texas Monthly*. 11 May 2016; *Press* 5 July 1925

24. *Chronicle* 5 November 2001; Pugh; City Reports; *Pos*t 24 October 1982

25. *Chronicle* 5 November 2001; Lomax

26. Digital Sanborn Maps 1924; *Post* 18 August 1912; City Reports; Lantrip Historical Marker. HCHC and THC;Wilcox

27. City Reports; Historical Marker; Chronicle 16 February 1941; Pugh

28. HISD websites; http://www.bloghouston.com/blog/2005/06/29/hisd-preserves-some-history-at-lantrip-elementary/ accessed 14 August 2009

29. *Houston City Schools Report* 1907-09

30. HC original 1876 schools ledger; County Treasurer ledgers

31. City Directories; City Reports; HISD websites; Pugh; Digital Sanborn Maps 1924; http://www.neighborhood-centers.org/locations/leonel-castillo-community-center accessed 7 January 2017

32. Lee High School Historical Marker HCHC and THC; Henson; GCCISD websites; *Big Spring Daily Herald* 5 April 1932; Scott

33. Kleiner, Diana J.. Handbook https://tshaonline.org/handbook/online/articles/hrlur accessed 19 July 2010; http://www.abandonedrails.com/Houston_to_Katy accessed 14 January 2017; US Census Harris County 1880; GDN 5 August 1885; *GDN* 18 September 1886; *GDN* 19 September 1886; County Treasurer ledgers; HAM N2N interview with Della Mouser.18 September 2006; http://forthosebefore.tumblr.com/post/95915936924/lily-white-texas accessed 14 January 2017

34. County Treasurer ledgers

35. County Reports; *Suburbanite* 8 March 1918; *Post* 29 March 1901; *Bellaire Texan*. 9 September 1959; *Post* 2 August 1910; *Post* 22 July 1916

36. Bush, David and Parsons, Jim. *Houston Deco.*

37. USGS 1914 maps; Black; *Chronicle* 9 May 1980; County Reports; HCCCM R439. 31 August 1914

38. *Houston Age* 1 October 1877; City Directories; City Reports; *GDN* 20 December 1883; *GDN* 27 August 1884; Pugh; *GDN* 27 November 1888

39. City Reports; *GDN* 27 November 1888; *Dealy & Baker Guide to Houston.* 1895; Digital Sanborn Maps 1896

40. Author interview with Sandra Cole Reiser. October 2006;

41. Reiser; HISD websites

42. http://www.brighthubengineering.com/structural-engineering/77511-water-chlorination-history-the-mid-1800s-through-the-early-1900s/ accessed 1 April 2016; http://apps.who.int/iris/bitstream/10665/58891/3/WHO_EPI_GEN_93.16_mod6.pdf accessed 01 April 2016;

43. http://polio.emedtv.com/polio/causes-of-polio.html accessed 01 April 2016; http://www.medicalnewstoday.com/articles/155580.php accessed 01 April 2016; *Southwestern Times* 27 May 1948

44. *Dallas Morning News* 14 October 1927

45. https://www.ncbi.nlm.nih.gov/pmc/articles/PMC1473032/figure/F1/ accessed 4 April 2016; https://www.ncbi.nlm.nih.gov/pmc/articles/PMC1473032/ accessed 4 April 2016;

46. Author interview with Sandra Cole Rieser 3 September 2006

47. https://en.wikipedia.org/wiki/History_of_poliomyelitis accessed 1 April 2016;

48. City Directories; HISD websites; Chronicle 11 November 1935; Post 24 November 1935

49. City Directories; City Reports; Pugh; *Post* 31 October 1919; *Post* 28 October 1922

50. Pugh

51. County Treasurer ledgers

52. City Reports; HISD websites; City Directories; Digital Sanborn Maps 1907, 1924

53. City Reports; *Post* 29 June 1913; HAM N2N interviews with Johnny Bonilla, Moises Villalpando and Robert Schleyer;

54. http://www.plumbworld.co.uk/the-history-of-the-toilet   accessed 15 November 2015

55. https://victoriaplum.com/news/a-brief-history-of-the-toilet%20accessed%2015%20November%202015 ;Panati, Charles. *Extraordinary Origins of Everyday Things*. Harper & Row (New York), 1987.

56. http://blogs.discovermagazine.com/bodyhorrors/2011/04/25/blood-money-hookworm-economics-in-the-postbellum-south/   accessed 15 November 2015

57. Harris County School Report 1913-14; Birdia Churchwell Interview by author 18 March 2016

58. Houston Chronicle 25 May 1913 *Improvements in City Schools for Four Years Are Detailed*.;

59. *City Report* 1916-17; *City Report* 1918-19

60. *City Report* 1893-94

61. Digital Sanborn Maps 1924; City directories; City Reports; Bryant; Calico Tees website accessed 2006; *Post* 17 December 1962; *Chronicle* 31 December 2024

62. https://web.archive.org/web/20030401141406/http://www.lutheransouth.org/History/history.htm   accessed 10 September 2017

63. USGS maps; https://tshaonline.org/handbook/online/articles/hll75   accessed 27 January 2014; County Reports; Author correspondence with Shelby Cantrell 2010-15; Original HC Schools ledger 1876; HC-CCM E98. 18 June 1884; HCCCM Q139. 12 January 1912; County Treasurer ledgers; United States Census Harris County 1880; HCHC website https://historicalcommission.harriscountytx.gov/Pages/Lynchburg.aspx   accessed 05 February 2017; Cartier & Hole

64. County Treasurer ledgers; Shelby Cantrell

Schools M

1. HISD websites; City Reports; *Chronicle* 1 May 1921; City Directories; Pugh

2. https://prezi.com/f0khnociiwzd/history-of-physical-education/   accessed 14 February 2016;

3. http://absolutelymemorial.com/2013/03/turnverein/   accessed 14 February 2016; https://tshaonline.org/handbook/online/articles/vnt02   accessed 14 February 2016

4. McCullough, David. *Mornings on Horseback*. Simon & Schuster (New York) 1982; Dayen, David. *How Teddy Roosevelt Saved Football*. Politico. 20 September 2014; Miller, John J.. *The Big Scrum: How Teddy Roosevelt Saved Football*. Harper Collins. (New York) 2011; http://www.ymca.net/history/1870-1890s.html accessed 14 February 2016;

5. *City Report* 1907-08

6. *City Report* 1909-10 *Report of Physical Director*;

7. *City Report* 1909-10

8. *City Report* 1909-10

9. ibid

10. *City Report* 1909-10; *City Report* 1910-11

11. *Harris County Schools Annual Report* 1912

12. County Report 1914

13. *City Report* 1917-18. Report of J.K. Staples.

14. *City Report* 1910-11

15. City Report 1910-11; City Report 1917-18

16. https://prezi.com/f0khnociiwzd/history-of-physical-education/ accessed 14 February 2016

17. Lavender; United States Census Harris County 1870

18. GCCISD websites; Baytown Museum; Henson

19. Chandler, Chuck. *Cedar Bayou Methodist Church, 1844 – 1897*. 2024; *Texas Wesleyan Banner* 22 May 1850

20. HCCCM E213. 9 June 1885

21. City Reports; Dealy & Baker 1895 Guide to Houston

22. City Reports; Fonville; Pugh; *Post* 22 February 1914; *GDN* 14 June 1922; *Post* 1 August 1948; *Chronicle* 21 May 2013

23. http://www.ohiohistorycentral.org/w/First_Junior_High_School_in_the_United_States?rec=2690 accessed 22 February 2016; http://www.faqs.org/childhood/In-Ke/Junior-High-School.html accessed 22 February 2016:

24. *City Report* 1908-09;

25. *City Report* 1910-11

26. ibid

27. *City Report* 1912-13

28. Horn, P.W.. *The Junior High School in Houston, Texas*. Elementary School Journal, University of Chicago Press. 1915

29. *City Report* 1919-20

30. *City Report* 1918-19; *City Report* 1919-20

31. *City Report* 1919-20; Horn

32. Carroll, B. H. Carroll Jr., ed. *Standard History of Houston: From a Study of the Original Sources* (Knoxville: H. W. Crew & Co., 1912); Keller; HMRC Bonewitz Papers MSS 25; *Telegraph* 23 December 1857; *Telegraph* 27 October 1862

33. http://mcgeechapelchurch.com/about-us/history/ accessed 19 February 2017; Beverly, Trevia. *Directory of Harris County Cemeteries*. Tejas Publication, 2001; Worrall; USGS Map 1914

34. HCHC Historical Marker Application; Beverly; Scott

35. City Reports; City Directories;

36. Pugh; City Directories; City Reports; *Chronicle* 15 July 1928;

37. City Reports; City Directories; Virginia Hancock research on Merkel family. April 2009' Freeman, Lucinda. *Historic Houston: How to See It*. iUniverse. 2011

38. City directories; http://www.trinitydt.org/apps/pages/index.jsp?uREC_ID=349189&type=d&pREC_ID=758490 accessed 9 October 2017

39. HC original 1876 schools ledger; CCISD websites; County Reports; County Treasurer ledgers; HCCCM E98. 18 June 1884; HCCCM F436. 14 May 1892; HCCCM R037. 22 December 1913; USGS map 1914; Interview with Jean West various dates, 2018

40. Pugh; City Reports; Chronicle 2 May 1933

41. HISD websites various; Author visit to Milby campus 2017

42. *Chronicle* 3 November 1939; *Post* 3 November 1939; *Chronicle* 28 November 1939; *Press* 3 November 1939; Gonzales, J.R.. *Bayou City History Blog*. 6 June 2007

43. Cypress Top; Notes of Darlene Roth on Solomon title abstracts; US Census Harris County 1930

44. HC 1876 original schools ledger; HCCCM D488. 1August 1882

45. HC Deeds. V326:630; County Reports; USGS Map 1914

46. Lavender; United States Census Harris County 1870

47. Keller; Hickman; City Directories; Chapman, Betty. HBJ 23 October 1998; Lavender; Johnston; United States Census Harris County 1870, 1880; *Post* 23 January 1927

48. Hack, Richard. *Hughes: The Private Diaries, Memos and Letters* (2007); Johnston

49. Hickman

50. Hickman; Johnston

51. City Directories; Digital Sanborn Maps 1924; *New York Times* 24 March 2002; Johnston; City Reports; Pugh

52. City Reports; Pugh; Author interview with Dr. Denton Cooley. HAM N2N. 1 August 2006; HAIF; *Chronicle* 1 October 1916

53. Montrose School History. HISD Collection. HMRC; Author interview with Dr. Denton Cooley. HAM N2N. 1 August 2006; HISD websites; *Chronicle* 10 March 2017; Broyles, William. *Texas Monthly*. February 2013

54. *City Report* 1909-10

55. *City Report* 1906-07;

56. *City Report* 1909-10; *City Report* 1908-09

57. Bryant; *Post* 16 August 1914; *City Report* 1919-20

58. *City Report* 1923

59. *Houston Chronicle* 16 May 1913

60. *Chronicle* 16 May 1913

61. *Post* 19 March 1899

62. *GDN* 12 September 1906; County Reports

63. Bryant; City Directories; Informer 5 March 192; City Reports; Goffney, Aaron P. *Dawson Lunnon Cemetery*. Houston History Magazine. July 2015

64. HC Deeds 294:160 10 September 1912; County Reports

65. SD 25 minutes ledger 1894

66. County Treasurer ledgers; HCCCM E372. 9 May 1887; HCCCM E625. 15 May 1889

67. *Telegraph* 21 October 1837; *Telegraph* 16 May 1838

68. *Telegraph* 17 November 1858

69. *Telegraph* 28 July 1838; Harris, Dilue Rose. Reminiscences. TSHA Quarterly V4:188

70. *Telegraph* 28 February 1851

71. The Heritage Society research; Chapman; Lavender; Bonewitz; United States Census Harris County 1860, 1870;

72. Chapman; Bonewitz

73. *Telegraph* 26 September 1872; Lavender; Bonewitz; *Houston Age* 1 October 1877; Census 1870; Aulbach

74. *Post* 30 April 1904; *Post* 3 May 1904; *Post* 4 May 1904; *Post* 10 May 1904

75. *Post* 15 May 1904

76. *Post* 7 May 1913

77. Post 8 May 1913; Records of Texas Medical Association; *Houston City Council Minutes* 27 March 2007;

78. *Post* 10 May 1913

79. ibid

80. Post 13 May 1913

81. Chronicle 13 June 1913

82. Houston Press 11 August 1913

83. *City Report* 1912-13

84. *Post* 15 October 1913

85. ibid

86. *Houston Business Journal*, Betty Chapman, 7 August 2009

87. *Telegraph* 26 September 1872

88. ibid

89. County Reports; HC Post Offices; Author site visit; *Post* 28 October 1922; *Chronicle* 31 December 2024

90. County Reports; Post 5 September 1907

Schools N - O

1. Meaux; County treasurer ledgers; Young, Nancy Beck. Handbook Online https://tshaonline.org/handbook/online/articles/eqh14 accessed 13 March 2017

2. HCCCM E98. 18 June 1884; Ledbetter; HCCCM F436. 14 May 1892; County Treasurer ledgers; Post 15 May 1897; CFISD websites; Post 19 March 1899; County Reports; Crews; Sullivan

3. County Treasurer ledgers; *Post* 19 March 1899

4. HCCCM C381-388. 2 December 1875; HCCCM C288 15 January 1876; HCCCM D630. 3 July 1883; HCCCM F419. 13 February 1892

5. County Treasurer ledgers

6. HCCCM E98. 18 June 1884; County Treasurer ledgers; SD 25 minutes ledger; HCCCM E 372. 9 May 1887; HCCCM E625. 15 May 1889; HCCCM F419. 13 February 1892; *Post* 15 May 1897; *Post* 19 March 1889; Perkins

7. McHugh, Sister Mary Sebastian "History of the Order of the Incarnate Word and Blessed Sacrament in Houston, Texas" (M.A. Thesis, University of Houston; 1948)

8. Henson; GCCISD websites

9. HISD websites; Post

10. HCCCM E98. 18 June 1884; County Treasurer ledgers; *Post* 15 May 1897; *Post* 19 March 1899; County Reports; USGS maps 1914; Severance

11. http://www.phrases.org.uk/meanings/328950.html accessed 28 December 2015

12. *Recollections of Early Schools*. Kenney, M.M.. Southwestern Historical Quarterly, Vol. 1, No. 4 April 1898. Pps 285-296

13. *Harris County Schools Report* 1912, L.L. Pugh, County Superintendent

14. *Press* 3 June 1925; *Chronicle* 9 June 1925; *Post* 9 June 1925; *Chronicle* 12 June 1925; *Press* 13 June 1925; *Post* 9 June 1925

15. https://www.aacap.org/aacap/policy_statements/1988/Corporal_Punishment_in_Schools.aspx%20 accessed 28 December 2015; http://www.economist.com/news/united-states/21632521-spanking-makes-your-children-stupid-spare-rod accessed 28 December 2015; http://statelaws.findlaw.com/texas-law/texas-corporal-punishment-in-public-schools-laws.html%20accessed%2028%20December%202015

16. HC Assessors Abstracts of Town Lots and Additions. Oak Lawn Annex. Block 4, lots 6 & 7. 1900-1905; City Directories; City Reports

17. HC original 1876 school ledger; County Treasurer ledgers; Beverly; Post 16 May 1937; HISD websites; United States Census Harris County 1880; TGLO land register. Harris County. 1839; HMRC SC38. Harrisburg Coroners books 1886-87; HCCCM E506. 19 May 1888; HCCCM E625, 15 May 1889; HCCCM F436. 14 May 1892; Post 19 March 1899; County Reports; 1954 History of Oates School. HMRC. HISD Collection

18. Valdez, Sister Mary Paul. *The History of the Missionary Catechists of Divine Providence* (The Missionary Catechists of Divine Providence, 1978): HCHC Historical Marker narrative; De Leon; von der Mehden, Fred R. ed. *The Ethnic Groups of Houston* (Houston: Rice University Studies, 1984)

19. Valdez; http://olgschoolhouston.org/about/history/ accessed 25 March 2017; de Leon

20. Archdiocese records

21. Sorrelle; Archdiocese records; http://www.ourmotherofmercy.net/history.html accessed 1 September 2017; Steptoe

Schools P - Q

1. *Dallas Morning News* 12 March 1940; *Chronicle* 24 December 1926

2. *The Aegis* (Sam Houston High School) 23 January 1941

3. Gainesville Daily News 26 July 1915; Pugh; HC Deeds 332:254. 17 August 1914; HISD websites

4. Lewis, Kirk. *A Century of Learning:. Pasadena School History.1898- 1998*; *Post* 19 March 1899; HCCCM M073. 9 January 1905; HCCCM P229. 23 April 1910;

5. Lewis; County Reports; *Chronicle* 10 February 1918

6. Lewis

7. Lewis; Chronicle 9 December 2006;

8. USGS Map 1914; County Reports; *Post* 16 January 1910; *Post* 28 October 1922

9. *Post* 19 March 1899

10. City Directories; City Reports; Pugh; *Big Spring Daily Herald* 18 April 1943; http://www.pershingms.org/info/pershinghistory.html%20accessed%2019%20May%202006 ; *Chronicle* 19 February 1929; *Post* 4 September 1949; Harris County Auditor Report 1925; *Southwestern Times* 27 May 1948; Pershing JHS history. HMRC. HISD Collection; *Southwestern Times* 15 August 1949

11. *Standard History of Houston from a study of the original sources*, Edited by BH Carroll, 1912, H W Crew & Co.; *Houston: The Unknown City 1836-1940*, Marguerite Johnston, 1991, Texas A&M Press, College Station; *Buffalo Bayou: An Echo of Houston's Wilderness Beginnings*, Louis Aulbach, 2012, Author, Houston

12. City Report 1906-07; City Report 1907-08; City Report 1908-09

13. City Report 1906-07

14. City Report 1907-08; City Report, Medical Inspector, 1914-15

15. Houston City Schools Report 1909-10; Houston City Schools Report, Medical Inspector, 1910-11; Transaction of the Annual Meeting of American Academy of Ophthalmology and Otolaryngology. 1921.; Journal of the American medical Association, Vol. 62. 1914

16. Houston City Schools Report 195-16; Houston City Schools Report 1918-19

17. Houston city Schools report 1914-15

18. HCCCM R:100, 30 March 1914

19. https://virus.stanford.edu/uda/ accessed 17 November 2015;

20. http://www.flu.gov/pandemic/history/1918/your_state/southwest/texas/ accessed 17 November 2015

21. *City Report* 1918-19

22. *City Report* 1918-19; *Houston Chronicle* 10 Oct 1918; *Houston Chronicle* 11 October 1918; http://bayoucityhistory.blogspot.com/2006/10/houstons-pandemic-panic.html accessed 17 November 2015

23. *City Report* 1909-10

24. ibid

25. Anderson, Mossele Athelia. *A Survey of the Health Records and Their Implications in the Negro Elementary Schools of Houston, Texas*. M.S. thesis. Prairie View A&M College (1947)

26. *Chronicle* 23 Oct 1929

27. Anderson

28. ibid

29. *Chronicle* 23 October 1929;

30. *Press* 2 March 1925

31. *Post* 23 August 1933; *Chronicle* 24 January 1934; *Post* 25 January 1934; *Post* 18 March 1934; *Chronicle* 10 September 1934

32. Anderson

33. Worrall; http://www.cityofpineypoint.com/default.aspx?name=about.history accessed 13 November 2016; USGS map 1919; County Treasurer ledgers;

34. Worrall; Bryant; County Treasurer ledgers; County Reports; Beverly; US Census Harris County 1880; HCCCM N208. 10 October 1906; Johnson; *Chronicle* 6 March 1994; Author interview with Jewel Simpson Houston and Debra Sloan 5 January 2010; Rasmus, Walter, Sr.. *History of Piney Point*. C2000; *Post* 13 October 1977

35. County Reports; City Reports; City Directories; US Census Harris County 1910, 1920; *Chronicle* 15 January 1914; *Post* 3 November 1931; Author interview with owner of Bissonnet Kirby Animal Hospital. 2 January 2007; *Post* 14 July 1937

36. County Treasurer ledgers; County Reports; SD 25 ledger; City Directories

37. *Chronicle* 15 September 1959; Post 16 September 1959; *Press* 15 September 1959; *Chronicle* 16 September 1959; *Chronicle* 29 January 2001; Pugh; City Reports; City Directories

38. County Reports; HISD websites; City Directories; *GDN* 5 April 1922; *Abilene Reporter-News* 28 January 1947; HISD News Blog 5 March 2014 accessed 2 April 2017;

39. County Reports; *GDN* 16 April 1892; *GDN* 21 April 1892; *GDN* 28 April 1912

40. SD25 Minutes ledger; County reports; City Directories

41. City directories; *Post* 3 April 1916; US Census Harris Co 1920

42. City Directories

43. Hickman; Alyssa Honette; Johnston; Hack, Richard. *Hughes: The Private Diaries, Memos and Letters* (2007); Sargent, Peter E. . *A Handbook of American Private Schools, An Annual Survey*. 6th ed. (Boston: Atlantic Printing Co, 1920); City Directories; Obituary of James Perkins Richardson in *Phi Gamma Delta* Oct. 1921, no. 1, vol. 44; Whitney, Carrie Westlake. *Kansas City, Missouri: Its History and Its People, 1800-1908, vol. 3*. Chicago: S. J. Clarke Publishing Co, 1908

44. City Directories

45. https://tshaonline.org/handbook/online/articles/fre07 accessed 15 March 2016;

46. Samuel C. Red papers, Briscoe Center for American History, University of Texas, Austin; Samuel C. Red Texas Death Certificate; https://tshaonline.org/handbook/online/articles/fre09 accessed 15 March 2016

47. http://digitalcommons.library.tmc.edu/ebooks/6/ accessed 15 March 2016

48. Houston City Directory 1932; United States Census 1900, 1910, 1920, 1930 Harris County

49. http://www.queenofpeacecatholicschool.org/index.php/about-us/history accessed 03 April 2016

Schools R

1. Author interview with Don Ramsey June 2008; Cole; USGS Map 1914

2. City Directories; Digital Sanborn Maps 1924; HISD websites; HISD reports; http://www.biography.com/people/horace-mann-9397522 accessed 08 April 2017; *Post* 27 February 1925; *Press* 1 April 1925; *Press* 3 April 1925; *Chronicle* 7 April 1925; *Press* 5 July 1925; *Chronicle* 7 July 1925; Press 9 July 1925; Post 8 July 1925; Post 14 July 1925; Chronicle 14 July 1925

3. *Chronicle* 15 July 1928; *Chronicle* 13 October 1929; Pugh; Sloan, Anne. *Houston Heights*. Arcadia (Charleston, SC) 2009; Post 22 February 1932

4. Pugh; Reagan Statesman 5 April 1940; Sloan

5. https://en.wikipedia.org/wiki/Cotton_Bowl_(stadium) accessed 30 March 2016;

6. *Dallas Morning News* 27 December 1932

7. ibid

8. *DMN*

9. ibid

10. http://www.baltimoresun.com/sports/ravens/bal-sp.manning20oct20-story.html accessed 30 March 2016; https://en.wikipedia.org/wiki/Cecil_Isbell accessed 30 March 2016; *Milwaukee Journal* 24 June 1985

11. Klein ISD websites; City directories

12. HCCCM C381. 2 December 1875; HCCCM C393. 1 February 1876; HCCCM E372. 9 May 1887. County treasurer ledgers; HCCCM G498. 15 June 1897; Post 15 May 1897; Author conversation with jean West

13. Archdiocese records;

14. County Treasurer ledgers; USGS maps 1914; Kleiner, Diana. https://tshaonline.org/handbook/online/articles/hrrsm%20accessed%208%20April%202017 ; Bullard, Robert D. *Invisible Houston*. Texas A&M Press. 1987

15. City Reports; *Press* 26 April 1928; *Post* 7 September 1928; *Post* 9 September 1928; City directories; http://www.geocities.com/riveroaksalumni/our_teachers.html%20accessed%2027%20July%202009 ; *Post* 1 December 1929

16. HMRC Hugh Potter Scrapbook.

17. HISD websites; http://www.texasmonthly.com/the-daily-post/lanier-middle-school-name-change/ accessed 25 February 2017

18. HISD websites

19. City reports; City directories; Pugh; *Big Spring Herald* 29 May 1950

20. Crews; Heritage of North Harris County; HCCCM February 1878; HCCCM D488. 1 August 1882; HCCCM E98. 18 June 1884; County Treasurer ledgers; County Reports

21. County Treasurer ledgers; Cypress Historical Society archives

22. Houston City Schools Report, Superintendent's Message, 1914-15

23. Department of Education. National Center for Education Statistics. *Digest of Education Statistics 2004*.

24. Houston City Schools Report 1916-17

25. Houston City Schools Report 1919-20

26. County Reports; Pugh; *GDN* 9 August 1920; *Suburbanite* 8 March 1918; Young; City reports

27. Author conversation with Margaret Mallot Smith; USGS map 1914

28. *Houston Age* 1 October 1877; *GDN* 20 December 1883; *GDN* 16 July 1885; City Directories; Digital Sanborn Maps 1890, 1896, 1907; City Reports; *Post* 19 September 1897; Mackey, Thomas Clyde. *Red Lights Out: A Legal History of prostitution, Disorderly Houses and Vice Districts 1870-1917*. Thesis, Rice University. 1984

29. City Reports

30. City Reports; City Directories; Bracey Block Book 1919; De Leon; *Post* 24 September 1912; *Post* 24 May 1913

31. City Reports; De Leon; *Chronicle* 22 February 1930; HISD websites; *Post* 17 May 1913

32. Capps, Robert, Fix, Michael and Nwosu, Chiamaka. *A Profile of Immigrants in Houston; the Nation's Most Diverse Metropolitan Area*. A Report for the Migration Policy Institute. March 2015; Wintz, Carey and Bleeth, Howard. *Black Dixie: Afro-Texas History and Culture in Houston*., Texas A&M Press (College Station). 1992; DeLeon, Arnoldo. Ethnicity in the Sunbelt. Texas A&M Press (College Station) 2001

33. Houston City Schools Report 1904-05

34. Houston City Schools Report 1906-07, Superintendent's Report

35. Houston City Schools Report 1909-10

36. Houston City Schools Report 1908-09

37. Houston City Schools Report 1912-13; Houston City Schools Report 1914-15

38. Houston City Schools Report 1920-21

39. HISD websites; City directories; HISD Directory 1942-43; *Chronicle* 13 November 2024

Schools Sacred Heart – Southland

1. Archdiocese Archives; Author interview with Don Ramsey

2. Digital Sanborn Maps 1924; City Directories; Johnston; Archives of Dominican Sisters; *GDN* 5 June 1904; GDN 2 June 1909; Unattributed internal history; http://www.sacredhearthouston.org/index.cfm?load=page&page=208 accessed 9 April 2017

3. City Directories

4. County Treasurer ledgers

5. HCHC marker Salem Lutheran School. 2005; http://salemlutheran.com/about/history/ accessed 9 April 2017; Klein, John A. *To You... My Legacy of Love*. 1969

6. GDN 18 October 1888; City Directories; City Reports;

7. Scott; Henson

8. DPISD websites; City Directories

9. City Reports; City Directories; Digital Sanborn maps 1924; *Post* 22 September 1914; *Post* 29 September 1914

10. Vance, Mike. *Houston's Sporting Life*. Arcadia. 2012

11. *Chronicle* 6 March 2013; City Reports

12. County Treasurer ledgers; Original 1876 county schools ledger; Cartier & Hole; Olmstead, Frederick Law. *A Journey Through Texas*. Reprint. University of Texas. 1978

13. ibid

14. Gould, Lewis. *The Progressive Era*. https://tshaonline.org/handbook/online/articles/npp01 accessed 25 February 2016

15. *County Report* 1910

16. *County Report* 1914

17. *County Report* 1913

18. ibid

19. County Reports; Kleiner, Diana. Handbook https://tshaonline.org/handbook/online/articles/hrs18 accessed 14 April 2017

20. Smith, Margaret Mallot; USGS maps 1914

21. *Post* 15 May 1897; *Post* 19 March 1899; County Reports; HCCCM M270. 19 June 1905; HCCCM Q138. 12 January 1912; Burke, Ruth and Holbrook, Dan. *Seabrook*. Arcadia (Charleston, SC) 2010

22. *Telegraph* 12 May 1860; WPA Guide

23. Perkins; *Texas Standard* V29:4. November – December 1955; *Texas Standard* V31:1 January – February 1957: USGS maps 1915

24. Cy-Fair web history; Crews; Cypress Historical Society archives

25. Hudson, Theresa. *A History of Sheldon*; USGS maps 1914; County Treasurer ledgers; County Reports; Post 15 May 1897; Post 19 March 1899; HCCCM E282. 11 February 1886; HCCCM E371-2. 9 May 1887; HCCCM F436. 14 May 1892

26. County Treasurer ledgers; Scott; Post 5 September 1907

27. City Reports; City Directories; Digital Sanborn Maps 1896, 1907; Dealy & Baker's Guide to Houston 1895; *Post* 2 December 1893

28. *Post* 19 September 1897; City Reports; Fonville; *GDN* 16 December 1903; *GDN* 29 September 1904;

29. http://swamplot.com/sherman-elementary-is-toast/2012-01-05/ accessed 10 October 2016; HISD websites including http://es.houstonisd.org/shermanes/school%20history.htm accessed 4 March 2008

30. *City Report* 1908-09

31. *City Report* 1918-19

32. *City Report* 1919-20

33. City Report 1920-21

34. Hickman; City Directories

35. Meaux; County Reports; HAM N2N Mary Lea Layton Taylor; Montgomery, T.S.."Report of the Summary of the Humble Public Schools" in *Bulletin of the Sam Houston State Teachers College*. May, 1926; Telegraph & Texas Register 4 July 1850

36. City Reports; *Post* 19 September 1897

37. *Chronicle* 22 February 1941; USGS maps; *Chronicle* 16 March 2008

38. http://www.gccisd.net/ashbelsmith/index.htm%20accessed%2017%20May%202008 ; GCCISD websites; Wanda Mitchell, Baytown Museum

39. City Reports; City Directories; *Chronicle* undated clipping 1986; History of E.O. Smith Junior High, HISD Collection, HMRC; *Houston Defender* 4 May 1934; Johnson; Handbook at https://tshaonline.org/handbook/online/articles/fsm83%20accessed%2025%20June%202017 ; *Chronicle 1* September 2014; *Chronicle* 8 September 2014; *Chronicle 13* September 2014

40. USGS Maps 1921; County Reports; City Directories; http://www.riveroaksgardenclub.org/Forum.cfm accessed 9 October 2011; HCCCM 16 August 1927; Research of Carol Butler

41. County Treasurer ledgers

42. Texas School Journal, September 1888; County Treasurer ledgers

43. County Reports; City Directories; PISD History

44. http://texasalmanac.com/sites/default/files/images/CityPopHist%20web.pdf accessed 20 November 2015; http://www.loc.gov/teachers/classroommaterials/presentationsandactivities/presentations/timeline/riseind/city/ accessed 20 November 2015

45. Harris County Schools Report 1913

46. Harris County Schools Report 1913; Harris County Schools Report 1914

47. Report of Roy Glasgow, South Houston School, 8 January 1913

48. HCCCM E372. 9 May 1877; HCCCM F419. 13 Feb 1892

49. County Treasurer ledgers

50. Pugh; City Directories; Southland School files. HISD Collection. HMRC; *Post* 7 January 1915; *Post* 22 February 1919; *Post* 6 October 1924; *Press* 18 April 1927; *Southwest Citizen* 6 October 1949; Chronicle 17 November 1952; Bayou City History blog September 2010

51. City Directories; Southland School files. HISD Collection. HMRC

Schools Southmayd - Sykes

1. City Directories; GDN 2 October 1936; Virginia Hancock N2N HAM; HISD websites; Walls, Laura Dassow. *Henry David Thoreau: A Life*. University of Chicago Press. 2017

2. County Reports; Rylander; Fields, Ross C., Freeman, Martha Doty & Kotter, Steven M. *Inventory and Assessment of Cultural resources at Addicks Reservoir, Harris County, Texas.* For Prewitt and Associates Archaeologists. June 1983; Email exchange with Marie Neuman Gray July 2017

3. County Treasurer ledgers; Blackmon; Spring ISD https://www.springisd.org/site/default.aspx?PageType=3&DomainID=375&ModuleInstanceID=1584&ViewID=6446EE88-D30C-497E-9316-3F8874B3E108&RenderLoc=0&FlexDataID=673&PageID=1000 accessed 12 August 2017; *Post* 5 September 1907

4. PISD History

5. HCHC Historical Marker narrative 2003; HC 1876 original schools ledger; US Census Harris County 1880; HCCCM E98 18 June 1884; Country Treasurer ledgers; *Post* 15 May 1897; *Post* 19 March 1899; HCCCM L325 13 February 1904; HCCCM N 463-4 14 May 1907; HC Deeds 19 December 1907; HCCCM O 15-6 30 September 1907; *Heritage of North Harris County*

6. County Reports; Smith; Unattributed manuscript Spring ISD; USGS map 1920

7. Chapman. HBJ, 24 Dec 1999; HCHC Spring Branch marker narrative; Herridge, Karen. Spring Branch Heritage. 1998; HCCCM 21 May 1854; Hickman; HC 1876 original schools ledger; HCCCM D145 14 February 1878; county treasurer ledgers; *Post* 15 May 1897; *Post* 19 March 1899; HCCCM N463 14 May 1907; County Reports' Slaughter, George. *Spring Branch*. Arcadia 2011; *Post* 22 October 1922

8. HAM N2N interview with Jim and Della Mousner and Pauline Hallard 18 September 2006; http://springbranchbears.com/ accessed 28 August 2017; *Lubbock Evening Journal* 15 October 1953; *El Paso Herald Post* 15 October 1953; *Big Spring Daily Herald* 27 October 1953; http://freepages.history.rootsweb.ancestry.com/~patsyandrews/SPRING%20VALLEY%20HISTORY%202009.pdf accessed 23 September 2017

9. *City Report* 1910-11; *City Report* 1911-12

10. *City Report* 1910-11

11. *City Report* 1913-14

12. HC 1876 original schools ledger

13. City Directories; Digital Sanborn Maps 1924; *GDN* 10 June 1906; Johnston; Moore, James T.. *Acts of Faith: The Catholic Church in Texas 1900-1950*; https://www.st-agnes.org/page/about-st-agnes accessed 29 August 2017

14. Archdiocese records; *GDN* 27 June 1931

15. http://www.sccs1939.org/about-sccs/history-of-sccs/ accessed 03 April 2016; Archdiocese records

16. *Chronicle* 1939

17. http://www.sjs.org/Page/About/History accessed 9 September 2016;

18. Ivins, Molly. *Molly Ivins Can't Say That, Can She?* Vintage. 1991.

19. McHugh; Archdiocese records; City Directories; Digital Sanborn Maps 1890, 1896, 1907, 1924; Author interviews with parishioners at Our Lady of Guadalupe

20. Archdiocese records

21. Archdiocese records; City Directories

22. Archdiocese records

23. McHugh; Archdiocese records; City directories; Sorelle; HCHC marker narrative St. Nicholas Catholic Church

24. McHugh; Archdiocese records; City Directories; Digital Sanborn Maps 1890, 1896, 1907, 1924

25. City Directories

26. Archdiocese records; http://stpacs.org/ accessed 30 August 2017

27. Archdiocese records

28. http://www.stroselima.org/school/history.html accessed 03 April 2016; Archdiocese records

29. Archdiocese records

30. McHugh; Archdiocese records; https://sttheresaschool.cc/about-our-school accessed 30 August 2017

31. http://sths.org accessed 30 August 2017; HCHC St. Thomas High School marker narrative; WPA Guide; City Directories; Digital Sanborn Maps 1907, 1924; *Chronicle* 3 August 1903;

32. WPA Guide; HCHC narrative; HAM N2N Lou Daleo;

33. WPA Guide; Archdiocese records; Lavender; City Directories; McHugh; Turner, Allen http://www.houstonchronicle.com/local/history/article/Houston-s-wild-days-in-the-1800s-birthed-churches-7723088.php%20accessed%201%20September%202017 ; *Telegraph* 21 December 1846; *Telegraph* 10 March 1856

34. McHugh; Archdiocese records; https://saintvincentschool.org/history accessed 30 August 2017

35. SD 25 minutes book; City reports; *GDN* 16 July 1896; *GDN* 14 August 1898; *GDN* 2 April 1904; *GDN* 18 September 1904

36. United States census. Harris County 1880, 1900; HCCCM E213. 9 June 1885; HCCCM E372. 9 May 1887; Post 15 May 1897; *The Heritage of North Harris County*. North Harris County Branch American Association of University Women. 1977;

37. HISD websites; City reports; City directories; *Post* 14 April 1915; *Post* 15 April 1915; *Post* 21 August 1915; *Post* 16 September 1915; *Chronicle* 9 December 1928; HC Auditor's report 1923

38. *City Report* 1909-10

39. *City Report* 1910-11

40. *City Report* 1918-19

41. ibid

42. Winegarten

43. *City Report* 1918-19

44. ibid

45. *Post* 8 April 1919; *Post* 16 April 1919; *Post* 26 April 1919; *Post* 29 April 1919

46. *City Report* 1919-20

47. *Chronicle* 14 June 1932; *Chronicle* 1May 1934; *Chronicle* 12 February 1935; *Chronicle* 13 February 1935; *Post* 14 September 1934; *Post* 8 February 1935; *Post* 12 February 1935; *Press* 14 September 1934; *Press* 17 January 1935; *Press* 12 February 1935

48. *Post* 5 February 1919; Texas Constitution, Section 67, Article XVI; Stevens, Traxel. *Vision, Vigilance and Victory*. Teacher Retirement System (Austin) 1986; https://tshaonline.org/handbook/online/articles/met01 accessed 19 February 2016

49. Hickman; *Post* 13 September 1932

50. Rylander; USGS Maps 1914; HCHC Katy Elementary marker narrative

51. Bryant; Whidby, Tina. *A Study of Sunnyside School, Its Pupils and Community*. Houston Negro College. 1938;

52. County reports; US Post Office records; City Reports; Suburbanite 8 March 1918; Author visits

53. City Directories

54. City Directories; HCCCM E98. 18 June 1884; HCCCM F285. 13-14 May 1891; HCCCM F436. 14 May 1892; County Treasure ledgers; Post 15 May 1897; Post 19 March 1899; County reports; HC Deeds 311:34. 27 July 1913; City Reports; Pugh

55. City Directories; Pugh; http://es.houstonisd.org/suttones/Sutton/History.htm%20accessed%2013%20March%202017 ;

Schools T - V

1. City reports; City Directories; Johnson; *GDN* 27 September 1884; *Post* 19 September 1897; Digital Sanborn Maps 1896, 1907; Pugh; HAM N2N interview with John Aden 2007

2. http://www.usarmyjrotc.com/jrotc-history accessed 2 March 2016; http://www.cadetcommand.army.mil/history.aspx accessed 2 March 2016; Lord, Gary. *Images of Its Past*. Harmony House (Northfield, VT) 1995

3. *City Report* 1912-13

4. ibid

5. Hickman; Press 21 April 1936

6. HMRC Vertical files; HCCCM O548 16 April 1909; County reports; Handbook online https://tshaonline.org/handbook/online/articles/hgt06 accessed 4 September 2017; Stanfield, Staci. Tomball ISD; Daniels

7. Standfield

8. SD 25 minutes ledger; County Reports; City Reports; City Directories; Pugh

9. SD 25 minutes ledger; City reports; City Directories; Digital Sanborn Maps; Pugh

10. *Post* 14 December 1913; *City Report* 1913-14

11. ibid

12. *City Report* 1913-14

13. City Directories; Chronicle obituaries various; http://www.chron.com/news/article/HISD-will-consolidate-three-schools-1494528.php%20accessed%204%20September%202017 ; HISD Directory 1942-43; https://tshaonline.org/handbook/online/articles/fcoau accessed 4 September 2017

14. Author interview with Ruth Taube Stoerkel, Trinity Lutheran historian; City directories; Digital Sanborn maps 1924

15. Heritage of North Harris County; Klein

16. County Treasurer ledgers

17. ibid

18. Sr. Agatha; City Reports; *Suburbanite* 18 August 1906; Bryant; HISD Directory 1942-43

19. Cole; Scott

20. HC 1876 original schools ledger; County Treasurer ledgers

21. HC 1876 original schools ledger; HCCCM E213 9 June 1885; County Treasurer ledgers

22. County Treasurer ledgers

23. HC 1876 original school ledger; US Census 1880 Harris County

Schools Waller - Whittier

1. HCCCM G151 13 August 1894; County Treasurer ledgers; Post 15 May 1897; Post 19 march 1899; County reports; HCCCM Q290 26 August 1912; A History of Waller Texas. Burman. 1997

2. Anderson, James D.. The Education of Blacks in the South, 1860-1935. University of North Carolina Press (Chapel Hill) 1988; US Census various 1900, 1910

3. City reports; City directories; Digital Sanborn maps 1896, 1907; Bryant; *Chronicle* 25 May 1913; Bracey Block Book 1919

4. City Reports; Young, Bryant; *Post* 19 September 1897; Sorrelle; Johnson; *GDN* 3 June 1905; Digital Sanborn maps 1907; Bracey

5. City reports; *Chronicle* 1 May 1921; *Informer* 26 January 1924

6. *Informer* 7 November 1925; Bryant; *Informer* 22 December 1923; Booker T. Washington Eagle Yearbook 1928; Author interview with Thelma Scott Bryant; Johnson; Chronicle 13 September 2007

7. City Reports; United States Census Harris County 1900;

8. https://tshaonline.org/handbook/online/articles/kdi01 accessed on 03 January 2016; *Houston City Schools Report* 1890-91

9. TSHA Handbook online; http://www.britannica.com/topic/Smith-Hughes-Act accessed 03 January 2016

10. *City Report* 1907-08

11. Anderson, James D.. *The Education of Blacks in the South, 1860-1935*. University of North Carolina Press (Chapel Hill) 1988; Du Bois, W.E.B.. *The Souls of Black Folk*. A.C. McClurg & Co. (Chicago) 1903; *City Report* 1907-08

12. City Report 1909-10

13. *City Report* 1916-17

14. *City Report* 1916-17

15. *City Report* 1916-17

16. Smith Hughes Act TSHA Handbook Online

17. *City Report* 1919-20

18. ibid

19. *Telegraph* 26 September 1872; City Reports; Bryant; *GDN* 27 September 1884; *Post* 19 September 1897; Digital Sanborn Maps 1907, 1924

20. Texas Historical Marker. St. Paul AME Church; Bryant; Chronicle 1986 clipping; US Census Harris County 1900; Gonzales, JR. Chronicle http://www.houstonchronicle.com/local/bayou-city-history/article/When-school-first-became-cool-Air-conditioning-11740303.php&cmpid=twitter-premium Accessed 9 August 2017

21. City Directories; Digital Sanborn Maps 1924; *Post* 7 February 1926; *Post* 9 February 1926; City Reports; Pugh; http://blogs.houstonisd.org/news/2016/10/06/high-school-for-law-enforcement-and-criminal-justice-celebrates-groundbreaking-for-new-campus/ accessed 12 September 2017;

22. City directories; County Treasurer ledgers

23. HC 1876 original schools ledger; http://www.cityofwebster.com/index.aspx?NID=2 accessed 17 April 2009; https://tshaonline.org/handbook/online/articles/eqg07 accessed 12 September 2017; HCCCM E98 18 June 1884; County Treasurer ledgers; HCCCM E371 9 May 1887; HCCCM E625 15 May 1889; HCCCM G454 12 May 1896; HCCCM H028 19 November 1896; *Post* 15 May 1897; *Post* 19 March 1899; *GDN* 21 September 1904; County reports; *Post* 13 December 1923; *Post* 23 April 1924; *Post* 4 May 1924; *Post* 23 April 1924; HC Auditor's report 1923

24. County reports; Post 5 September 1907

25. Bush, David & Parsons, Jim. *Houston Deco*. UT Press; Maple, Amber. Clear Creek ISD. Memories of Ralph Parr & Darwin L. Gilmore; http://clearview.ccisd.net/ accessed 12 September 2017; *Post* 13 December 1923;

26. HISD websites

27. City Directories; City reports; Digital Sanborn maps 1924; Post 15 May 1904; GDN 23 August 1914;

28. HC Auditor's Reports 1925; *Chronicle* 19 February 1929; City Reports; Author interview with Sandy Cole Reiser October 2006; *Post* 4 September 1949; http://www.houstonpress.com/news/what-went-wrong-at-the-rice-school-6570776 accessed 17 September 2017

29. Chisholm, Hugh. *Jean Frederic Oberlin*. Encyclopedia Britannica. Cambridge University Press 1911; http://www.nycgovparks.org/parks/poppenhusen-park/monuments/1208 accessed 5 March 2016; http://www.stlouiswalkoffame.org/inductees/susan-blow.html accessed 5 March 2016; Eby

30. *Post* 10 January 1899

31. Kirkland; Chapman; *Post* 26 December 1895; *Post* columns September – November 1902, various; *Post* 12 October 1902

32. http://path.coe.uh.edu/seminar2002/week1/tour.html   accessed 5 March 2016; *Informer* 25 August 1923

33. *City Report* 1906-07

34. *City Report* 1911-12; *City Report* 1912-13; *City Report* 1915-16

35. City Report 1916-17; Chapman;

36. Stone, Irene Glass. *The Influence of Kindergarten Experience on Selected Pupils at Blackshear School, Houston, Texas, September, 1950 to February, 1953*. M.S. thesis, Drake University, 1953

37. HC 1876 original schools ledger; HCCCM D360 18 November 1881; HCCCM E98 18 June 1884; HCCCM E625 15 May 1889; County Treasurer ledgers; *Post* 15 May 1897; *Post* 19 March 1899; County reports; Author correspondence with Mark McKee; *Heritage of North Harris County*

38. Winegarten, Ruthe and Schechter, Cathy. *Deep in the Heart: The Lives and Legends of Texas Jews*. Eakin Press. 1990; *Post* 3 August 1905

39. City directories; *Chronicle* 24 October 2007; City reports; *Press* 26 April 1928; *Post* 15 July 1928; *Chronicle* 11 September 1928; Pugh; Beverly, Trevia. Harris County Cemeteries

40. *Informer* 7 November 1925; Bryant;

41. City Reports; Bryant; *Informer* 20 October 1945; *Chronicle* 25 March 1997; Steptoe

42. Informer 20 October 1945; Bryant; HMRC RG D072; Koush, Ben http://www.houstonmod.org   accessed 19 September 2017; Hurd, Michael. *Thursday Night Lights*. University of Texas Press. 2019; Texas State Historical Marker files

43. Koush; *Chronicle* 11 December 2014; HISD websites

44. *Houston City Directory* 1867; *Houston Telegraph* 9 September 1871;

45. *City Report* 1904-05

46. *City Report* 1909-1910

47. *City Report* 1914-15

48. *City Report* 1917-18. Report of Supervisor of Music

49. https://tshaonline.org/handbook/online/articles/fal56 accessed 15 February 2016; *Post* 30 April 1921

50. *Post* 31 July 1919; *Post* 13 October 1919; *Post* 5 January 1923; *Post* 14 September 1923; *Post* 31 August 1922; *Post* 29 October 1924; United States Census Harris County 1930, 1940; Texas Death Index

51. HC 1876 original schools ledger; https://www.youtube.com/watch?v=7jnSRrYFMfo accessed 22 September 2017; Hickman; *Post* 15 May 1897; *Post* 19 March 1899; US Census Harris County 1880; HC-CCM E98 18 June 1884; County Treasurer ledgers

52. Cole; HC 1876 schools ledger; United States Census Harris County 1880; HCCCM F285. 14 May 1891

53. Jacinto City history; City directories

Schools Willow - Z

1. US Census Harris County 1880; Upchurch; *Heritage of North Harris County*; Crosby Historical Society archives; County reports; County Treasurer ledgers; Hickman; HC 1876 original schools ledgers; *Post* 15 May 1897; *Post* 19 March 1899; HCCCM F436 14 May 1892

2. City Directories; Digital Sanborn Maps 1924; City reports; Pugh

3. http://www.archive.org/stream/teachingthroughu00courrich/teachingthroughu00courrich_djvu.txt accessed 12 February 2016; http://onlinebooks.library.upenn.edu/webbin/book/lookupname?key=Strayer%2c%20George%20D%2e%20%28George%20Drayton%29%2c%201876%2d1962 accessed 12 February 2016

4. Strayer, G.D., Englehart, N.L.. *Standards for High School Buildings*. Teachers College, Columbia University (New York) 1924.; Strayer, G.D., Englehart, N.L.. *Standards for Elementary School Buildings*. Teachers College, Columbia University (New York) 1923

5. HISD Report 1924-30; Bryant

6. *City Report* 1910-11

7. Sorelle; *City Reports*

8. City Reports; *Texas Almanac: City Population History from 1850–2000*, https://texasalmanac.com/sites/default/files/images/CityPopHist%20web.pdf accessed September 15, 2016

9. Young

10. *Press* 21, 27, 29 and 30 October 1925; *City Report* 1924-30

11. ibid

12. Sorelle; Young; *Houston Informer* 15 March 1924

13. *Freeman* 31 October 1925

14. *City Report* 1924-30

15. Bryant; *City Report* 1924-30; Young

16. County Reports

17. Cypress Historical Society archives; Hickman; County Treasurer ledgers; Texas Historical Marker. St. John Lutheran Church. 2002

18. HCCCM E283. 11 February 1886; HCCCM E587. 12 February 1889;

19. Cypress Historical Society archives; Cy-Fair ISD websites; HCCCM F436. 14 May 1892; HC Deeds 53:28. 25 August 1890; Labay; HC Deeds 921:161. 6 October 1900; HC Deeds 99:256. 22 July 1897; County Treasurer ledgers; United States Census Harris County 1880; HCCCM E98. 18 June 1884

20. Sullivan; Crews; HC Deeds 3794:239. 20 August 1959

21. City Directories; Digital Sanborn Maps 1924; Bryant; HISD Directory 1942-43, 1948-49; *Post* 7 October 1949

22. Meaux; USGS maps 1914; County reports; Humble Museum; Montgomery; *GDN* 14 May 1911

23. County Treasurer ledgers; HCCCM G225. 9 April 1895; HCCCM G454. 12 May 1896; HCCCM G498. 15 June 1896; *Post* 15 May 1897; *Post* 19 March 1899; County Reports; Author conversation with Trevia Wooster Beverly 1 July 2009; Texas Historical Marker. Wooster Common School No. 38 1990; *Chronicle* 22 April 1988; Letter of Quincy A. Wooster 1894

24. Beverly; Historical marker file

25. Spring ISD websites

26. City Reports; Bryant; *Chronicle* 22 October 1925; *Informer* 24 October 1925; *Informer* 31 October 1925; *Post* 7 February 1926; *Post* 9 February 1926;

27. Bryant; Young; HMRC Yates Collection; HMRC MSS 397

28. https://asalh100.org/origins-of-black-history-month/ accessed 15 March 2016

29. *Teacher Recalls First Study of Negro History in Texas. Houston Informer*. Date unknown.; asalh;

30. *Texas Standard* Vol. 22, No. 3, May-June 1948; *Texas Standard* Vol. 23, No. 1 January-February 1949

31. King, Judy. Except the Lord Build. 1989; US Census Harris County 1870, 1880; Lavender; Hickman; City directories

32. ibid

33. Lavender; City directories; Johnston

34. *Post* 15 May 1897; *Post* 19 March 1899; US Census Harris County 1910;

A Few Final Stories

1. Rules and Recommendations of the Public Schools of the City of Houston 1877. James T D Wilson, mayor

2. *Houston City Schools Report* 1904-05, 1905-06, 1907-08

3. *City Report* 1906-07

4. *City Report* 1907-08

5. *City Report* 1909-10

6. *City Report* 1909-10

7. *City Report* 1910-11

8. *City Report* 1911-12

9. *City Report* 1911-12, 1913-14

10. *Houston Post* 3 April 1914; *City Report* 1913-14

11. *City Report* 1913-14

12. *City Report* 1919-20

13. *City Report* 1916-17; *Houston Post* 13 September 1932

14. *Post* 6 December 1924

15. *City Report* 1916-17

16. *Chronicle* 12 March 1928; *Press* 12 March 1928; Olsen, Margaret N. SHQ Vol 110:4. October 2006. *Teaching Americanism: Ray K. Daily and the Persistence of Conservatism in Houston School Policy, 1943-1952*.; *Press* 14 March 1928; HMRC Digital Archives. Interview with Dr. Ray K. Daily by Don Carleton. 10 December 1974

17. Olsen; Abram, Lynwood from Weiner, Hollace Ave and Roseman, Kenneth, Ed.. *Lone Stars of David: The Jews of Texas*. UPNE. 2007

18. Olsen; Abram; Daily

19. ibid

Index

A

Adams, *84*
Addicks, *27*
Albert, Kate, *48*
Aldine, *40–41, 196, 201*
Alessandro, *200*
Alexander, *54, 99*
Alief, *101*
Allen, *6, 24–25, 105, 108, 195, 198*
Allen, Charlotte, *24–25, 195*
Alvarado, *71*
Ammerman, *39–40*
Anderson, *28, 36, 104, 107, 224–225*
Andrews, *79*
Archer, *120*
Armstrong, *4, 225*
Asbell, *116*
Ashford, *133*
Atherton, *24–25, 182*
Atwood, *110*
Austin, *44, 48, 55, 57, 61, 184, 224*

B

Baker, *78, 111, 226*
Banks, Nathaniel P., *3*
Barnett, *110, 124*
Barrett, *27*
Bass, *110*
Bastian, *124*
Bay View, *34*
Baytown, *24, 36, 46, 130, 160, 209–210*
Beauchamp Springs, *44, 85*
Bell, Archie, *25, 197*
Bell, Isabella, *73*
Bellaire, *36, 50, 99, 105*
Bender, *40, 79*
Benitia, *93*
Berry, *1, 68*
Beth Yeshurun, *47*
Beuchley, *4*
Beyonce, *25*
Big Cypress, *207*
Blackshear, *56*
Blaffer, *28, 159*
Blalock, *202*
Bochow, *110*
Bolinger, *68*
Bonner, *69*
Booker, *4, 6, 47, 76, 107, 169, 181,*

i

187–188
Boone, *53*
Bowers, *27*
Boyd, *68*
Brackenridge, *42, 114*
Bradford, *4*
Bradley, *110*
Braun, *178*
Brays Bayou, *52, 114, 118, 180*
Brinkley, *187*
Brock, *188*
Brown, Jewel, *211*
Browne, *73–74*
Browning, *209*
Bruce, *76*
Brunner, *67, 69, 115*
Bryant, *207, 225*
Burbank, *20*
Burke, *36*
Burnett, *64*
Burrus, *14*
Bush, *159*

C

Cage, *30, 78, 83*
Calabar, *6*
Campbell, Ben, *83*
Campbell, Sybil, *10, 103*
Cane Island, *26–27*
Capshaw, *79*
Cascara, *136–137*
Castillo, *65*
Catchings, *185*
Cato, *36*

Cedar Bayou, *141*
Central High School, *16, 186, 200*
Chadwick, *110*
Chaneyville, *153, 189, 192*
Charlton, *84*
Chidsey, *159*
Christen, *87*
Clark, *111, 123, 149, 214*
Clayton, *14, 23, 28*
Clayton, Nicholas J., *14*
Cleveland, *111*
Cline, *124*
Clinton, *88*
Cobb, *25–26, 197*
Cobb, Arnett, *25, 197*
Cole, *19*
Colored High School, *7, 24, 76, 129, 182–184, 188*
Compton, *135*
Convent of the Good Shepherd, *159*
Cook, *184*
Cooley, *29, 131, 137*
Crapper, *54*
Crawford, *13, 59, 73, 76, 137*
Crews, *135*
Crockett, *69, 185–186*
Cronkite, *203*
Crosby, *27, 32, 64, 114, 128, 135, 153, 202, 207, 209*
Cunningham, *214*
Cushman, *110*
Cy-Fair, *208*
Cypress, *31, 42, 47, 72, 87–88, 90, 121, 132–133, 135, 150, 153, 207–210*

D

Daggett, *27*
Daily, Ray K., *220*
Davis, Eva Margaret, *119*
Davis, Fannie, *209*
Davis, Jeff, *72*
Davis, W. B., *188*
Dawson-Lunnon, *78*
Deady, *92*
DePelchin, *44*
DeWalt, *33–34*
DeZavala, *69, 125*
Dickey, George E., *22*
Dishman, *26*
Dodson, *56, 187*
Dominican, *113, 128, 157–158, 161*
Douglass, *56, 185, 213*
Dow, *32, 44, 55, 181, 185, 200*
Du Bois, *6, 225*
DuBois, W.E.B., *6*
Dudley, *1*
Duggan, *116*
Dullahan, *92*
Dunbar, *184*
Dunman, *15*
Durkee, *1*
Dwyer, *84*
Dyersdale, *139*

E

East Houston, *79*
Eckhardt, *90*
Edison, *64, 96*
Eichler, *74*
Elena, *202*
Ellerbee, *36, 42*
Elmore, *135*
Elsbury, *110*
Elysian, *23*
Emancipation Park, *56*
Englehart, *204, 206*
Ewell, *6*
Ewing, *53, 77, 82–84*

F

Fannin, *55, 76, 173*
Farmer, *68, 132, 152*
Feldman, *170*
Fidelity, *78*
Fifth Ward School, *22*
Figueroa, *56*
Finck, *28*
Finn, *36*
Fisk, *5–6*
Flake, *110, 224*
Fleet, *110*
Flickwir, *50*
Forshey, *48, 110*
Forshey, *48, 110*

Foxall, *211*
Foxworth, *36*
Fraga, Felix, *11*
Franklin, *13, 63–64, 73*
Franzheim, *36*
Freedmen, *3–4, 6, 27, 43, 224–225*
Fretz, *38–39*
Fullerton, *56, 62*

G

Gaines, *197*
Gallegos, *71*
Galveston, *3, 13, 27, 160, 167, 224*
Gammage, *71*
Gannon, *157*
Gardentown, *190*
Gentry, *110*
Glasgow, *145*
Glen Cove, *146*
Glover, *36*
Gonzo247, *56*
Goose Creek, *64*
Gorgeous George, *71*
Grady, *109*
Grant, *4, 167*
Gregg, *59, 69*
Gregory Institute, *4*
Gribble, *110*
Grimes, *121*

H

Hambleton, *79*
Hamilton, *22, 63, 79, 123–124*
Hampton, *4, 6, 225*
Hanna, *97, 132*
Hanner, *105*
Harbor, *1, 39, 109, 118, 209*
Hardy, H.C., *6*
Hargis, *214*
Harper, *25, 76, 138, 141*
Harris, *4, 7, 9, 26–27, 30, 45, 50–52,
   54–55, 62, 66, 68, 79, 88, 91–92, 100,
   106–107, 110, 112, 114, 118, 129, 132,
   135, 137–139, 141, 144–146, 149–152,
   154, 164–165, 169, 181, 189, 197, 205,
   224, 227*
Harrisburg, *26, 51, 53, 62, 71, 92, 115,
   131–132, 136, 148, 153*
Hart, *92*
Hartman, *16, 36*
Hawthorne, *28, 55, 188, 195, 205*
Heyer, *77*
Hidalgo Escuela Mexicana, *33*
Higginbotham, *16*
Higgins, *124*
Higgs, *195*
Hillebrandt, *20–21, 153*
Hiriart, *17*
Hodges, *116*
Hofheinz, *42*
Hogg, *42, 44, 69, 111, 119, 142, 221*
Hohl, *1, 153*
Holcombe, *148, 220*
Holden, *185*
Holland, *65, 68, 212*

Holley, *176–177*
Hollywood, *141, 184*
Holmes, *36, 168*
Hopkins, *197*
Horn, *1–2, 7–8, 19, 37, 61, 66–67, 76, 84, 98, 102, 122, 124, 126–127, 157, 164–166, 184, 195, 205, 217*
Howard University, *6*
Howard, Oliver O., *6*
Hufsmith, *164*
Hughes, Howard, *74, 111, 131*
Humble, *15, 28, 46, 87, 138–139, 153, 191, 193, 209*
Humble Oil, *28*
Hunter, *28*
Hurley, *110*
Hutcheson, *104–105, 219*
Hutchins, *110*
Hutchinson, *110*

I

Ideson, *44–45*
Immaculate Conception, *12*
Immaculate Heart of Mary, *12*
Immanuel Lutheran, *12, 226*
Incarnate Word, *13–14, 158, 160–162, 164, 226*
Independence Heights, *14, 79, 169, 206*
Indian Hill, *15*
Industrial ES, *15*
Irvington, *15, 51*
Isaacks, *15*
Isbell, *116–117*
Issac, *15, 118*

Ivins, *160*

J

Jacinto City, *15*
Jackson, *15–16, 19*
Jacquet, Illinois, *25*
Jaeger, *202*
Jamison, *180*
Janowski, *20, 153, 206*
Jefferson, *20–21*
Jensen, *123*
Jeppesen, *38–39, 72*
Johnson, Charles E., *41*
Johnson, Conrad, *25, 211*
Johnston, *21–22, 227*
Jones, Anson, *11, 23*
Jones, J. Will, *24*
Junker, *25*

K

Kaiser, *26*
Kamrath, *198*
Kashmere Gardens, *26*
Katy, *26–27, 148, 168*
Keaney, *129*
Keeton, *61–63*
Kellum, *80*
Kelly, *80*
Kenney, *91*

Kenning, *27*
Kent, *148, 225*
Kettleson, *40*
Kidd, *214*
Kiddoo, *27–28*
King, Lesta, *30*
Kingsley, *28*
Kinkaid, *28–29, 145, 159*
Kirby, *30, 142*
Kirksey, *110*
Kleb, *90*
Kleiber, *124*
Klein, *30–31, 90, 154, 179*
Kobs, *121*
Kohrmann, *32*
Kohrville, *31–32*
Kolb, *155*
Kolbe, *31*
Kolter, *108*
Kothman, *32*
Krahl, *32*
Krenek, *32*
Krichamer, *116*
Kruse, *32*

Lantrip, *15, 43–44, 75*
Laws, *45, 122, 187, 189*
Lee, *4, 36, 40, 45–46*
Lewis, *41, 227*
Lily White, *46–47*
Link, *74–75*
Little White Oak, *20*
Little York, *47*
Lockett, *47*
Lockhart, *47*
Lomax, *47–48*
Longfellow, *32, 48–51, 55*
Looscan, *15, 51, 73*
Looscan, *15, 51, 73*
Love, William G., *52*
Lowell Street, *52*
Lubbock, *44, 53, 56, 75, 124*
Luckie, *56–57, 76*
Lutheran, *12, 57, 70, 129, 159, 161, 178–179, 208, 226*
Lynchburg, *57–58, 64, 209*

M

MacGregor, *59–60, 148*
Magnolia City, *63*
Magnolia Park, *12, 33, 64*
Male and Female Select, *64*
Manayunk, *64*
Mancuso, *71*
Mann, Horace, *64*
Mannazank, *64*
Market House, *2, 23, 64*
Marrs, *41, 65*
Marshall, *7, 65, 225*

L

La Porte, *33–35, 47–48, 78, 160*
Laird, *36*
Lamar, *36–37, 39–40, 48, 56, 74, 115*
Lampson, *167*
Lane, *40*
Langford, *41*
Langston, *41–42, 106*
Lanier, *16, 42–43, 120*

vi

Marshall, Thurgood, *7*
Martin, W.H., *9*
Masonic Hall, *68*
Maxey, *40*
McCarter, *168*
McClanahan, *116*
McDavid, *197*
McDonald, *68*
McGee, *68*
McGhee, *68–69*
McGowen, *69*
McKinney, *75, 179*
McReynolds, *65*
Meadowbrook, *69*
Memorial, *38, 69, 156, 161–162*
Mendenhall, *36*
Merkel, *44, 69*
Mexican School, *125*
Meyerland, *22, 72*
Mico, *6*
Middle Bayou, *70*
Milam, *71, 192*
Milby, *71–72*
Miller, *22, 72, 110, 209, 211*
Miller, Doris, *209*
Mills, *72, 173*
Milo, *73*
Minnetex, *73*
Mistrot, *62, 111*
Mitchell, *110*
Montgomery, James Arlie, *108*
Montrose, *36, 42–43, 74–77*
Moon, *195*
Mooney, *78*
Moonshine Hill, *78, 209*
Moore, *68, 110*
Moreland, *22*
Morgan, *33, 78*

Morris, *42, 73, 110*
Moses, *183*
Mother M. Gabriel, *13*
Mount Gillian, *78*
Mount Houston, *79*
Mount Pleasant, *79*
Mt. Pilgrim, *79*
Munger, *97*
Murphy, *214*
Myers, *168*
Mykawa, *73, 85–86*

N

Namendorf, *49*
Narrow Gauge, *26, 87*
Navarro, *16*
Neidorff, *87*
Nelms, *119*
Neville, *28*
Newman, *88, 153, 169–170*
Niday, *136*
Noble, Z.M., *80–81*
Nold, *160*
Norsworthy, *88*
North Houston, *47, 89*
Northside, *20, 45–46, 65, 136*
Novitiate, *89*
Nutini, *110*

O

Oak Addition, *89*
Oak Forest, *90*
Oak Grove, *90*
Oak Lawn, *92*
Oakwood, *92*
Oates, *92–93*
Oberholtzer, *148*
Oldham, *110*
Ollie Lorehn, *129*
Orgeron, *108*
Orman, *98–99*
Our Lady of Guadalupe School, *12, 93–94*
Our Lady of Perpetual Help, *94*
Our Mother of Mercy, *95*
Owens, *197*

P

Palmer, *56, 84*
Park J H S, *64, 96*
Park Place, *96, 159*
Parker, *4*
Pasadena, *19, 32, 97–98, 143, 153–154, 161, 227*
Pastoriza, *84*
Patillo, *23*
Patterson, *211–212*
Pauline Gray, *41*
Payne, *36, 38–39, 46*
Peine, *102*

Pemberton, *103*
Penn, *64, 98*
Penn City, *98*
Pereir, *110*
Perry, *98*
Pershing, *98–99, 193*
Pierce, *50, 129, 138, 146, 183*
Piney Point, *29, 68, 106*
Pitchman, *107*
Pittschumann, *208*
Platte, *107, 153*
Pleasant Ark, *108*
Pleasant Grove, *87*
Pleasant Hill, *108*
Poe, *108–109*
Port Houston, *109, 152*
Post Oak, *109, 153*
Potter, *119*
Prairie Hill, *110*
Prairie View, *4, 6*
Pratt, *110*
Prentiss, *36*
Prewett, *110*
Priday, *110*
Prince, A.B., *34*
Prosso, *111*
Pugh, *62, 132–133, 144–145, 227*
Punchard, *27*

Q

Quan, *71*
Queen of Peace, *113*

R

Ralston, *100*
Ramier, *114*
Ramsey, *114*
Rasmus, Adam, *107*
Rather, Dan, *52*
Ray, *41, 220*
Reagan, *101, 114–116*
Recreation Acres, *117*
Red Bluff, *118*
Red, S.C., *82, 112*
Reddish, *48*
Reid, *72*
Reiser, Sandy, *226*
Resurrection, *118*
Rice, Ella, *74*
Rice, Horace Baldwin, *84*
Riceville, *118*
Richardson, *111, 206, 211*
River Oaks, *118–119, 159*
Roberts, *69, 119–120*
Robinson, *80, 132*
Roche, *162*
Rogers, *120*
Rone, *164*
Roosevelt, *60, 120*
Rose Hill, *73, 121, 129, 152*
Roseboom, *110*
Rosedale, *59, 160, 170*
Ross, *123*
Roth, *123*
Rowland, *36*
Rowlett, *48*
Rowls, *89*
Runge, *194*

Rural High School, *31, 123*
Rusk, *10, 123–126*
Russell, *27*
Ryan, *127*

S

Sacred Heart, *128–129*
Saengerbund, *129*
Salem, *129*
Sam Houston, *81, 96, 116–117, 173, 201*
Sample, *25, 197*
San Esteban, *162*
San Felipe, *26, 68, 106, 129*
San Jacinto, *130–132*
Sanderson, *129*
Sator, *85*
Satsuma, *133*
Schlipf, *26*
Schneider, *191*
Scholibo, *84*
Schroeder, *155*
Schultz, *134*
Seabrook, *118, 134, 153, 191*
Second Ward, *4, 41, 53, 134–135*
Settegast, *38, 135*
Settlement House, *10, 124*
Sewell, *135*
Sharp, *15, 74, 111, 119*
Sheldon, *135*
Shepler, *74*
Sherman, *39, 44, 55, 65, 69, 125, 136–137, 200*
Shiloh, *138*
Shirar, *138*

Shofstal, *65*
Shoylin, *110*
Shumate, *120, 193*
Sibley, *59*
Sikes, *138*
Sills, *26*
Simmons, *110*
Singleton, *109, 138–139*
Sister Mary Paul, *13, 226*
Sisters of Divine Providence, *12, 161*
Sisters of Divine Providence, *12, 161*
Sisters of the Incarnate Word and Blessed Sacrament, *13, 94, 158, 162*
Sixth Ward, *139, 160, 162, 187*
Slataper, *102*
Smiley, *23, 132, 139–140, 149*
Smith, Ashbel, *112*
Smith, E. O., *141–142, 187, 197, 218*
Smith, Jaclyn, *36*
Smith, John, *142*
Smith, Katherine, *201*
Smokyville, *142–143*
Smythe, *98*
Solomon, *72*
South End, *39, 59, 65, 67, 84, 130, 143, 156–157, 187*
South Houston, *19, 98, 143–146, 153, 169*
South Mayde, *27, 148*
South Shaver, *154*
Southland, *128, 146–147*
Southmayd, *148*
Southmore, *47, 59, 148*
Southwell, *149, 155*
Sparks, *56*
Spring, *31–32, 47, 77, 81, 96, 108, 110, 123, 132, 134, 145, 149, 153–157, 180*
Spring Branch, *47, 155–156*
Spring Creek, *157, 180*

St. Agnes, *157*
St. Anne, *158*
St. Christopher, *158–159*
St. Euphrasia, *159*
St. John, *159–160, 201, 208*
St. Joseph, *160*
St. Mary, *160*
St. Nicholas, *161*
St. Patrick, *161*
St. Peter, *155, 161*
St. Pius, *161*
St. Rose, *162*
St. Stephen, *162*
St. Theresa, *162*
St. Thomas, *162–163, 188*
St. Vincent, *163*
Stansfield, *214*
Staples, *11, 62–63, 164*
Steubner, *31, 123, 164*
Stevens, *199*
Stevenson, *71, 164–165*
Stewart, *47, 168*
Stiles, *214*
Stockdick, *27, 168*
Strack, *90*
Strayer, *204, 206*
Sullivan, *163*
Sumners, *159*
Sunniland, *110*
Sunnyside, *118, 147, 168*
Sunset Heights, *1, 153, 168–169*
Sutton, *23, 169–170*
Sykes, *20, 148, 170*
Szabo, *81, 171*

T

Tallman, *42, 197*
Tautenhahn, *32*
Taylor, *48, 75, 164, 171, 185, 200, 206*
Textile Mill, *120, 173*
Third Ward, *48, 56, 173, 197, 211*
Thompson, *56, 133, 146–147, 174, 190, 206*
Thurbur, *174*
Tomball, *129, 153, 164, 175*
Tompkins, *57, 64*
Travis, *53, 175, 195, 214*
Trinity Gardens, *177*
Trinity Lutheran, *70, 178–179*
Tucker, *85*
Tune, Tommy, *36*
Turkey Point, *179, 191*
Turner, *170*
Tuskegee, *4*
Twain, *179*
Twenty-Third, *179, 206*

U

Ulrich, *179*
Union Hill, *180*
Urwitz, *109*

V

Volmer, *180*

W

Waldo, *74*
Waller, *98, 181, 215*
Waltrip, *192*
Washington, *4, 6, 47, 69, 76, 107, 163, 181, 183–185, 187–189, 192, 201, 206*
Washington Road, *189*
Washington, Booker T., *4, 6, 47, 76, 188*
Washington, George, *163, 189*
Waters, *9, 169*
Watkin, *75*
Watkins, *82, 109*
Watson, *110*
Webster, *49, 153, 190–192*
Websterville, *190, 192*
Wesley, Carter, *7*
Wesley, Mabel, *47*
West End, *37, 56, 62, 67, 69, 71, 98, 110, 192*
West River, *193*
West U, *98, 194*
West University, *36, 50, 98, 105, 193*
Westfield, *195*
Westheimer, *36, 42, 106, 158–159, 196*
Wharton, *196*
Wheatley, *69, 183, 197–198, 207*
Whidby, *168*
Whisand, *175*

White Oak, *201*
White Settlement, *202*
White, Lulu, *7*
White, Mark, *42, 203*
Whitmire, *131*
Whittier, *181, 202*
Wiess, *28*
Wilberforce, *6, 56*
Williams, *97, 169*
Williams, Willoughby C., *97*
Willow, *153, 203*
Wilson, *43, 71, 75, 198, 203–204, 207*
Wilson, William A., *43*
Winkler, *47, 107, 159, 207–208*
Wolfe, *36*
Woodcrest, *72, 209*
Woodland, *209*
Woodson, *213*
Woodward, *78, 209*
Wooldridge, *110*
Wooster, *209–210*
Wunsche, *154, 210*
Wynns, *110*

Y

Yates, *211–212*
Young Ladies School, *214*
Young, S.O., *108*
Younger, *25, 34, 102, 197, 200, 217*

Z

Zeiss, *215*
Zeus, *129*

www.ingramcontent.com/pod-product-compliance
Lightning Source LLC
Chambersburg PA
CBHW082022050526
44107CB00100B/621